AMERICAN LEGAL AND CONSTITUTIONAL HISTORY ★ A Garland Series of Outstanding Dissertations

Edited by

HAROLD HYMAN
William P. Hobby Professor of History,
Rice University

STUART BRUCHEY
Allan Nevins Professor of American
Economic History, Columbia University

WHAT GOD HATH WROUGHT ★ The Embodiment of Freedom in the Thirteenth Amendment

George H. Hoemann

Garland Publishing, Inc.
New York & London ★ 1987

Library of Congress Cataloging-in-Publication Data

Hoemann, George H., 1952–
What God hath wrought.

(American legal and constitutional history : a Garland series of outstanding dissertations)
Originally presented as the author's thesis (Ph.D.)
—Rice University, 1982.
Bibliography: p.
1. United States—Constitutional law—Amendments—13th—History. 2. Slavery—Law and legislation—United States—History. 3. Afro-Americans—Civil rights—History. 4. United States—History—Civil War, 1861–1865. I. Title. II. Series: American legal and constitutional history.
KF4757.H63 1987 342.73′C873 86-31986
ISBN 0-8240-8271-0 347.302873

All volumes in this series are printed on acid-free, 250-year-life paper.

Printed in the United States of America

WHAT GOD HATH WROUGHT:

THE EMBODIMENT OF FREEDOM IN THE THIRTEENTH AMENDMENT

George H. Hoemann

A Thesis Submitted in Partial Fulfillment
of the Requirements for the Degree of
Doctor of Philosophy

Department of History

Rice University

May 1982

CONTENTS

ACKNOWLEDGMENTS

Anyone who has written a dissertation knows that, in many ways, he is only one of its authors. The debts I owe to others, intellectual as well as personal, loom large in the final product of these many years of study.

My indebtedness begins with my mentor, Harold M. Hyman. With much patience he listened when appropriate, guided when possible, and never failed to encourage me in my research. Much of what I have written only begins to trace insights he shared with me. For all his help, my sincere thanks.

Similarly, I thank Sara D. Jackson of the National Historical Records and Publications Commissions for helping me to explore the National Archives, Kay A. Flowers of the Rice University library for invaluable aid in locating obscure sources, and my colleagues and friends Caludine Ferral, John Hughes, Tom Mackey, Evelyn Nolen, and Dee Pipes for reading drafts of this manuscript and offering their insights, suggestions, and encouragement. I also want to thank my colleague at the *Papers of Thomas Jefferson*, J. Jefferson Looney, whose help in typesetting this dissertation was invaluable and the *sine qua non* of its present appearance. Of course, any errors within the text are mine.

There are several other people who deserve special thanks. Without their support and encouragement, I would never have finished this work. My mother and father showed great patience with me, as did my friends and co-workers at the *Papers of Jefferson Davis*, Lynda L. Crist and Mary S. Dix. I also include with my warmest feelings Alice and Frank Hagen, Angelica Menta, and Nancy and Ray Nowak.

Finally, I thank Gary L. Adams, OP, who taught me many things, but especially that the fullness of life is the glory of God. To him, I dedicate this dissertation.

INTRODUCTION: THE MEANING OF WORDS

Sumter.

Seldom in American history has a single word stirred such a range of emotion. Seldom has one word summed up so well the essence of a time. Sumter the moment of independence, Sumter the fulfillment of treason. Men of reason and insight accepted the word with resignation or greeted it with joy–Sumter a blessing was also a curse.

There was another word that also captured the time, the moment, the condition of men. It, too, brought forth the extremes of reaction. Defended, attacked, blessed, and cursed.

Slavery.

The two words, Sumter and Slavery, are linked in American history. Today we see the connection almost as one of causality, but it was not seen so clearly then. Abolitionists, anti-slavery extensionists, Unionists, secessionists–all agreed on the gross outlines of the April crisis. Slavery (conceived alternately as the cornerstone of a civilization, or as a malevolent, sinful force antithetical to Civilization) would be limited and subject to wounding and destruction. The crisis occurred when each group decided upon the virtue of that event.

On the whole northerners accepted slavery's decline. On the whole southerners rejected it. The remedy southerners selected–Sumter–placed many border state men in a quandary. Residents of the border states were southern by birth, tradition, and culture, but the separation of South from North left these natural seekers of compromise with little ground to stand on, for they did not approve the secession solution. Yet neither were they happy with the prospect of warring with their cultural cousins–of coercing them back into a Union growing increasingly inimical to their most profound views of right and order.

Some border state men followed their section–former Vice-President John C. Breckinridge–while others followed the nation, as future Vice-President Andrew Johnson. Although most remained loyal to the Union, they were never comfortable with the leadership provided by Republicans, who were antislavery from the beginning and dangerously open to experience as a teacher. Border state representatives in Congress would have the Union remain as nearly as it had been before Sumter; slavery would not be harmed at all. This policy, officially adopted in July 1861 in the Crittenden-Johnson Resolutions,[1] pleased border state men who thought that they had confined antislavery feelings and principles in congressional concrete. With slavery protected, a reunion of the states through negotiations would be practical, and the fear of the unknown avoided.

But that policy suited secessionists not at all, since they were well on the road to creating (or ratifying?) a distinct and separate self-view, devoid of attachment to a Union they no longer trusted or respected. On the other hand, Republicans were always willing to employ the least government action to affirm the integrity of the Union, whole, complete, and indivisible. But to accomplish that goal Republicans would do what was necessary, remaining open to the prospect of discovery so they could determine what means would achieve their end. Abolitionists were uneasy with Republican pragmatism and caution, yet joined them to prosecute the war, more fully aware of the possibilities the circumstances allowed. In the tension of conflicting expectations it became clear that the gulf that separated radicals from conservatives was not constitutional ideology so much as psychology: would the nation meet the future with fear or with confidence?[2]

During the first months of the struggle, another word quickened in the American conscience, paralleling the experience and expectations of the times. By the end, this word overshadowed Slavery, and made sense of Sumter, even as it was itself made possible by their convergence.

Freedom.

The great, ironic result of Sumter was the birth of a new freedom, a more substantive freedom, an embodied freedom. The accomplishment of the embodiment of freedom is the history of the war itself, and the Thirteenth Amendment constitutes that history. The sad, tragic result of Sumter was the decline of freedom, the enshrinement of legality, and the triumph of a slavery more insidious than ever, lacking little of its old self, save its very name.

Introduction–Notes

1. Co-sponsored by John J. Crittenden and Andrew Johnson, the resolutions bearing their names blamed disunionists for the civil war and pledged the federal government not to interfere with the domestic institutions of the states, that is, slavery. *Congressional Globe*, 37th Congress, 1st Session, 222-23, 243, 265; Herman Belz, *Reconstructing the Union: Theory and Policy During the Civil War* (Ithaca, New York: Cornell University Press, 1969), 24-28; Albert D. Kirwan, *John J. Crittenden: The Struggle for the Union* (Lexington, Kentucky: University of Kentucky Press, 1962), 441. As Belz points out, the ambiguous language of the resolutions lent itself to opposite interpretations: Andrew Johnson thought it prohibited interference with slavery. John Hale noted the lack of specific language and believed the issue was open. Belz, *Reconstructing the Union*, 24-28.

2. See Lawanda Cox, *Lincoln and Black Freedom* (Columbia, South Carolina: University of South Carolina Press, 1981), 3-5, for a similar view, although Cox discounts the impact of war itself. And see generally, Harold M. Hyman, *A More Perfect Union* (New York: Alfred A. Knopf, 1973), Michael Les Benedict, *A Compromise of Principle* (New York: W. W. Norton, 1974), and Benedict's "Preserving the Constitution: The Conservative Basis of Radical Reconstruction," *Journal of American History* (1974), 61:65-90.

I

THE SHOCK OF WAR

Sumter's surrender on April 14, 1861 forced upon the North the decisive issue of war or peace. How would the nation react; what constitutional rules would it follow? Would slavery be affected? The shock of Sumter's surrender, binding agent though it was, did not and perhaps could not alter life-long conceptions of nation, government, power, and morality. Sumter's more apparent meaning, the unity of North against South, was only a superficial expression of solidarity. Expectations of the ensuing war, tactics used and even the reasons for the conflict itself, were areas of bitter disagreement and division. To be sure, the war was for the Union, but ideas of exactly what the Union was varied sharply among members of the emerging war coalition.

In the months of indecision preceding Sumter the debate over secession had steadily escalated. Variant perceptions of Union emerged even as the Union itself disintegrated. With the secessionists gone, the 36th Congress–the Congress of the secession crisis–provided the first leadership of the Union coalition. And though the war motivated all to find a solution, possibilities remained only dimly seen and little changed by the new circumstance of civil war. As the war lengthened and victory proved elusive, leaders gradually responded to changed expectations. In what was desirable or, more grimly, what was necessary, the first months of war resembled the last months of peace.

Border states reacted cautiously to the firing on Sumter, even blaming the Confederacy for the incident. Yet Lincoln's April 15 call for 75,000 troops to suppress the rebellion prompted Virginia, Arkansas, Tennessee, and North Carolina to forget their moderation and see federal coercion of sister states rather than national measures to save the Union.[1]

In the North people did not focus on the use of federal force, but on the South's resistance to federal authority. The April 15 proclamation was the first war reaction to southern intransigence. The day before the call for troops, Ohio senator John Sherman expressed the North's weariness of suspense, giving in to the relief of decision. Putting aside his previous pro-compromise views, Sherman welcomed the resolution of months of tension. "For me, I am for a war that will either establish or overthrow the government and will purify the atmosphere of political life."[2] But others did not react with relief. Months of uncertainty had shaped the opinions of many northern leaders. With Sumter it was as if something had snapped; the restraint that always was bent but never broken, now gave way in a flood of passion. War had come to America; was it not God's will? If so, a refusal to furnish volunteers would be "flying in the face of His Omnipotence."[3] And so one editor offered his meditation on the theme, "War as a Means of Grace."

> So, bowed with sadness that it must be, we bend to the necessity of war, believing that it is best for us. Honorable war is better than dishonorable peace. Honorable war is better than corrupt peace. War that stirs us and calls us for self-abnegation and self-sacrifice–war that makes heroic lives of common-place men–war that binds the hearts of men together as with bands of iron–war that brings forgetful men and women to their knees, and leads them to the acknowledgement of the God of nations–war that inspires with noble motives the brutal elements of society–war that makes us forget the schemes of personal gain in devotion to the country–war that recalls and emphasizes the trials of the fathers of the republic–war that shows us what a true peace is worth–such a war is not the greatest of evils. . . . Let it come then; and may God in His mercy make it the blessing to us which he means it to be![4]

Sumter's importance as a revolutionary force in northern thought cannot be overestimated. While divisions remained, the nation's momentum went over to the Republicans as they united behind the standard of a Union militant, and hoped for the triumph of antislavery principles. In their eyes the war for the Union became a holy crusade.[5] Young men were called to sacrifice their lives upon the "altar of our country" in the great battle between "anarchy and law, between rebellion and government."[6] Secession was treason and treason anarchy. As Columbia law professor Theodore Dwight observed immediately before Sumter, "the flag of the Union is not merely the symbol of freedom; it is as well the symbol of law." Law was the rudder for society not only in peace, but most especially during war. The "heathenish maxim" that the law became silent during wartime had to be rejected; traitors were not the only enemies by this reckoning. An even greater enemy were those who would succumb to war's passion. Dwight urged his audience to "insist that even a traitor's doom shall be settled in strict accordance with law." Liberty and law were Siamese twins, for one could not be assured without the other. Such was the faith in legal forms; such was secession's threat.[7]

While emphasizing the overriding goal of restoring order to

the nation, Republicans were careful not to limit themselves too closely to narrow interpretations some might place upon law and Constitution and Union. Indeed, they were leading the fight for law and Constitution and Union, arguing that "the necessities of war–especially civil war–are above all technical forms." The necessity of war was the just reward for southerners who dared disrupt the nation. In their effort to crush out rebellion, some Republicans even acknowledged the possibility of dictatorship.[8] Sumter posed the question whether America should use force to settle its disputes. The dedication to the rule of law might have provided a negative answer; the challenge to entire concepts of Union compelled an affirmative response.[9]

From the beginning many abolitionists saw the war as a chance for the eradication of slavery. Most abandoned whatever pacific ideals they may have once held, to join the Union coalition. Wendell Phillips explained his changed view when he remarked that "civil war is a momentous evil. It needs the soundest, most solemn justification." Phillips found justification in Lincoln's sincerity and in Phillips' belief that slaves would soon view the Stars and Stripes as a pledge of emancipation. William Lloyd Garrison joined Phillips in urging pacifist abolitionists to "stand still and see the salvation of God."[10]

Henry Ward Beecher focused his sermons upon the necessity of the conflict. Denouncing war in general, he nonetheless maintained that it was "ten thousand times better to have war than to have slavery." As if gifted with foresight, and against continuing denials by most responsible officials, Beecher saw the war as God's instrument, not for reunification with the South, but for a true reconstruction of the nation's spirit. Freedom for the slave and mutual respect between the reconstructed sections would become the new national anchors. Until that happier time, Beecher urged strong measures against the South. Far from cursing the war, he recommended its utility, and argued that opposition to the Union should be seen as treason against both nation and God.[11]

Disunion and the dynamic of war began an evolutionary process. Those Republicans, northern Democrats, and border state men who did not accept secession were forced by circumstance into alliance–an alliance that meant something different to each group. The Republican press attempted to hide these deep divisions, but without success.[12] Many conservatives chose the North and a pro-war platform. Yet their concept of Union meant that they would be forever watchful, temporizing where they could, to keep the Union in war as nearly as it had been in peace. Rather than seeing war as a means of grace, conservatives lamented the resort to force. As one Philadelphia editor wrote, "it is as if Hell had been transplanted into Eden."[13] As war-related problems arose and the nation dealt with substantive issues, the coalition regularly divided, and with Republican victories, reunited. Republicans led the Union coalition in only the narrowest of senses; no one foresaw the future.

Those who held Union as the highest good were, on the whole, less strident in tone and more moderate in policy. The conflict was termed "this unhappy war"; calmness of spirit and moderation of temper were the rule. These Unionists sought reunification with the South, not reconstruction of the section. Their only purpose was to "uphold the Constitution [and] to reinvigorate the Union."[14] They reassured themselves that their partners in war did not fight to abolish slavery and that national political unity was the common goal.[15] Above all, conservative Unionists meant to let Republicans and abolitionists know that they had not been swallowed up in the reaction to Sumter. While they might support a war for reunification, they did not endorse a platform of antislavery principles.[16] Virtually from the beginning of the conflict, these Unionists realized that their's was a two-front struggle–against secessionists who dissolved political bonds, and against Republicans who might transform the nation: "The question is this: Is the war in support of the Government, the Constitution, the Union and dearly-purchased rights of a free people, or a negro crusade for the abolition of slavery?"[17]

On the whole antislavery advocates did not heed conservatives' warnings, but neither did they rush to emancipation. There was no consensus about the goals or methods within the antislavery portion of the Union coalition. Republicans and abolitionists realized that they stood for some ideals, loosely defined as "antislavery," but the ready answers of "no" to the slave power, and "yes" to the Wilmot Proviso had little relevance now. Rather, men like Benjamin Butler began a long pilgrimage of improvisation. Renouncing compromise with the South, they offered little in its stead save a fight to sustain the government.[18]

The Republicans' first strategy relied upon border state unionism, but throughout the secession crisis they had misconceived the nature of that unionism, missing entirely the ambiguity within border state sentiment. The secession of North Carolina, Virginia, Arkansas, and Tennessee might have informed Republicans that border unionism was far from absolute. Nevertheless, it is unclear whether they ever fully believed during the first months of war that a majority of southern people really wanted secession.[19] Lincoln's concern for maintaining an alliance with border state unionists contributed to his "go slow" approach on most war issues; nothing could be done to alienate this necessary part of the war coalition.[20] As long as antislavery forces were unsure of themselves and the war's outcome unpredictable, the Union coalition remained fairly harmonious. As the war daily created new questions, requiring new answers and as tactics and goals subtly changed, so conservatives' resistance increased. They were not blind to what was happening; indeed, they understood all too well. Past compromise formulas had always been based upon a protection of southern rights within the Union of states. With war, that position changed little, yet the situation was radically different. The more tinkering with slavery, the more difficult would be the restoration of political unity, conservatives thought. And so, their goal remained reunification of slave and free states–and not reconstruction. Yet the more that new circumstances called forth new answers, the more irrelevant old formulas became. These men were caught in the unfolding of history.

One reason northerners so readily accepted war in April 1861 was their supreme confidence in a quick victory over treason. Within that general belief, though, were many different estimates for the actual length of the conflict. John Sherman discussed this with his brother William, noting the South's better organization, armament, and general unity. The North might suffer initial defeats for those reasons, but Sherman still looked for a quick triumph over the South. A better prophet was New York Democrat Daniel S. Dickinson. Not venturing an exact estimate of the war's duration, Dickinson unknowingly grasped the nature of the war long before most even began to suspect: "The war, for aught I can discover, must go on [to] its bitter end,–bitter it must be, but the end I wot not of."[21]

If many opinions existed about the length of the war, even more offered their view on how the war should be waged. Although Sumter was in many ways a revolutionary break in American history, tradition still shaped and constrained. Charles Sumner offered the use of his international law books to Benjamin Butler as the latter moved down to Fortress Monroe, Virginia. Attorney General Edward Bates hoped to force the South's capitulation by economic blockade rather than military engagement. But so limited a view did not long endure. When Baltimore citizens fired on Union troops moving through the city on April 19, killing and wounding several soldiers, Bates realized his error, decrying the lack of strong military reaction.[22] Vice-President Hannibal Hamlin echoed the sentiment in a letter to the President:

> Does our government feel its full strength? I fear they cannot. The only course now to pursue is one of promptness, energy, and power. The whole power of the government should be exerted. *There is safety in no other course.*[23]

By this time other government leaders were serving notice of their displeasure with Lincoln's war actions–or inactions. When the

President called for 75,000 volunteer, Massachusetts' Republican senator Henry Wilson urged the number be increased to 300,000.[24] Two other Republican senators, Zachariah Chandler of Michigan and Benjamin Wade of Ohio, voiced their desire for tougher actions. Wade particularly disliked Lincoln's decision not to severely discipline Baltimore citizens for their attack on the federal troops. The Ohioan wanted southerners to be punished, and while he hoped that the war would be conducted "by assent of the President in a constitutional way" Wade warned that "the stern demand for justice of a united people cannot and must not be baffled by the perverseness of one man though he be the President of the United States."[25]

Numerous issues received public attention during the first weeks of the war, but never far from the forefront of public thought was the issue that many labeled the cause of the war–slavery. Besides abolitionists few spoke of the institution's overthrow. Yet some already realized that, whether a goal or not, slavery could not remain unaltered.[26] Three days after Lincoln's call for troops, one Republican editor predicted:

> Slavery, foul, loathsome, man-cursing, and heaven-defying slavery–in this mortal struggle will go down–down like a millstone in the ocean–even though, under the Providence of God, it should be called to make its exit amid the glare of burning cities and the shock of armies."[27]

As abolitionists abandoned pacific principles in hopes of an antislavery crusade and as the war's length defied even the most pessimistic forecasts, government leaders began to look at new possibilities under the cloak of military necessity. The abolitionist wing of the Union coalition increased its power as circumstances played into its hands. Movement toward his goal prompted William Lloyd Garrison to comment on his support of the war: "when I said I would not sustain the Constitution because it was a covenant with death and an agreement with hell, I had no idea that I should live to see death and hell secede."[28] The *National Anti-Slavery Standard* spoke of slavery itself as a state of war, and while the best way to abolish it might be through Christian non-violence, the editor quickly pointed out that "war, bad as it is, is innocence itself compared with the sort of peace which, in this case, is its only alternative."[29] Even Lincoln's otherwise conservative friend (later United States senator from Illinois) Orville Browning contemplated the creation of a "negro republic" upon the ruin of the conquered cotton states.[30]

The situation never became desperate enough for Browning's vision to gain significant support. And as conditions were not disastrous, conservatives continued to work for as little change as possible in slavery's status. Yet, the war had stopped the effective enforcement of the fugitive slave law; slaves were fleeing their Maryland masters in ever-increasing numbers, and many northerners feared slave insurrections.[31] Lest the war give bondsmen any encouragement, some urged protection for southern whites against slaves. The rule of civilized warfare demanded as much, and Attorney General Bates hoped for the least possible disturbance of the South's "accustomed occupations."[32]

A clear example of the ambivalence over slavery is found in an exchange between Benjamin Butler (commanding the contingent of Massachusetts volunteers in Baltimore) and Massachusetts governor John A. Andrew. Not yet the "beast" of later reputation, Butler promised Maryland governor Thomas Hicks that he would aid state forces in suppressing any slave rebellion. Butler argued that he was not in Maryland to interfere with its laws, but to restore peace within the Union. Governor Andrew and abolitionists, on the other hand, denied any obligation to uphold Maryland slave laws. Slavery-related questions were no longer to be regarded as political, but only military issues. In other words, the risk of slave uprisings was a danger the South had incurred as a military liability and a cost of secession. As a matter of good tactics, the North might not encourage, but neither should it prevent slave insurrection.[33]

The difficulty with Andrew's reasoning was that Maryland, though the home of many secessionists, had not left the Union. His solution was incompatible with her loyal status. Moreover, Butler had other reasons for opposing Andrew's suggestions. The general argued on moral grounds that arming slaves or promoting rebellion could endanger southern white women and children. Since his own troops would not target them, Butler could not allow slaves to harm these whites. Recalling, too, that British use of Indians during the Revolutionary War had embittered Americans, he believed that Andrews' tactic would prevent the speedy reunification of North and South. Yet Butler was not entirely sanguine about possible southern tactics. If the South continued to employ assassins or poison soldiers, as Butler believed them to be doing, then (but only then) would he retaliate by utilizing the "potent means" for slaughter within southern lines–slave insurrection.[34]

As April became May, northern confidence continued to be reflected in calls for a quick victory. Pennsylvania congressman Galusha Grow, soon to be Speaker of the House, urged any measure "no matter what the cost" to quell the insurrection,[35] and one Republican newspaper stated that "[w]e do not want peace, now, nor do we desire a slow or merely defensive war. We want war, swift and overwhelming: The more terrible the war is made, the shorter it will be, and the more humane the policy." The New York *Evening Post* suggested that traitors ought to "look out for themselves."[36] This civilian brauvara notwithstanding, military men like William Sherman realized that the war could not be won before the next winter, at the earliest. And new estimates of the war's length posed new questions for government leaders.[37]

Projections for troops and supplies increased accordingly. Some commentators guessed that as many as 500,000 men under arms might be required, and by early May, government recruiters began emphasizing three year enlistments. Few really believed the war would last that long, but in other times Americans had exhibited the disturbing habit of leaving the battlefield when their enlistments expired.[38] Just how many Americans appreciated the need for a stable supply of soldiers is unclear especially as the number of northern volunteers continued to pour in. For a time the government found itself in the embarrassing position of having too many troops. With the policy of limited engagements, there was little need for replacements. Rather than turn away volunteers for which no organization, weapons, or supplies were available, Lincoln's insight proved entirely correct and prophetic: "The enthusiastic uprising of the people in our cause, is our great reliance; we can not safely give it any check, even though it overflows, and runs in channels not laid down in any chart."[39]

For the moment, however, the public continued to resent the administration's "masterly inactivity," despite military assessments in its support. Lincoln's policy aimed toward keeping border states in the nation, but such delicacy seemed particularly inappropriate. "The strongest battalions are always on the side of the defense of principles which alone make government august and civil society possible."[40] Fighting that did occur at this time was designed partly, at least, to quell dissatisfaction with military moderation.[41]

In the back of abolitionists' minds was the possibility of dramatic changes in the nation's social and political arrangements as northern armies prepared to meet the enemy. The editor of the *National Anti-Slavery Standard* observed that the future of the rebel states (and by implication slavery) had certainly been called into question. No one, it was true, could predict the future. Still, "the question will turn rapidly from Abstract into the Concrete as the armies advance into the enemy's country."[42] This convergence of federal armies and southern property happened early in the conflict, and incidents of this kind would inevitably raise profound policy issues. One of the first encounters occurred in mid-May. In his proclamation to the people of Baltimore, Benjamin Butler affirmed the sanctity of private property, pledging his army's respect and excepting only munitions and other articles used to aid the rebellion. When found, these would be confiscated under the law of nations.[43]

Slave property was not mentioned, and legal questions about military confiscation were not addressed. Confiscation could be justified within areas in rebellion, or traitorous states. In Maryland, however, the army meant to single out individual traitors in a state still in the Union. Cautious northern consciences were salved, apparenly, by the South's apparent disregard for public and private property (as represented by sequestration of northern debts and the seizure of federal property during secession). Perhaps this explains how one newspaper could suggest a mass seizure of southern real estate and a redistribution to northerners, converting the land from one of "treason and barbarism into one of law, order and civil liberty."[44] August Belmont, conservative Unionist and future chairman of the Democratic party, shuddered when Republicans spoke in these terms. If the war lasted more than one year, Belmont sadly remarked, its goal would surely change from mere reunification to basic reconstruction. Abolition would then become the war's aim, and the Union as it was would have little chance to return.[45]

Belmont had good reason to fear a change in the war's goal. Ambivalence about slavery and the war continued, but sentiment was growing for some attack, however indirect, upon the institution. Repeating his call for such an attack, Henry Ward Beecher fanned the flames of patriotism, hoping to channel its fervor for abolition's end.[46] William S. Robinson, the New York *Tribune*'s Boston correspondent, condemned Benjamin Butler's ideas of suppressing slave revolts as an "old fashion and foolish notion, of comity and Constitutional obligation which is bad enough in times of peace, but absolutely intolerable in times of rebellion."[47] That language was remarkable, even for antislavery leaders. Perhaps more remarkable was the fact that Butler himself began the first chipping away at the peculiar institution.

Butler was transferred from the Department of Annapolis to Fort Monroe in Virginia at mid-May, and was in close contact with Confederate military forces. When three slaves made their way to his lines, they sought asylum from their masters. After questioning them, Butler discovered that the slaves had been used by the Confederates in building military fortifications. Since he was himself in need of laborers, the general improvised a policy, declared the slaves to be "contraband of war," and put them to work for the North. Butler's policy, termed a "happy fancy" by abolitionists, was limited indeed. Slaves fleeing from loyal states were returned and even Virginia slaves were sent back if their masters took an oath to support the Union. Butler's overall policy toward private property closely resembled his

Baltimore proclamation. The army would seize property only when necessary, and then only by proper officers, according to specific procedural standards.[48]

Almost immediately, circumstances forced Butler to modify his policy concerning fugitive slaves. His rationale–confiscating the *labor* of slaves used against the United States for military purposes–collapsed when southern masters began sending slave women and children southward. Not surprisingly, many escaped and sought protection behind Union lines. These slaves had not been used against the federal government to further the insurrection, and did not meet the requirements for confiscation. But Butler did not return these slaves either. Instead, he put the able-bodied to work, fed all, and kept a record of work done against food eaten, so the government would not have to finance his venture at a loss. From a humanitarian point of view, Butler had no doubt that what he did was correct. Yet he was unsure about the political ramifications of his actions, and so requested guidance from Washington.[49]

Butler's query came before the Cabinet for discussion and, according to Postmaster General Montgomery Blair, the President was concerned about the problem. Blair wanted to limit the contraband umbrella to working slaves, letting the South bear the burden of care for women and children. Blair revealed his own views rather than the Cabinet's when, in a letter to Butler, he explicitly reminded the general that his business was "war not emancipation." Realizing the delicate position that Butler was in, however, the Postmaster General suggested congressional action: "I think that Congress should amend the law of treason so as to admit, in the less aggrivated [sic] cases, of punishment, by fining so as practically to work confiscation." Blair also urged the general to use slaves as spies because they knew the land and their "sly tricks" would allow them to learn a great deal of military intelligence.[50] Official word came when Secretary of War Simon Cameron informed Butler on May 30 that the Cabinet had approved his *ad hoc* policy for dealing with fugitive slaves from seceded states. The Lincoln administration authorized the general to use slaves and not to return them to their masters. But legal title to the slaves was not abolished nor even transferred to the government. Rather, final disposition was reserved for some future determination.[51]

Butler's policy exemplified the northern attitude about the conflict: "This war is in truth a war for the preservation of the Union, not for the destruction of slavery. . . on the other hand, no pledges can be given that slavery shall receive no damage from a Union triumph."[52] Abolitionists predicted that sheer numbers of escaping slaves would soon overwhelm Butler's stop-gap strategy, and require a systematic approach to the problem of slavery's status in time of war.[53]

The Administration's idea of holding the Unionist coalition together through military inactivity no longer sufficed. Cabinet members added their voices in criticism of General-in-Chief Winfield Scott, a prime proponent of the policy. Montgomery Blair hoped northern armies would be "pushed into action by the indignation of the people." In London, American commentator Samuel Goddard had only contempt for qualms about shedding fraternal blood.[54] Underlying this uneasiness was the untested belief in swift northern victory. Estimates continued to put the end of the war at next winter; Scott himself thought victory would come in February, 1862. And some observers blamed the encouragement given the Confederacy by British and French neutrality for the lack of a speedy conclusion of the conflict.[55]

Nevertheless, by June the optimistic forecasts about the war's early end had already been disproved and Americans began to realize the scope of the war in which they were engaged. Lincoln's original call for 75,000 troops seemed laughable against new estimates that that number alone would be necessary to capture Richmond. And as troop numbers increased, so did the amount of money needed for the war. By late June, some guessed that the government would need $150 or $200 million before the conflict's end. A dawning sense of a tough fight ahead was reflected by Henry Adams in a letter to his brother, Charles Francis, Jr. "The cotton states," Adams wrote, "would rather annex themselves to England or Spain than come back to us." A once common belief in quick victory was dissolving into uncertainty. A week and a half before Congress convened on July 4, Iowa's senator James Grimes confided to his wife that he knew nothing more than any one else about when the war would end. And even as estimates changed and perceptions became more acute, the ever-present conern of conservative minds remained the relationship between the war's length and its effect on slavery.[56] That was the rub. As armies advanced, more and more slaves would come into Union lines. What to do with hundreds, then thousands of slaves (let alone slavery) was a frightening, perplexing question for an Administration fearful of driving the upper South into the eager arms of their southern cousins.

So the quest for action collided with ingrained American restraint, and fears that Congress would do little more than talk were joined with fears that it would do too much. The uneasiness that Grimes, for example, felt over Lincoln's "usurpations" had not lessened. Yet in his uneasiness, Grimes, too, could see the new tool the Union would use for its purposes. Unwilling to "clothe the President with the utmost potentiality of this great people," as was his colleague Timothy Howe of Wisconsin, Grimes nonetheless anticipated the enactment of a direct tax and conscription–significant departures from peacetime practice and a telling comment upon the increasing universe of possible federal actions.[57]

American dedication to order and restraint was evident not only in the Administration's strategy, but in martial conduct as well. Calls for hanging Confederate privateers as pirates were conspicuous for their unusualness. Whether captured rebels should be treated as prisoners of war or traitors was a genuine puzzle. In theory, the government regarded Confederates as traitors, but punishment was never as severe as theory allowed. More representative of how the war was actually being fought were prisoner exchanges and safe conduct passes; "civilized warfare," was still the norm. In a communication with his Confederate opposite, Butler carefully explained federal policy on private property, emphasizing the limited scope of military seizure. All non-contraband property would be returned to Virginians when they demonstrated their allegiance to the United States. An indemnity would be paid for destroyed property. And as proof of his good word, Butler court-martialed several soldiers who had plundered private property without cause.[58]

While conservatives worried about the connection between the war's duration and slavery, antislavery advocates seized upon it. Francis Lieber, former South Carolina College professor of history and political economy, was willing to accept "all the struggle and heart-burning . . . if and only [if]" slavery would be abolished in the border states.[59] Such an admitedly radical sentiment for the time was not shared by all. Attorney General Bates opposed slave confiscation throughout December 1861, and pushed for enforcement of the fugitive slave law. Montgomery Blair hoped to remove the unwanted contraband to Haiti and let Congress tie up loose ends of legal title and transfer either by confiscation or compensated emancipation.[60]

Yet by the time Congress convened on July 4, there was a consensus to strike at slavery some how, some way. Questions of tactics would continue to haunt the Administration, but it was precisely tactical questions that proved decisive for understanding the shape and force of the freedom unleashed by war. The crucial first question was settled in July–attack slavery, accept the abolitionists' argument that the war was the product of malignant slave power; recognize the intimate connection between slavery and southerners' treason and the necessity of striking at treason's heart in order to preserve the Union. Philadelphia lawyer Sidney George Fisher put it well: "It has been discovered that laisser aller won't do in politics at any rate, and that society must be armed for self-defense."[61] Republicans adopted abolitionist arguments;

the best self-defense was an attack upon the war's cause. On July 4, Congress began the search for an effective weapon against slavery.

NOTES FOR CHAPTER ONE

1. Donald E. Reynolds, *Editors Make War: Southern Newspapers in the Secession Crisis* (Nashville: Vanderbilt University Press, 1970), 201-204.
2. Rahcel S. Thorndike, ed., *The Sherman Letters* (New York: Charles Scribner's Sons, 1894), 113.
3. Howard C. Perkins, ed., *Northern Editorials on Secession* (New York: D. Appleton-Century Company, 1942), 735.
4. Ibid., 1066-67.
5. August Belmont, *Letters, Speeches and Addresses* (New York: Private, 1890), 57; Samuel A. Goddard, *The American Rebellion* (LondonL Simpkin, Marshall & Company, 1870), 10-11.
6. Perkins, *Northern Editorials*, 1067.
7. Philadelphia *Legal Intelligencer*, June 7, 1861. A judge in Pennsylvania common pleas court remakred that even if the enemy were within the city [Philadelphia] the court would be protected int he adminsitration of justice. The *Legal Intelligencer*'s editor agreed, Ibid., April 26, 1861. Lawyers were also concerned that people know their contribution to the war effort–either by enlistment in thearmy or through continued legal activity. Legal practice was neceesary to continue the civil justice system and therefore give security necessary to function and produce the wealth required for the war, Ibid., May 3, 17, 1861.
8. Perkins, *Northern Editorials*, 732.
9. Phillip S. Paludan, "The American Civil War Considered as a Crisis in Law and Order, " *American Historical Review*, (1972), 77:1019.
10. *National Anti-Slavery Standard* April 27, 1861; Wendell P. Garrison, *William Lloyd Garrison, 1805-1879* (New York: The Century Company, 1885-1889), 4:21.
11. Conrad Cherry, ed., *God's New Isarel: Religious Interpretations of American Destiny* (Englewood Cliffs, New Jersey: Prentice-Hall, 1971), 168-74, quoting Henry Ward Beecher.
12. Perkins, *Northern Editorials*, 756, 811, 813, 827.
13. Ibid., 946.
14. G. M. D. Bloss, *Life and Speeches of George H. Pendleton* (Cincinnati: Miami Printing & Publishing Company, 1868), quoting Pendleton May 18, 1861.
15. Daniel S. Dickinson, *Speeches, Correspondence, etc., of the late Daniel S. Dickinson, of New York* (New York: G. P. Putnam & Sons, 1867), 2:15, 28.
16. Perkins, *Northern Editorials*, 762.
17. Ibid., 830-31.
18. John L. Motley, *The Causes of the American Civil War* (New York: J. GH. Gregory, 1861), 35; Benjamin F. Butler, *The Private and Official Correspondence of General Benjamin F. Butler ...* (Norwood, Massachusetts: The Plimpton Press, 1917), 1:90-91.
19. As late as June some northerners believed in such a latent unionism throughout the South, Goddard *Letters*, 8. 19; Belmont, *Letters*, 57. See also Abraham Lincoln, *The Collected Works of Abraham Lincoln, edited by Roy P. Basler* (New Brunswick, New Jersey: Rutgers University Press, 1953), 4:437. Northerners' faith in the future and hope about the present is captured in Motley's interesting comment, "The Union is omnipresent," Motley, *Causes*, 29.

20. Albert D. Kirwan, *John J. Crittenden: The Struggle for the Union* (Lexington: University of Kentucky Press, 1962), 433-48.

21. Perkins, *Northern Editorials*, 527, 816, 1052-54, 1057-58; Sidney George Fisher, *A Philadelphia Perspective: The Diary of Sidney George Fisher Covering the Years 1834-1871, edited by Nicholas Wainwright* (Philadelphia: Historical Society of Pennyslvania, 1967), 387, 389 (hereafter cited as Fisher, *Diary*); Thorndike, *Sherman Letters*, 112; Dickinson, *Speeches*, 548.

22. Butler, *Correspondence*, 1:21; Edward Bates, *The Diary of Edward Bates, edited by Howard K. Beale* (New York: Da CApo Press, 1971), 183-85.

23. Charles E. Hamlin, *The Life and Times of Hannibal Hamlin* (Cambridge [Massachusetts]: Riverside Press, 1899), 401, as quoted therein.

24. Richard H. Abbott, *Cobbler in Congress: The Life of Henry Wilson, 1812-1875* (Lexington: University of Kentucky Press, 1972), 114.

25. Hans L. Trefousse, *Benjamin Franklin Wade: Radical Republican from Ohio* (New York: Twayne Publishers, 1963), 148, as quoted therein.

26. James Russell Lowell, *Political Essays* (Boston and New York: Houghton Mifflin Company 1888), 91.

27. Perkins, *Northern Editorials*, 744.

28. Carleton Mabee, *Black Freedom: The Nonviolent Abolitionists from 1830 through the Civil War* ([New York]: Macmillan Company, 1970), 336-44; Garrison quoted in Oscar Sherwin, *Prophet of Liberty: THe Life and Times of Wendell Phillips* (New York: Bookman Associates, 1958), 443 (Garrison spoke in 1862).

29. *National Anti-Slavery Standard*, APril 27, 1861.

30. Maurice G. Bacter, *Orville H. Browning, Lincoln's Friend and Critic* (Bloomington, Indiana: Indiana University Press, 1957), 119-20.

31. Fisher, *Diary*, 387.

32. Perkins, *Northern Editorials*, 527.

33. Butler, *Correspondence*, 1:26-27, 37-38; *National Anti-Slavery Standard*, May 11, 25, 1861.

34. Butler, *Correspondence*, 1:38-41.

35. James T. Dubois and Gertrude S. Matthews, *Galusah A. Grow, Father of the Homestead Law* (Boston and New York: Houghton Mifflin Company, 1917), 243-44.

36. Perkins, *Northern Editorials*, 756; *National Anti-Slavery Standard*, May 11, 1861. See also Thomas S. Perry, ed., *The Life and Letters of Francis Lieber* (Boston: J. R. Osgood, 1882), 318; Sherwin, *Prophet of Liberty*, 455.

37. Thorndike, *Sherman Letters*, 121.

38. Goddard, *Letters*, 22; Butler, *Correspondence*, 1:74; Thorndike, *Sherman Letters*, 122-23. For examples of evolving congressional opinion on the cost of the war and eventual army size, see the *Congressional Globe*, 37th Congress, Special Session, 1460, 1446, and 37th Congress, 1st Session, 72, 123-24, 148.

39. Lincoln, *Coll. Works*, 4:375.

40. Butler, *Correspondence*, 1:63-64; Lowell, *Essays*, 88-89.

41. Thorndike, *Sherman Letters*, 116.

42. *National Anti-Slavery Standard*, July 13, 1861.

43. Butler, *Correspondence*, 1:83.

44. Belmont, *Letters*, 48; Perkins, *Northern Editorials*, 605-606; John Syrett, "The Confiscation Acts: Efforts ar Reconstruction During the Civil War," (unpublsihed Ph. D. dissertation, The University of Wisconisn, 1971).

45. Belmont, *Letters*, 53.

46. Perkins, *Northern Editorials*, 812-13, 821-22, 824, 833-34; Goddard, *Lettes*, 14, 27; Henry Ward Beecher, *Patriotic Addresses in American and England from 1850 to 1885, edited by John R. Howard* (New York: Fords, Howards & Hulbert, 1887), 297, 299.

47. As quoted in Butler, *Correspondence*, 1:77.

48. Ibid., 105-110; *National Anti-Slavery Standard*, Juńe 8, 1861.

49. Butler, *Correspondence*, 1:112-14. Louis S. Gerteis argues that Butler changed his policy for political reasons, having been chastised by Governor Andrew, Gerteis, *From Contraband to Freedman: Federal Policy Toward Southern Blacks, 1861-1865* (Westport, Connecticut: Greenwood Press, 1973), 12-13.

50. Butler, *Correspondnece*, 1:116-17; Gerteis, *From Contraband*, 14.

51. Cameron to Butler, May 30, 1861, in *The War of the Rebellion: A Compilation of the Official Records of the Union and Confederate Armies...* (Washington: Government Printing OFfice, 1880-1900), Series III, 1:243 (hereafter *OR*); Gerties, *From Contraband*, 13-14.

52. Perkins, *Northern Editorials*, 834, 835.

53. *National Anti-Slavery Standard*, June 8, 1861.

54. Blair, quoted in Butler, *Correspondence*, 1:129-30; Goddard, *Letters*, 34.

55. Trefousse, *Wade*, 146; Willard H. Smith, *Schuyler Colfax, the Changing Fortunes of a Political Idol* (Indianapolis: Indiana Historical Bureau, 1952), 155; Belmont, *Letters*, 64.

56. Goddard, *Letters*, 36-37; Belmont, *Letters*, 61, 62-63, 71; Henry Adams, *Letters of Henry Adams, edited by Worthington C. Ford* (Boston and New York: Houghton Mifflin, 1930-38), 1:92-94; William Salter, *The Life of James W. Grimes* (New York: D. Appleton & Company, 1876), 141.

57. Salter, *Grimes*, 141.

58. Fisher, *Diary*, 394; Belmont, *Letters*, 67; Butler, *Correspondence*, 1:123, 139-41, 150-51.

59. Perry, *Lieber*, 320. See also Belmont, *Letters*, 77; Charles Sumner, *The Works of Charles Sumner* (Boston: Lee & Shephard, 1872-83), 5:497-98. Secretary of State William Seward refused to grant a Massachusetts black a passport, citing the *Dred Scott* decision which denied United States citizenship to blacks. Sumner then went to Seward's office and personally filled out the passport application. The Secertary of State thereupon granted the passport, saying that he would accept anyone Sumner certified to be a citizen.

60. Marvin Cain, *Lincoln's Attorney General: Edward Bates of Missouri* (Columbia, Missouri: Unversity of Misouri PRess, 1965), 160-61, Butler, *Correspondence*, 1:130.

61. Fisher, *Diary*, 393.

II

A STERN AND SERIOUS REALITY

In the first months after Sumter the reality of war encroached on the traditional paterns of thought and behavior of Americans. Changes in attitudes were subtle, gradual, but constant.[1] Often those with a tenuous commitment to the Union, clung tenaciously to careful schema defining relationships between government and citizens. Before hostilities had begun, many conservatives had proclaimed the soundness of the rock upon which slavery was built, invoking the law of nations as well as positive local law for its protection.[2] Many did not believe that war made a dfference or meaingfully altered the situation. When citizens of Norfolk, Virginia complained about damage done to their property during the fighting, they must have been surprised at the Union commander's reply: "Gentlemen, this is War. I hope that you considered the full menaing of tha word before you seceded."[3]

But in truth few Americans had changed their views or possibilities they envisioned. Iowa's Senator James Grimes worried about the expanded military and feared violations of the Constitution, even as the Confederacy ignored the document entirely. Democratic representative John McClernand, later a Union general, commented that no serious person proposed the abolition of slavery in the states where it existed.[4] Abolitionists' calls aside, the political truth, the reality of the possible, almost justified the Norfolk citizens' outrage that the war had gotten in the way of their lives.

Or so it must have appeared to Republicans who gathered in Wasington on July 4 to attend the special session of Congress. Lincoln had fought the war since April without without congressional sanction, but that would never be the case again. And never afterward would antebellum reality completely dictate the realm of possibilities.[5] The full meaning of war emerged not only on fields reclaimed by body and blood, soul and humanity, but in the precincts of Congress and President. These men perceived the hope of victory in the embrace of heretofore impossible federal action, and by that embrace, began the long climb through reconstruction.[6]

Such a climb would not be easy, nor barely perceived at the beginning as a climb at all. A correspondent of the *National Anti-Slavery Standard* predicted prematurely that the Congress of July 4, 1861 would be compared to the Congress of July 4, 1776, because it, too, would end up deciding upon the question of freedom. When the House of Representatives assembled, it disclaimed any abolition aspirations by explicitly confining its business to measures affecting the war effort. Rumors abounded of compromise along the lines of the old Crittenden formula, and an even inquiry about the possiblity of repealing the fugitive slave law lost overwhelmingly.[7] Gerrit Smith wrote to the repeal's sponsor Owen Lovejoy of Illinois and labled the distinction between war measures and slavery an absurdity, noting, "the slave question is the war question." Yet that was truly a minority view.

Despite some Republicans' hopes for a short session that would skirt the slavery issue, there was at least a willingness to consider, if only in the abstract, circumstances in which slavery might die for the sake of the nation. Republican senators James Dixon and Kinsley Bingham both accepted in principle the demise of slavery if became necessary for the Union's preservation. To crush out the rebellion any means needed would be used, Dixon declared, even those "which seem to us terrific in their consequences." Secretary of War Cameron and Kansas Republican James Lane invoked Fate, a tone terrifying to conservative Unionists, as they commented on the inevitable fall of slavery in the face of advancing federal armies.[8] When Republicans raised the specter of abolition either through war necessity or as an intrinsic product of the war itself, it was another signal that slavery's strongest defense had been breeched. A question of "whether" was suddenly becoming questions of "how, when and where." The psychological impediment that constrained thinking and acting during the secession crisis and early war began to give way. A constitutionalism that had, barely four months before, brought forth a thriteenth amendment that forever prohibited the abolition fo state slavery, was becoming anachronistic.[9]

During those hot July days of 1861, members of the conservative wing of the Unionist coalition intetly maintained the constrained constitutionalism of the pending thirteenth amendment. As the Senate considered a bill for the organization of the vastly expanded army, Lazarus Powell, a Kentucky Democrat, introducted an amendment that would prohibit federal interference with slavery in the states.[10] To be sure, no serious man, as John McClernand had said, now proposed slavery's abolition. But the key word was "now," and Powell wanted to commit Congress and the nation to the *status quo antebellum* regarding slavery. Contemplation of a wholly free Union was too unsettling an abstraction, too clearly an idle fancy, and too worrisome a possibility not to stop immediately–if possible.

Powell's amendment highlighted the division between realists and romantics.[11] Unionist senator John S. Carlisle, representing the few square miles of loyal Virginia, argued that the war was for the Union and had nothing to do with slavery. But he opposed Powell's proviso, because he thought it raised a false issue. Yet Powell was not raising a false issue or seeing something that was not there. He had detected the subtle shift in Republican perceptions. When as conservative a Republican as Illinois' Orville Browning was willing, at least in theory, to abolish slavery to save the nation, then the slavery issue was already intimately linked with the prosecution of the war.[12] When Samuel Pomeroy (R, Kansas) spoke of the great sacrifices in men and material the North was making to fight the war, he concluded with a neat hook. If, in the process of beating back treason, slaves were taken from their masters (he used the word confiscated), it was an "incidental result." And after all, the sacrifices would have to be shared.[13] Powell was not raising a false issue.

Later in the debate Kansas' other senator, James Lane, asked Carlisle whether in the event of a slave insurrection, the army ought to return slaves to their masters. When Carlisle answered yes, Lane remarked that this might obtain with loyal masters, but never with rebels. There, plainly stated, was the the difficulty of distinguishing loyal southern whites from rebels. And Carlisle warned that an assault upon slavery would lead southern Unionists to reconsider their allegiance. Powell asked Browning if he could "uphold constitutional government by putting the Constitution of his country under his feet?" Behind that query (really an indictment) lay the assumption that some Republicans wanted to save constitutional form by destruction of constitutional substance, that is, the protection of southern property rights. Army-sponsored confiscation (for Powell and others a synonym of abolition, although certainly not the same thing) would make Congress "national robbers, national freeboooters" in the name of constitutional preservation.[14]

Powell's amendment had created a potentially embarrassing predicament for Republicans. How could they vote against a commitment not to abolish state slavery, especially when the Administration worried so about border state reaction to federal policy? John Sherman, another conservative Republican, suggested a way out of the difficulty. Sherman's substitute language stated merely that the army's purpose was the preservation of the Constitution, and omitted explicit mention of slavery altogether. Although Powell and two allies, Democrats Jesse Bright and John C. Breckinridge (both later expelled from the Senate) favored a direct vote on Powell's amendment, Sherman's substitute passed overwhelmingly. With the embarrassment removed, the Senate then rejected the substitute. The entire question was dropped.[15] All this occurred on July 18, just two days before the Senate began consideration of a bill for the first tentative but official congressional attack upon state slavery. Border state and Democratic senators had registered their views against federal intrusions on state slavery. But Republicans were not deterred, and a confiscation bill came before the Senate on schedule.

Although others made proposals, Judiciary Committee chairman Lyman Trumbull's (R, Illinois) plan became the basis for debate on confiscation.[16] His measure's comparatively limited scope was clear from the first, for it only consifacted that property that was specficially used for insurrectionary purposes.[17] On July 20 the Senate began consideation of Trumbull's bill, S. No. 25. Confiscations were only to be handled through civilian courts. Originally, Trumbull had wanted the condemnation proceedings to be held in the appropriate district, circuit, or admiralty court having jurisdiction where the property's was seized. But this presented a problem since most seized property would be in rebel-held areas where civilian courts were not functioning. Rather than allow the military to control the process, a Judiciary Committee amendment (readily agreed to by Trumbull and approved on July 22) directed that condemnation proceedings be held "in any district in which the property may be seized or into which they may be taken and proceedings first instituted."[18] Thus, confiscated items could be taken to an area where civilian courts were functioning before formal proceedings were initiated and legal title transferred. So far Trumbull's bill conceived property in general terms, but the senator proposed an amendment that explicitly dealt with slave property. With the introduction of that amendment, both the nature of the bill and the debate changed.

When war was less than a month old, President Lincoln's secretary John Hay had considered the question of what to do with slaves that came into Union hands. In contradiction to the policy then followed by commanders at Fort Pickens and Madison, Hay believed that the government ought not return fugutive slaves if their masters were in rebellion:

> nothing would bring [masters] more to their senses than a gentle reminder that they are dependent upon the good-will of the Government for the security of their lives and property. The action [confiscation] would be entirely just and eminently practicable &elip. What we could not have done in many lifetimes the madness and folly of the South has accomplished for us. Slavery offers itself more vulnerable to our attack than at any point in any century and the wild malignity of the South is excusing us before

God and the World.[19]

Abolitionists were echoing Hay's view and going a step further, deploring the irony that slavery was safer within the Union than without. Constitutional protections and obligations ruled during peacetime, but with rebellion and a *de facto* rupture of the Union, those guarantees ought to lapse, or so they argued. Non-abolitionists were also making the connection: "The war is to be no child's play," the Springfield *Republican* reminded its readers, and this presumably meant a willingness within the Unionist coaltion to reevaluate notions of obligation and the rendition of fugitive slaves.[20]

What to do with fugitive slaves was a more pointed concern in Washington, D. C. Slaves began to escape to the Distirct from Virginia shortly after the war began. Rather than extend Butler's contraband theory, Lincoln ordered that fugitives not be harbored in the District. The President's policy was born from his deep concern to reassure border states and his inaugural pledge to enforce the Fugitive Slave Act. But this policy was not announced until mid-July, and never became general army practice. Butler had been holding slaves since late May and continued to do so. By the end of July, the general reported nearly 850 slaves at Fort Monroe, almost a third of the Elizabeth City county's prewar slave population. According to Lincoln's secretary, the President consciously allowed this contradcition in order to meet local situations and military necessitities.[21]

The actual situation at the time of congressional debate on confiscation, then, contained precedents for limited "slave holding," if not confiscation, and also for rendition of fugitive slaves. The difference between holding and confiscating was important, as Secretary Cameron realized when he postponed the question of title transfer in his May instructions to Butler. Lincoln's policy of diversity to the contrary notwithstanding, a more uniform policy toward runaways and captured slaves was needed.[22] In one sense, Trumbull's amendment concerning slave property was an attempt to formalize a policy already being implemented in a haphazard way.

On July 15 S. No. 25 went to the Judiciary Committee and was reported to the Senate on the 20th, debate beginning on the 22nd. The Battle of Bull Run intervened on the 21st, and was one of the first major military clashes of the war and a major Union defeat. The North had been so confident of victory that many congressmen had gone to the battlefield near Washington to view the engagement. The disaster's impact on the members of Congress was profound. One reporter told of a Democratic congressman who went out to the field as an old line Breckinridge Democrat, but who came back a fighting abolitionist. Such a dramatic reversal was reportedly shared by thousands, but could hardly have been usual. Yet the defeat had a tremendously disturbing effect, dislodging many from safe if archaic notions. Government leaders who had avoided the plaguing question of slavery, now began some "hard thinking" about the institution. Sidney George Fisher noted that "everyone is impressed with the conviction that the war is a very stern and serious reality."[23] In the shock of defeat, Trumbull's slave confiscation amendment came before the Senate.

Linking slave confiscation directly with reaction to the defeat at Bull Run, however, is problematic. Although debate occurred after the battle, Trumbull had introduced the amnemdnet the day before the fighting. His motivation for presenting the amendment was not Bull Run. The defeat does suggest, on the other hand, some reason for the Senate's subsequent action.[24]

Before the battle it appears that Trumbull's colleagues on the Judiciary Committee were unwilling to cross the line and make confiscation government policy rather than *ad hoc* military tactic. Trumbull offered the slave confiscation clause solely as a personal amendment, not as chairman of the Judiciary Committee. Nor did it have the committee's endorsement. Indeed, Senator John Ten Eyck (R, New Jersey) observed that he had voted against the amendment in the committee's discussion. Trumbull apparently could not find a majority among his four Republican and two Democratic colleagues on the committee for the slave confiscation amendment.[25]

Trumbull's amendment was consistent with the rest of the bill. In other words, all slaves would not be confiscated, but only those used for insurrectionary purposes. Slaves used to aid the rebel war effort would be subject to seizure, but loyal slaveholders' property rights in slaves were carefully safeguarded.[26]

Despite the bill's cautious approach to confiscation, some Democratic senators remained unalterably hostile. Although realizing that prolonged debate was futile because of Republican strength in the upper chamber (32 Republicans against 17 opposition members), Democrats nonetheless did all they could to stake out their philosophical opposition to confiscation. Not surprisingly they aimed their remarks at the violation of slave property rights contemplated in Trumbull's amendment. Maryland Democrat James Pearce questioned the practicality of the legal apparatus envisioned for condemnation proceedings, the effect the bill mgiht have on the border states, and the measure's constitutionaltiy. Above all, he saw Trumbull's amendment as an irritant to the South and the border, maing suspect the North's war motives. From a war to preserve the Union,

Pearce saw an evolving hybrid goal of Union with emancipation.[27] Similarly, Kentucky's Breckinridge looked beyond the letter of the lsave confiscation amendment to what he perceived as an underlying trend. Instead of a restrained war measure, Breckinridge labeled slave confiscation as the first step toward total emancipation.[28]

And that was that. The remarkable thing about the Senate debate was the lack of it. Pearce and Breckinridge provided the only real opposition to Trumbull's amendment and the bill in general. The size of the Republican majority was not the only reason for lack of debate, however. The idea of confiscation in general and slave confiscation in particular had gained unexpected support because of the defeat at Bull Run, for the Confederacy had used slaves in support of their troops during that battle.

Lyman Trumbull was too good a politician not to take advantage of the new situation, especially when other senators picked up the refrain. Henry Wilson declared that if the southern traitors used slaves against the government, then the government ought to "convert those bondsmen into men that cannot be used to destroy our country."[29]

Many saw the sue of slaves in combat as unjustified and illegitimate. The new Confederate tactic was so disturbing that the House of Representatives formally asked Secretary Cameron to report on the subject.[30] Again, abolitionists had anticipated politicians' realization. In May the Oneida, New York *Weekly Herald* remarked that slaves armed under the banner of rebellion ought to be met by black men under the flag of loyalty. Any slave fighting with the North ought to secure not only his own freedom, but that of his family as well. In April Wendell Phillips had called for the North to summon "justice, God and the negro to [its] side."[31]

Until the Battle of Bull Run nothing had been done about the legal status of confiscated slaves. But with the stunning Union defeat, men everywhere began to look at the war in a different and more somber light. The Washington correspondent for the *National Anti-Slavery Standard*summed up the new realization. The conquest of rebellion would not be easy, he said, "It is, in fact, a gigantic job for the government to conquer it. IT cannot be done without striking at the heart of the monster."[32] It is quite possible that had the North won at Bull Run, the Confederacy's use of slaves might not have been seized upon or cared about so deeply. If the Union had won, however, the necessity for confiscation would not have been as apparent. Defeat at Bull Run and the use of slaves to engineer that outcome changed at least one senator's mind. Ten Eyck, who had opposed Trumbull's amendment in committee, announced his conversion during debate on the Senate floor. Reality confronted his belief that the South would not "make use of such means as the employment of persons held to labor or service in their armies." Ten Eyck declared:

> God knows that we do not want them [freed slaves] in our own section of the Union. But, sir, having learned and believing that these persons have been employed with arms in their hands to shed blood of the Union-loving men of this country; I shall now vote in favor of that amendment with less regard to what may become of these people than I had.[33]

The vote was anti-climatic. Thirty-three senators favored the slave confiscation clause, and only six opposed it. Thirty-one of the affirmative votes were cast by Republicans; no Republican voted against the amendment. The bill as a whole passed without a division. Within a day of Bull Run, the Senate had acted (reacted?) swiftly and forcefully.[34]

On the next day, July 23, the House received the confiscation bill, and sent it to its own Judiciary Committee. When the measure came back to the floor on August 2, a substitute amendment amendment was in the place of Trumbull's language. Ohio Republican John Bingham was in an awkward position as committee chairman. He reported the the substitute amendment, but personally opposed the change. The primary difference in between the two versions was the substitute's more explicit limitation on slave confiscation–applying only to thsoe slaves actually engaged in military activities against the Union. The Senate's language might be interpreted to allow confiscation for other than military use of slaves, that is, indirect support of the Confederate war effort. Bingham argued strongly against the substitute because of its mroe cautious treatment and conception of southern tactics. Bingham was against showing any "tenderly regard [for] the property of these rebels in arms."[35]

Even so, the chairman and other supporters of slave confiscation continually emphasized the limited scope of the proposed measure. All slaves who aided the rebellion were not subject to confiscation, but only those whose masters knowingly consented to their use in rebel activity. Bingham made this explicit in a reply to a Kentucky congressman's apprehensions:

> I will undertake to say that no just court in America will ever construe this fourth section . . . to the effect that, because it happens that citizens of the United States residing in a seceded state hold slaves, this law amounts to an emancipation of their slaves. I deny that that was the intention of law, or that it will bear any such construction by a court of justice.[36]

But under the Senate language, "insurrectionary use" might mean something besides military action. Henry Burnett (D, Kentucky) asked whether the slaves of a Tennessee slave-holder used to produce staple crops would be subject to confiscation if thsoe crops were sold to the rebel army. Bingham asnwered that they would, because "a traitor justly forfeits both life and property."[37] When the House decided to accept the committee's substitute language, they placed a major limitation upon an already limited policy.

Senators had passed the confiscation bill without serious attention to a connection betwen slave confiscation and emancipation. But former senator and now congressman John J. Crittenden, described by abolitionists as a "defunct politician" and "a corpse set up for show, galvinized at time to go" focused precisely upon that conection.[38] Ignoring the question of Congress' real authority in the seceded states, Crittenden addressed the question of congressional power to act upon slavery at all:

> It has been conceded that [slavery] was a subject for state legislation only. Does war change the powers of Congress in this respect? It is the absence of all power upon the subject which has prevented your legislation. Absence of all power of legislation in time of peace must be the absence of the same power at all times. The constitutional power of this House does not come and go with a change in circumstance.[39]

Crittenden's argument was on two levels. First, he took a static view of the Constitution; it superseded the environment. The Constitution was meant to control poltiical circumstances, not be controlled by them. But on the second level, Crittenden was uphodling essentially the special nature of slave property. His colleagues' attempts to trap him in inconsistency failed to note this distinction. Two members from Illinois, Democrat John McClernand and Republican William Kellogg, asked Crittenden whether the government had the right to confiscate a horse if the owner were a traitor. Crittenden replied that he was not concerned about any increase of power during war, nor with international law. Rather, he was interested in the constitutional sanction against interference with slavery.

Kellogg tried to recoup by emphasizing the limited nature of the proposed law; slavery was not being abolished, no state law on slavery was, in fact, being touched at all. Only specific slaves were being confiscated. According to Kellogg, Congress was not legislating on slavery *per se*, but merely punishing treason:

> I repeat that we have no more power to legislate on the subject of slavery in time of war than we havce in time of peace. If a citizen of the United States commits high treason, or any other crime known to the law, it is competent for the United States legislature, if the crime be within its cognizance (and treason is), to provide

> for the forfeiture and confiscation of the offender's property . . . yea, his right to service in another shall be confiscated; not annulling the law by which he holds it: for that is a matter which neither in war nor in peace can we reach. But because of the crime, we may either in war or peace impose the penalty of . . . confiscation.[40]

Crittenden replied by denying that necessity sanctioned the assumption of pwer. Morover, in the final round of this exchange, he argued that slave confiscation would allow the South to misrepresent the North's war aims and that the use of slaves in war was an insignificant military matter.[41] The Kentucky congressman did not refute Kellog's argument distinguishing confiscation from abolition. But many border state men seemed to have equated the two terms. That Crittenden felt constrained to deny the significance of the military use of slaves is further evidence of the importance this issue had assumed.

Another conservative Unionist, congressman Alexander Diven (R, New York) maintained that confiscation of property would hardl y be worht the price to advance the Union cause. Breaking with the Republican tactic of considering slaves as "property" in order to confiscate and free them, Diven consistently referred to slaves as men. The ironic consequence of his position was continued enslavement for men he was unwilling to confiscate as property. Diven proposed to treat all persons captured by Union forces as prisoners of war. Rather than freeing slaves thus encountered, Diven wanted to hold captured slaves for possible prisoner exchanges. Diven emphasized the impracticality of the confiscation bill, yet his own suggestions seem hardly less unworkable. Because of his unwillingness to ackowledge the growing trend among Republicans and follow it, abolitionists later questioned Diven's commitment to the antislavery cause, remarking that a Democrat would hardly act differently.[42]

Objections to the confiscation bill centered upon southerners' rights.[43] This plainly irritated Republican House members, especially Thaddeus Stevens, one of its most influential number. Stevens' response to the bill's opponents contained one of the clearer statements in favor of confiscation. At first, his appeal wa snot to the Constitution, but to international law as authority for confiscation. Stevens ridiculed the notion of constitutional rights for rebels. "Who pleads the Constitution," Stevens asked, but the same traitors who were fighting to overthrow it? But when one of his colleagues asked whether Stevens addmited that confiscation was, in fact, unconstitutional, the Pennsylvanian retreated quickly. Confiscation was both constitutional and sanctioned by internatioanl law, he argued. The special situation in which the nation found itself clothed the government with powers it did not possess during peacetime.

But Stevens did not make the usual distinction between rebel property in general and that specially used for military purposes. Stevens' principle was broader than almost any other voiced during debate on the 1861 Confiscation Act. By his rule, all rebel property, regardless of tis use, was confiscable. Despite a formalistic "reassurance" given to his southern colleagues, Stevens' views on confiscation surely confirmed their worst suspicions.[44]

After parliamentary maneuvering, the bill came before the Hosue on August 3 with substantially the same language it had had the previous day. Chairman Bingham, however, refused to allow more debate on the bill, and after defeating a motion to table (66 to 47), the House accepted the committee's more limiting substitute amendment without a division. The lower house then narrowly passed the confiscation bill as amended, 60 to 48; eleven of the forty-eight negative votes were cast by Republicans.[45]

When the House version came back to the Senate on August 3, Trumbull quickly accepted the substitute amendment, saying only that it made the same limitations he had attempted to include in the original text. Two days later, the Senate approved the bill, 24 to 11, and President Lincoln signed it into law on August 6.[46]

The Confiscaton Act of 1861 was not born in the isolated arena of legal precedent but in the aftermath of defeat and gorwing commitment. But commitment to what? Viewed from one perspective, the Union was laready near death and death not inflicted by the South, but by zealous abolition fanatics using opportunity to their advantage. Members of Congress more moderate and open to anti-abolition pressure struggled to justify to themselves the course they had chosen. Constitution, international law, common sense–all were appealed to as sanctions for what a majority agreed had to ber done. Yet each source seemed to have its own deficiency.[47]

With this diversity, why confiscation? Why any attack upon slavery? A clue emerges from looking at the question Unionists asked themselves and each other. Preeminent was the simple question of wht was necessary to win the war, or rather, what was enough. The process of learning, of growth through experience, depends upon a gradualistic approach to problems and circumstances. A coalition made up of widely disparate groups could never uniformly agree upon an answer. Unionists' answers to what was enough could not be plotted as a point upon a graph, but more as an elliptical range of opinions. Some elements tended to hold back as others moved forward with rapidity. The great middle, by and large Republican congressmen, moved far too quickly for the tastes of Crittenden, and far too slowly for the imperatives of Garrison. And yet, in certain narrow and exceedingly legal paths, they did move against slavery.[48] What had been unthinkable six months before became not only thinkable, but possible—and accomplished. Through the experience of war and rebellion, Republicans accepted that portion of abolitionist thought and program (constitutionalism) that seemed to be "enough."[49]

What abolitionists hoped, conservatives feared, and no one knew, was that there could be no stop-gap measures. Enough was enough only when the Unionist coalition accepted the heart of abolitionist thought–abolition itself. The prophets in the wilderness were those members of the coalition who called the country forward to the uncharted realms of freedom. For as most Unionists asked themselves what was enough, abolitionists had already moved beyond that question. They answered their partners (enough was the end of slavery), but also began the more precise task of coping with abolition's aftermath. As slaves came forward to Union lines, abolitionists asked, "What shall be done with the Slaves?"—and for those who would listen, they gave their answer.[50]

Abolitionists were deetermined that emancipation, when it came, would not mean freedom and then abandonment. Government protection—national protection—for freed men's and women's rights was part of the abolitionist vision as early as July 1861. And the major purpose for protection of freedmen's rights was to prevent their re-enslavement, to create a public climate that would prevent such a calmity from ever occurring. Abolitionists knew the intransigence of southern whites. They themselves had often been the victims of southern white reaction. They expected whit southerners to resist abolition, to gith it at every turn. Certainly Republicans were not unaware of potential (and already active) southern opposition to war measures. Yet Republicans did nto have the experience of thirty years of fighting the Slave Power. They soon realized the lengths to which southerners, unionist and secessionist, would to to save slavery. Abolitionists had too long been the victims of southern hostility. THey did not propose to leave the ex-slave alone to keep his freedom as best he could. Republicans also learned this lesson through the months of fighting intransigence on battlefield and in Congress' halls.[51]

The Confiscation Act of 1861 was the first substantive congressional action against slavery, and one of the first signs that Congress understood the stern and serious reality that war imposed upon the country. As the war went on it continued to call forth new responses to new circumstances, drawing government leaders ever closer to the abolitionist perception that, in the end, slavery must die if the nation were to live.

NOTES FOR CHAPTER TWO

1. In his diary Attorney General Edward Bates noted on April 15, 1861, that while the nation was now in "open war," he hoped to keep in close control and to "disturb as little as possible, the accustomed occupation of the people," Edward Bates Papers, Library of Congress (hereafter, DLC).
2. *Cong. Globe*, 37:Special Session, 1486.
3. As quoted in the Philadelphia *Legal Intelligencer*, May 10 1861.
4. Salter, *Grimes*, 140; *Cong. Globe*, 37:1, 77.
5. Abolitionists' predictions, though unheed at the time, provided accurate: "Our main hope must stil be in EVENTS, as the moving spring of action," *National Anti-Slavery Standard*, July 13, 1861.
6. Before the assault on Fort Sumter, the *National Anti-Slavery Standard* editorialized against the new word "reconstruction" which it took to mean a series of compromises engineered for Virginia and other border states to secure their allegiance, and to woo back the seceded South, *National Anti-Slavery Standard*, April 13, 1861.
7. Ibid., June 29, July 13, 20, August 7, 1861; *Cong. Globe*, 37:1, 24-25.
8.*Cong. Globe*, 37:1, 119, 142, 187; *National Anti-Slavery Standard*, June 8, July 20, 1861.
9. The text of the prposed thirteenth amendment is as follows: "No amendment shall be made to the Constitution which will authorize or give to Congress the power to abolish or interefere, within any State, with the domestic institutions thereof, including that of persons held to labor or service by the laws of said State." The proposed amendment (usually referred to as the "Corwin Amendment" after its author Thomas Corwin of Ohio) is treated tangentially in the standard works on the secession crisis. See especially Dwight L. Dumond, *The Secession Crisis, 1861-1861* (New York: Macmillan, 1931), David Potter, *Lincoln and His Party in the Secession Crisis* (New Haven: Yale University Press, 1962), and Kenneth Stampp, *And the War Came* (Baton Rouge: Louisiana State University Press, 1950). The only treatment of the Corwin Amendment itself that I am aware of is an article by R. Alton Lee, "The Corwin Amendment in the Secession Crisis," *Ohio Historical Quarterly*, 70:1 (1961), 1-26. No study has centered on the Corwin Amendment's significance during the first year of the war, although Ohio, Maryland, and Illinois all ratified the proposition. For the text, see *Cong. Globe*, 36:2, Appendix, 350.
10. For the text of Powell's amendment, see *Cong. Globe*, 37:1, 186.
11. Note the following from Wendell Phillips' speech of APril 21, 1861: "The North *thinks*—can appreciate argument—is the nineteenth century.... The South *dreams*—it is the thriteenth and fourteenth century—baron and serf—noble and slave"*National Anti-Slavery Standard*, July 27, 1861.
12. *Cong. Globe*, 37:1, 187-88. Orville Browning and John Sherman expressed similar sentiments, *National Anti-Slavery Standard*, July 27, 1861.
13. *Cong. Globe*, 37:1, 189.
14. Ibid., 189-90.
15. Ibid., 192-94.
16. Ibid., 11, 78, 134, 194.
17. Ibid., 120. Although John Syrett's "The Confiscation Acts" deals with the first confiscation act, and notes its "revolutionary" character, it fails to set the context for the bill's enactment. Of much more use are Patricia

M. L. Lucie's "Confiscation: Constitutional Crossroads," *Civil War History* (1977) 23:307-21, and the relevant chapter in her dissertation, "Freedom and Federalism, Congress and Courts, 1861-1866," (unpublished Ph.D. dissertation, University of Glasgow, 1972, now printed in the present series), both of which have influenced my treatment of the 1861 confiscation law. Standard works on confiscation are James G. Randall, *Constititional Problems Under Lincoln* (New York: D. Appelton, 1926), his "Some Legal Aspedts of the Confiscation Acts of the Civil War," *American Historical Review*, (1912), 18:79-86, and Henry D. Shapiro, *Confiscation of Confederate Property in the North* (Ithaca, New York: Cornell University Press, 1962).

18. *Cong. Globe*, 37:1, 218.

19. John Hay, *Lincoln and the Civil War in the Diaries and Letters of John Hay, edited by Tyler Dennet* (New York: Dodd, Mead and Company, 1939), 22.

20. *National Anti-Slavery Standard*, April 27, 1861, reprinting the Springfield [Massachusetts] *Republican.*

21. John G. Nicolay and John Hay, *Abraham Lincoln: A History* (New York: The Century Company, 1890), 4:389-92; Gerteis, *From Contraband*, 15.

22. Nicolay and Hay, *Lincoln*, 4:395. See also Joshua R. Giddings' letter to the editor of the New York *Tribune*, reprinted in the *National Anti-Slavery Standard*, June 22, 1861. Giddings concluded that Butler's passive policy ought to be changed to one more aggressive in confiscation fo slaves. See also the Philadelphia *Legal Intelligencer*, May 10, 1861, for early efforts to confiscate the Pennsylvania non-slave property of James Mason.

23. *National Anti-Slavery Standard*, August 3, 1861; Fisher, *Diary*, 397.

24. Shapiro, *Confiscation*, 6-7. For an example of too easy a connection, see James G. Blaine, *Twenty Years in COngress* (Norwich, Connnecticut: Henry Bill Publishing Company, 1884), 1:342; *Cong. Globe*, 37:1, 216-17. See also Ralph J. Roske, *His Own Counsel: The Life and Times of Lyman Trumbull* (Reno: University of Nevada Press, 1979), 74-76. Roske, however, confuses the chronology regarding Trumbull's slave confiscation amendment.

25. *Cong. Globe*, 37:1, 217-19. The members of the committee were Republicans Trumbull, Lafayette Foster, Ten Eyck, Edward Cowan, and Ira Harris; Democrats James A. Bayard and Lazarus Powell.

26. Ibid., 218.

27. Ibid., 218-19. Pearce argued that even if slaves were emancipated by this act, state slave law would not be abolished and state authorities would only reenslave anyone freed. Without the slave confiscation clause, Pearce indicated, he would vote for the confiscation bill.

28. Ibid., 219.

29. Ibid., 218-19.

30. *OR*, Series III, 1:340. Cameron replied on July 25, "I have the honor to state that this Department has in its possession no information on the subject."

31. *National Anti-Slavery Standard*, April 27, 1861, reprinting from the Oneida, New York *Weekly Herald.*

32. *Cong. Globe*, 37:1, 219; *National Anti-Slavery Standard*, August 3, 1861.

33. *Cong. Globe*, 37:1, 219.

34. Ibid. The two Democrats voting in favor of the amendment were James McDougall of California and Andrew Johnson of Tennessee.

35. Ibid., 409; House, *Journal*, 37:1, 197-99.
36. *Cong. Globe*, 37:1, 410-11.
37. Ibid., 411.
38. *National Anti-Slavery Standard*, July 6, 1861.
39. *Cong. Globe*, 37:1, 411.
40. Ibid.
41. Ibid., 411-12.
42. Ibid., 413-14; *National Anti-Slavery Standard*, March 1, 1862.
43. *Cong. Globe*, 37:1, 413-14; Randall, *Constitutional Problems*, 285-87.
44. *Cong. Globe*, 37:1, 414-15.
45. Ibid., 415, 431.
46. Ibid., 427, 434, 455. McDougall voted yes, while Cowan voted agaisnt acceptance of the House version. Seven of the eleven opponents were from border states.
47. Blaine, *Twenty Years*, 1:343; Leonard Curry, *Blueprint for Modern America* (Nashville: Vanderbilt University Press, 1968), 78, quoting the San Francisco *Daily Alta Californian*, August 18, 1861: "Constitutions are made for peace. We are at war, and we must make war and do it effectively, without regard to paper Constitutions."
48. The difficult congressmen had in finding grounds to justify confiscation illustrates the tenacious hold legal principles and categories exercised throughout the war. Competing views of the war's nature, whether rebellion or international conflict, shaped what powers the government might exercise over its traitorous citizens or, by the alternate view, enemy aliens. Confiscation of citizens' property, without conviction for treason, appeared unconstitutional and illegal on its face; confiscation of enemy aliens' property was a generally accepted right under international definitions of belligerent rights. Yet that stance also appeared to grant tacit recognition of the South's successful separation from the Union—the exact issue upon which the war was centered. The ambiguity and tension between the two views was accepted by government authorities both in the President's blockade proclamation and his July 4, 1861 message to Congress, Shapiro, *Confiscation*, 3-4; Randall, *Constitutional Problems*, ch. 13. See also the discussion in chapter four, below.
49. As Herman Belz rightly obdserves the slave confiscation clause did not "free" any slave, but denied legal title to the former master. Abolitionists emphasized the prevnetion of re-enslavement, noted below. But also note the tentative movement toward antislavery goals. Belz notwithstanding, the fact of first attack against slavery retains its importance, Herman Belz *A New Birth of Freedom* (Westport, Connecticut: Greenwood Press, 1976), 4-5.
50. "What Shall be done with the Slaves?" extract from the discourse of the Rev. W. J. Potter, Unitarian Church, New Bedford, Massachusetts, reprinted in *National Anti-Slavery Standard*, July 27, 1861.
51. Ibid., July 13, 27, 1861.

III

WHAT GOD AND NATURE DECREE:

ABOLITION IN THE DISTRICT OF COLUMBIA

Liberty for the slave remained more an abstract hope than an experienced reality when Congress reassembled on December 2, 1861. During the four months of recess from August through November, General George B. McClellan organized and polished his Army of the Potomac, eventually succeeding the elderly Winfield Scott as General-in-Chief. The *Trent* affair began with the capture of Confederate emissaries James Mason and John Slidell, a Union army met defeat at Balls Bluff, Virginia, and John C. Frémont lost his command in Missouri. Perhaps the most significant fact was the appreciable lack of military engagement, and the knowledge that a great offensive to end the war must now wait upon the spring. Even so, a spirit of possibilities greeted members of Congress as they returned to the seat of government—or rather, that spirit was upon them as they resumed their stewardship of the war effort.

The seat of government, the see city of the republic, presented the question: what spirit—liberty or slavery—would rule the city and, by implication, the country? Slavery could remain dominant by continued inaction, for Washington was a southern city, and slavery in the community was older than the city itself. Slavery's spirit would be manifest if rebeldom ever enlarged its territory northward by a mere few miles. And so, shortly after assuming the post of Secretary of War in January 1862, Edwin Stanton would write of his strong faith in the government's future—a faith not founded upon guns so much as upon the rock of God's will. "The powers of hell cannot prevail against it," Stanton proclaimed, hoping perhaps that his quotation of Matthew might engraft upon the government a bit of the permanence that the Christian Church had received.[1]

Congressmen shared Stanton's "undoubting faith" in the government's survival. Already members of the Unionist coalition were beginning to realize that to sustain the government, their faith had to be placed in a kind of country that had not heretofore existed.

Military necessity might demand novel responses, events might demand reactions. The remedies Congress considered were not always initiated because of their intrinsic merit. But the substance of America was already altered in the response to war.

As before the news from Fort Monroe, Virginia, continued to highlight the interaction between Union armies and fleeing slaves. Benjamin Butler, transferred to the Department of New England on October 1, had made arrangements with the American Missionary Society to begin the education of the contrabands held at the encampment. The society, founded upon the principle of preaching the Gospel "free from all complicity with slavery and caste" jumped at the chance to implement its philosophy—grounded in mutual respect, qualitative freedom, and racial integration. This fit well with the previous efforts Butler had encouraged among his troops. One of the Massachusetts volunteers at Fort Monroe, Edward L. Pierce, a lawyer and abolitionist, became superintendent for the contrabands. Watching over their work, securing food and housing, Pierce became an outspoken advocate for the contrabands.[2]

Upon completing his three month enlistment, Pierce returned to New England and prepared an article for the November issue of the *Atlantic Monthly*, detailing the contrabands' situation at Fort Monroe and giving his assessment. Pierce's legalistic analysis explored the varying perspectives with which the fleeing slaves might be viewed, noting that the question, what to do with the fugitives, was a "new question, and a grave one." Although the question of sojourner slaves (*Dred Scott v. Sandford*) and fugitive slave rendition (*Prigg v. Pennsylvania*) had received much attention, the "new question" Pierce referred to was the massive increase of slaves fleeing from traitorous masters. According to international law, slaves used in an auxiliary way to military operations might be prizes of war. Seizure by this method usually resulted by contact between a belligerent and a neutral power. The issue revolved around property caught between two belligerents. Pierce observed that under the law of nations all enemy alien property might be seized. Lest this grant too much to rebel claims of sovereignty, he noted also that the common law allowed the forfeiture of all traitors' property. These last alternatives, though strictly legal, were not in accord with modern, more humane practice. Nevertheless, the right to confiscate property "immediately auxiliary" to military purposes was unquestionable, in Pierce's opinion. Regarding slaves as property, Pierce concluded they could be confiscated, thereby sustaining the 1861 Confiscation Act. If, however, more delicate souls balked at the expedient of calling slaves property for the opportunity of freeing them, Pierce provided another answer. By their approach to Union lines, the fugitive slaves proved themselves loyal to the federal government. They were among the few loyal persons in the South, and asked for the government's protection. With this view of the contraband, Pierce gave a most hopeful definition for the fugitives. Contrabands were "negroes who had been held as slaves, now adopted, under the protection of the government."[3]

By defining contraband Negroes as slaves, Pierce seemed to hedge about their final legal status. The more significant part of his rule, however, lay with the protection the federal government now exercised over them. State authority was nowhere to be found, and in its stead was a striking new, direct link between the federal government and the individual.

Moreover, Pierce's reluctance forthrightly to declare contraband Negroes to be "freemen" appears to have been more a matter of political expedience. Noting that conservatives preferred to confiscate slaves rather than emancipate, and to call blacks contraband rather than freemen, Pierce thought "contraband" a useful, legal term that helped to move public opinion along when it might otherwise balk at a noble formula.[4] The 1861 Confiscation Act directed the civil authority in its dealings with fugitive southern slaves, and legitimized the military's practice, but did not, in Pierce's opinion, limit in any way actions derived from the war power. "That law," he wrote, "founded on *salus reipublica* [sic], transcends all codes, and lies outside of forms and statutes." Fears of border state reaction prompted restraint, like the revocation of Frémont's emancipation edict in Missouri, strong from the Union coalition's reluctance to shed the "fine-drawn distinctions of peaceful times." Unionists allowed themselves the power to kill or imprison a rebel but not to "unloose his hold on a person he has claimed as a slave. . . . This reverence for things assumed to be sacred, which are not so, cannot long continue."[5]

Divergent elements within the Unionist coalition were coming to agree with Pierce that slavery, more often recognized as the underlying cause of the rebellion and war, had to be dealt with. Slavery was the "Goliath of the Rebellion," according to Charles Sumner. Yet what to do and exactly how to strike at the mainspring of treason remained complex and controversial. The Washington *National Intelligencer*, a conservative organ and no friend of the freedman, pinpointed the problem early in December 1861. Any solution to the slavery problem involved a "question of race as well as a question of political and civil status. . . . " Even with slavery gone, the *National Intelligencer*'s editor believed, race "imbedded as it is in great historical laws" would continue to keep black subordinate to white. The *National Intelligencer* prominently featured articles on Liberia and Negro colonization during this time, expressing the view that the "Negro question" was unsolvable within America. Freedom for blacks would create horrible problems between the races. Emancipation, if it came, would have to be accompanied by colonization, for the good of both races.[6]

The contrast between that view of the future and Edward Pierce's was striking. Pierce recalled the courage that the contrabands at Fort Monroe had exhibited. Whatever the war's ultimate conclusion, Pierce firmly believed that every fugitive slave who defended the Union "had vindicated beyond all future question—for himself, his wife, and their issue—a title to American citizenship, and become heir to all the immunities of Magna Charta [sic], the Declaration of Independence, and the Constitution of the United States."[7]

Thus were the two choices presented. The hope of liberty did not only confront the spirit of slavery, but also that of race. Long before there was consensus to strike forthrightly at the heart of rebellion, the subsidiary and, in truth, more profound question of the quality of freedom emerged. In the process of attacking slavery, the coalition that could agree to attack, often disintegrated when faced with the consequences of its intended victory. What was freedom—what would the war mean—what did the Constitution allow—demand? The Constitution did not expressly say. So experience would have to.[8]

Different conceptions of the Union, what it was, what it ought to be, necessarily led to competing views of what the Constitution allowed and demanded. Conservatives, border state men and northern Democrats, continued to emphasize the pre-war distinctions Edward Pierce found anachronistic. Government, especially the federal government, was not an innovator, protector, or locus of power. The Bill of Rights was a lits of wrongs that the federal government could not commit against the states or their citizens. At the other extreme of the Unionist coalition were abolitionist war advocates. They had had little use for the Constitution before the war, and now they perceived events opening the way for radical changes in constitutional substance. Wendell Phillips wryly commented on his own, rather abrupt, conversion from castigator to defender of the Union and Constitution: "Do you supposed I am not Yankee enough to buy union when I can have it at a fair price?"[9] They key was Phillips' belief that the nation's reality had to have a bearing upon the Constitution's meaning. Months later he would make the point explicit:

> Now, I love the Constitution, though my friend . . . who sits besides me, has heard me *curse it* a hundred times, and I shall again if it does not mean justice.[10]

Radical abolitionists often commented on their coalition partners' reverence for the Constitution. They just called it idolatry. The Union founded upon the Constitution of 1787 was a pro-slavery union, and as long as the North clung to the Constitution's strictures and spirit, it would also fight for the slave power. All of which prompted Gerrit Smith to write that the North's first concern ought to be saving the country. What Smith meant by country became clear when he continued, "that saved, and we can restore the old Constitution or make a new one, but that lost and we shall have no need of either."[11] Constitutional form seemed less important than the country's fundamental moral stance, and with that corrected, any constitution might do.

Not all abolitionists were as flippant with form nor so willing to distinguish it from substance. Henry Ward Beecher, accepting a prewar view of constitutional allowances, wished that Congress could abolish slavery. But Beecher did not believe the North should violate the letter of the Constitution in order to defeat those who would destroy it. To violate its rule would be an admission of the failure of American institutions. If events proved the Constitution unworkable, then the war was already lost, and the nation lost.[12]

Somewhere in the middle of spectrum, too antislavery for conservatives, and much too moderate for radicals, was the President. Profoundly respectful of the Constitution and aware of his oath to "preserve, protect and defend" it, Lincoln had neither the blind, unswerving faith in form of the conservative, nor the firey exhilaration of the radical prophet. He was by nature and by constitutional opinion, a man of principle willing to deal with realities. Writing in January 1861, before the tremendous events later that year, Lincoln observed how the Constitution and Union were necessary to the United States, and yet, were not the primary reason for the nation's great prosperity. "There is something back of these, entwining itself more closely about the human heart. That something, is the principle of 'Liberty to all.' "[13] Lincoln clearly preferred to keep government practice as closely as that of peace as possible. Just as clearly, he was willing to modify or abandon tradition and opinion for sufficient reason. Lincoln sought consensus among the divergent viewpoints represented with the Unionist coalition that he led. No doubt disturbing to him, and positively terrifying to conservatives, consensus continued to emerge further and further down the road that radicals advocated. Gradually but perceptibly, the middle range of coalition opinion became increasingly radical. Lincoln was not "driven" to emancipation, but no one denied that was there the government was "drifting."[14]

Nevertheless, emancipation without regard to Constitution and law gained little support. leaders of government, most of whom were lawyers, were unwilling to journey too far beyond accustomed form.

Law defined liberty, as Harvard College student Eldridge C. Cutler suggested: "O Law, fair form of liberty, God's very light is ont hey brow—O Liberty, the soul of law, God's very self art thou."[15]

It was the latter senitment that radicals had the greater difficulty believing. Too often had they seen lawyers exhibit a soul of subservience to interest and financial reward rather that to the spirit of liberty. They were distrustful of those in power who might well use their expertise to steal the soul of freedom from congressional action, leaving a hollow and debilitating husk in its place. Still, abolitionists recognized that it was Congress that had to act upon war, slavery, and freedom. Like the President, congressmen also demonstrated willingness to synthesize new answers for new situations. But life-long dedications and familiar concepts and language could not be jettisoned, only adapted. Student Cutler was correct when he wrote of law and liberty. "Friends whom we cannot think apart, seeming each others foe—Twin flowers upon a single stalk, with equal grace that grow." The war had to be fought and win on the context of law and Constitution, not from mere adherence to form, but from a genuine faith that liberty had no meaning outside of a legal framework. America defined herself in a legal medium. Thus to save the country "the majesty of law must be vindicated and upheld."[16]

The experiment of abolition began in the District of Columbia. The Confiscation Act of August 1861 only affected slaves used for insurrectionary purposes, and then only as they came within Union lines. Whether those blacks were freedmen or contraband was left too much to public sensibilities, as Edward Pierce observed. Even if confiscated slaves were freed, even if all rebel-held slaves were freed, the system of slavery remained. Emancipation of specific slaves did not abolish the legal arrangement or holding property in human beings. The realization that slavery caused the rebellion referred not just to the act of holding slaves. Slavery was also the social, political, economic, and spiritual power slaveholders exercised over the nation. To defeat the South, slavery as an act and as a system had to be attacked. How this might be accomplished in the least disturbing way was the question congressmen faced within their own day to day hearing and seeing. Long a target of abolitionists, the end of slavery at the seat of the American government began in December 1861. Possessing clear power to legislate in "all cases whatsoever," Congress made the District of Columbia an experiment for the nation. There slavery was attacked directly; there it was first destroyed.[17]

Slavery in the District of Columbia existed more as a symbol of a larger reality than as a major institution in itself. Of the 14,316 blacks living within the District in 1860, only 3185 were slaves. Surrounded by Maryland and Virginia, the District's importance to southerners and northerners was apparent. Southerners feared an oasis of freedom in the midst of bondage, as abolitionists had long dreamed, would surely reduce the District to a fugitives' haven. Even now during the war, with Virginian sensibilities not in high regard, Marylanders worried over the possiblity of a freedom too close for comfort. The border land sentiment of defeating the rebellion but not disturbing social arrangements was aptly mimicked by an antislavery wag when he produced new lyrics to the tune "Yankee Doodle":[18]

Old Fogies sing on every hand—
The little men and bigger;
Wage war against the rebel band,
But do not touch 'the Nigger!'

Strike any other mortal blow
And use extremest rigor
But, lest you 'irritate the foe,'
Oh, do not touch 'the Nigger!'

Circumstance, however, demanded congressional attention, and the House of Representatives signaled its willingness to accept responsibility by its pointed refusal to reaffirm the Crittenden-Johnson Resolutions of the previous July. Those resolutions pledged the government not to overthrow or interfere with the "rights or established institutions of the States," that is, slavery. Confiscation had breached the principle in any event, and upon Thaddeus Stevens' motion, the House tabled and killed the attempted renewal of the resolves. On the same day, December 4, Henry Wilson introduced n the Senate a joint resolution aimed at releasing some 60 fugitives interned in the District's jail, charged with no crime, but held only on suspicion of being fugitive slaves.[19]

What to do with fugitive slaves was a key question in early December. Antislavery men in Congress had little desire to put the army in the fugitive slave business, arresting slaves they ought to be confiscating. The Administration had directed General McClellan to confiscate escaping slaves reaching his lines, but District officials continued to arrest fleeing slaves as fugitives. Responding to this, Secretary Seward ordered that persons arresting escapees as fugitives be themselves arrested by the army. Slavery might yet exist in the District of Columbia, but neither the Administration nor antislavery congressmen wanted the fugitive slave law rigorously enforced in the nation's capital. Neither did they want the District's jailers to negate confiscation. Jails were intended for criminals and, despite the efforts of the District marshal and warden, not to control the slave and freedmen population.[20]

Senators Wilson and Sumner were particularly intent upon questioning the whole system of justice as practiced in the District. They cited the black codes then in force as an example of the system's inherent evil, and Wilson offered a resolution reviewing all laws regarding blacks, suggesting the expediency of abolition within the District of Columbia. William P. Fessenden, a moderate Republican from Maine, agreed that a complete overhaul of the system of justice at the seat of government was in order. Because of the proximity of thousands of potential contrabands, and because the marshal of the District continued to presume blacks to be slaves, Congress had to address the question of slavery in the District.[21]

At precisely the same time, leading antislavery figures in and out of Congress were more forcefully making their argument against slavery. With President Lincoln in attendance on December 11, Charles Sumner eulogized his former colleague Edward D. Baker, a Union officer killed at Balls Bluff. There was no need to appoint a committee to discover Baker's killer, Sumner declared. The guns and the men at the battle were of little importance in his friend's death. It was the power behind the men and guns, behind the rebellion, that had taken Baker's life. That power was slavery. In the President's hearing Sumner named the killer—no, the murderer. So heinous an evil, slavery was now also taking the lives of white men, as it had always oppressed the lives of blacks.[22]

Gerrit Smith wrote Representative John Gurley (R, Ohio) criticizing the special powers Gurley wanted the government to assume over the liberated slaves. "The greatest sin of our country," Smith wrote, " . . . is the assumption of special powers by her white race over her other races." A mass removal of freedmen to the unfavorable climate and soil of southern Florida, as Gurley advocated, would doom the freedmen to failure and ordain future oppression. Rights should be equal regardless of race, Smith emphasized. Congress must not only abolish slavery, but entrust blacks with "all the rights of manhood."[23]

No longer could leaders presume to make rules for freedmen without some acknowledgment of their right to be consulted and to decide about their own future. Antislavery leaders began regular lectures at the Smithsonian Institution in Washington, featuring Horace Greeley and Wendell Phillips. The government ordered Washington police not to capture fugitive slaves. All the antislavery arguments, speeches, and hopes reached a central conclusion: slavery was based upon, and had become in itself, a dehumanizing philosophy. It enslaved millions. In slavery's attempt to attain absolute supremacy, it dehumanized whites, first by leading them into the sin of racism, and then by killing them in civil war. Charles Sumner's point was exactly this—rebels did not kill northern soldiers, slavery did. Treason did not threaten the Union, slavery did. Slavery was anti-human and had become malignantly anti-Union. Lincoln pondered what he had heard, what went on around him, and sought a scalpel for the cancer.[24]

In January 1862, fugitive slaves were again the medium by which Congress discussed slavery in the District. James Grimes of Iowa called up a resolution reforming the District's system of justice and discharging all unindicted persons in the District jails. Kentucky's Lazarus Powell tried to amend the resolution by excluding fugitive slaves from the dismissal order. In answer to Powell, Grimes pointed out the injustice of the existing system that gave cash incentives to District officials to capture and imprison every Negro they saw as a fugitive. Fellow Republican Lot Morrill observed that the judicial reform resolution was not emancipation by simply a dismissal from imprisonment. Conservative Maryland senator James Pearce agreed Morrill, asking for a more precise wording to clarify the resolution's meaning. Yet the resolution's relationship to slavery in the District was clear to all.[25]

Powell travelled remarkable lengths (at least rhetorically) to safeguard slavery. The Kentuckian argued that a black suspected of being a fugitive slave, and therefore imprisoned, could always sue for a writ of habeas corpus to secure a hearing on his freedom. Jacob Collamer (R, Vermont), in disbelief at what he had just heard, rose and inquired whether Powell accepted the *Dred Scott* decision, in which Chief Justice Roger B. Taney had declared that a black person had no rights that white men were bound to respect. Powell's answer, surprising in light of contemporary thinking and subsequent events, was to distinguish political from civil rights. The Court referred only to political rights in its 1857 decision, Powell maintained. Civil rights were unmentioned and, presumably, unimpaired. The distinction, though plausible, must have sounded disingenuous to congressmen, for the Senate overwhelmingly defeated Powell's amendment to exclude suspected fugitive slaves from the discharge order. White southern endorsement of civil rights for free blacks was barely imaginable, and not from Lazarus Powell. With slight modification, the bill to discharge the jail's occupants passed the Senate 31 to 4.[26] Although the measure was soon lost in the House, subsequent congressional attention to slavery in the District was more determined. By its adoption of Grimes' bill, the Senate had demonstrated its willingness to legislate on the subject of slavery. Yet District marshal Ward H. Lamon had not noted the changed feeling regarding slavery. His behavior, which had heretofore been the expected, now was found insolent and unacceptable. As the possibility and desirability of "transforming every slave into a man and a freeman, henceforth to be protected as such under the national ensign" was openly stated and advocated, even those who did not agree with such a far-reaching proposal sensed the changed atmosphere that allowed the proposal to be made in the first place. Commenting on Dr. Henry T. Cheever's antislavery lecture at the Smithsonian, the *National Anti-Slavery Standard*'s Washington correspondent summed up the situation: "It will seemd hard to go back to the Old Union, if the slavemasters and their manners are to come back with it!"[27]

Several bills to abolish slavery in the District of Columbia were introduced at the beginning of the session. Attention focused immediately upon the fugitive slave issue both for its more emotional appeal and its safety. Lazarus Powell had been only partially correct in his objection to the Grimes' resolution discharging fugitives in area jails. The discharge would have been only a glancing blow at slavery, and Republicans were only willing to take that tentative step. Outright abolition was a momentous step, and the fear of border state reaction dampened antislavery initiative.[28]

As January passed into February the general feeling was that the time was approaching when the government must crush the rebellion or acknowledge the separation as final. Abolitionists still welcomed the war for the possibilities it brought forward, but they showed increased concern that compromise might yet deny the necessity of striking at slavery. This danger of a "miserable patch-up" with the Confederacy doubtless spurred antislavery leaders in Congress to act while they were able. As with the fugitive slave dischargement bill, the Senate was more willing to act against slavery than the House. On February 13, the upper chamber reported Henry Wilson's bill to abolish slavery in the District, and began consideration as in Committee of the Whole.[29]

The bill was slightly altered from Wilson's original, first introduced on December 16. Its major feature remained intact, however. S. No. 108 abolished slavery in the District and granted compensation to slave owners. Some Republicans opposed compensation, yet it was generally conceded that payment to loyal masters was a necessary provision to secure passage in the more conservative House. The Senate took up Wilson's bill on February 27, and scheduled debate for the following week.[30]

Wilson introduced another bill at the same time, and it is important to understand his abolition measure. On the 24th of February Wilson called up his bill to repeal "certain laws and ordinances in the District of Columbia relating to persons of color," that is, the District's black code. The Maryland state law on slavery and color discrimination had been extended over the District when it was first founded, thereby sanctioning slavery. It was used later to discriminate against District blacks, both slave and free. Wilson's bill repealed it outright, and would have specifically withdrawn authority from the Washington and Georgetown city councils to legislate about blacks. Previously enacted municipal race laws would, thereby, also be voided. Finally, the measure required equal treatment before the law for whites and blacks.

Wilson's language aimed toward repealing the effects and concomitant attributes of slavery rather than positively secure rights for blacks. The races would be equal before the law as the logical result of the black code's repeal. Abolitionists outside government had already raised the issue of the post-slavery status of blacks, positing a somewhat hazy vision of a color-blind society. They noted Wilson's proposal to repeal the black code, and called it "of full equal importance" with his abolition bill. The repeal of the black codes, linked with Wilson's abolition bill, was the first attempt to give legal force to the abolitionist vision, to legitimate a policy spoken of only in radical circles. It gave an important definition of freedom for the freedmen and confirmed the long-held view that slavery could not exit without positive law to protect it. Freedom, on the other hand, was natural and required no special legislation. Wilson's two bills suggested that the abolition of slavery meant something more than a limbo world of free and not equal.[31]

Before the Senate debated Wilson's abolition bill, the President sent to Congress his solution for the slavery problem. Briefly, Lincoln invited the individual states to begin gradual, compensated emancipation, with the federal government paying the cost. Two serious differences between this proposal and Wilson's, aside from the national reach of Lincoln's idea, were the locus of power, and the time required for that power to work. Under Lincoln's proposal, the states, and not Congress, were the agents of emancipation; the federal government's presence would be limited to that of accountant only. This hardly created the protector's role that abolitionists contemplated. Perhaps of more importance, state-sponsored emancipation would require years to complete, so as not to disturb unduly the social and economic fabric of the border states. Lincoln's proposal was marked by constitutional principles and a need to assert control over events. Yet, if anything was true about the first year of the war, it was the power of events to shape and force change from often unwilling participants. Abolitionists recognized this and applauded; conservatives recognized and trembled.

"The power of events more might than President or Congress" were at work. Lincoln's gradual, compensated, state-sponsored emancipation plan was duly noted, commented upon, and sent to the states. The same powerful events that had allowed any attack upon slavery, allowed Lincoln to propose this plan. And yet, Lincoln's plan of gradual, compensated emancipation only obscured the horizon; in a real sense, it was irrelevant.[32]

In the renewed bitterness that the antislavery measures engendered between radicals and more conservative members of the Unionist coalition, Congress finally debated the District abolition bill. The New York *Times*, in support of Lincoln's gradualism, assured its readers that slavery would never resume its former power, although the *Times* did not assume slavery's total destruction. The *Liberator* warned against an evasion by the President or Congress of the solemn duty to proclaim liberty. And a great emancipation meeting at the Cooper Institute in New York heard letters read from senators Sumner, Wilson, and David Wilmot (R, Pennsylvania) calling for new vigor in the fight against slavery, the "omnipresent traitor."[33] Wilmot, the man who had lent his name to the anti-extension of slavery proviso which became the heart of Republican pre-war ideology, boldy stated Congress' duty to "uproot and eradicate forever any local institution, law, custom, usage" that endangered the country. He meant slavery. Sumner, already proposed a theory of reconstruction, remarked that if slavery had not died by the rebel states' suicide, Congress might prohibit the peculiar institution by using the language of the Northwest Ordinance.[34]

As debate on Wilson's abolition bill began, the Senate agreed to the first amendment proposed by the District committee, rephrasing S. No. 108 to emancipate those person held to service "by reason of African descent." Then, using the Northwest Ordinance as a model, ordering that "neither slavery not involuntary servitude" would be allowed within the federal district. Compensation was set at $300/slave for loyal maser who filed for payment. Other committee amendments included making attempted re-enslavement a felony (with a five to twenty year prison sentence), and a repeal of all acts of Congress or Maryland (extend over the District) inconsistent with the abolition of slavery.[35]

Immediately upon the Senate's consideration of the bill, Garret Davis (D, Kentucky), a noted conservative, moved to amend the proposal by forcing colonization of all District freedmen. Claiming that he knew well the "negro nature," Davis argued that freedom would guarantee freedmen's indolence and lead to a race war. Fearing the general policy of emancipation without compulsory colonization, the border state senator prophesied a future time when southerners would deal with liberated slaves remaining in the United States: "the moment you reorganize the white inhabitants of those [southern] States as State of the Union, they would reduce those slaves again to a status of slavery."[36]

There was no concern for ex-slaves in Davis' remarks; the obvious intent of his amendment was to kill District abolition by attaching to it mandatory colonization. The importance of Davis' prophecy lay in the educational value it held for Republicans. The intransigence with which Davis and others fought any attack upon slavery and the forthright announcement of southern intentions to overturn, at the end of the war, whatever antislavery measures had been taken, must have deeply impressed congressmen in 1862. Davis' and other similar predictions, together with subsequent actions in Congress and across the nation, helped to shape Republican attitudes about abolition and the quality of freedom for freed blacks. Davis' one remark might have appeared isolated and been forgotten, had not a long four year history of war and post-war actions confirmed southern intransigence in every detail.

The Senate resumed consideration of S. No. 108 on March 18. Davis' amendment for compulsory colonization was itself amended by James Doolittle (R, Wisconsin), whose addition made the colonization feature subject to the freedman's choice. Senator John Hale (R, New Hampshire), a long-time antislavery leader in Congress, urged the senators around him to do what was right and not draw back from abolition because of possible negative consequences. Fear was no reason to forestall freedom.

These three senators, Davis, Doolittle, and Hale, saw the District abolition bill as an experiment for the nation, yet each approached the experiment's consequences with different expectations and predictions. Davis opposed abolition. Hale favored it. But the issue was not so clear cut for James Doolittle. He strongly supported freely chosen colonization, but also accepted in great degree radical notions about the quality of freedom. The Wisconsin senator declared that the freedom given the slaves ought to be more than "a thing in name, it should be a thing in substance, freedom in fact." For that kind of freedom the slave had to be freed from his master and from the control of white racism. This was a succinct statement of the abolitionist theory and program. Yet Doolittle also accepted the reality of Garret Davis' America, believing that the qualitative freedom he desired for the ex-slave could not be created within the United States. The antagonsim between the races was too great, southerners' intransigence too pronounced, and Doolittle's own faith in the future too weak, to allow him to believe in the possibility of freedom for the black in America. Even those who wanted substantive freedom for blacks had to reckon with the "negro hate" endemic to the American political and social environment. Antislavery men had to deal with conservatives who wanted the Union preserved as the time-tested means of protecting slavery. To drive hate from them would take a might act. "Not even death or hell could do it," wrote one abolitionist, "in fact only God alone by a miracle can do it."[37] In the absence of that miracle, James Doolittle abandoned hope.

Despite warnings from border state men that abolition at the seat of government would drive their constituents out of the Union, the Senate adopted Doolittle's amendment to Davis' colonization proposal. It was a compromise to bring into the abolition coalition some conservative elements. Members of the most conservative and most radical camps opposed Doolittle's amendment. Yet, once having adopted Doolittle's ameliorating language, the Senate defeated the entire colonization proposal in a tie, with Vice-President Hannibal Hamlin casting the deciding vote. But the episode showed the Senate's sympathy for some form of colonization, and its less than full endorsement of immediate, unconditional abolition.[38]

Although losing the first round, Garret Davis and his conservative colleagues were unwilling to concede the issue. The goals of the war were changing, Davis charged, in direct contradiction to the pledge of the old Crittenden-Johnson Resolutions. Republican senators were experimenting with the District to see how far moderate men might go along the radical path; abolition in the District was only the "entering wedge" for universal abolition. "You want to get the head in, and then you intend to push the monster through," Delaware's Willard Saulsbury declared. Representing the least populous slave state and the state with the fewest slaves, Saulsbury demonstrated his unqualified commitment to the idea of slavery by introducing an amendment to require freed District slaves to emigrate to free states within thirty days of their release from servitude. Clearly, this was a delaying tactic, and one meant to embarrass Republicans by pointing up northern racism.[39]

Republican perceptions and expectations for abolition were interesting in the light of conservative opposition. There were apparent divisions between radical and moderate elements within the party. Henry WIlson spoke against a Washington city ordinance that presumed color as a sign of slavery. Abolition, Wilson argued, would convert personal chattel into free men and wipe out hateful laws that oppressed all blacks, slave or free. Remembering Wilson's sponsorship of the anti-black code bill, his view of freedom appeared broad and comprehensive.[40] Thus, his repealer of the black code would only make explicit what he believed abolition itself would achieve.

On the other hand, there was James Doolittle, already discussed. Men like Iowa Republican occupied a middle position. Harlan carefully emphasized the limited scope of freedom gained by abolition, particularly noting the lack of political rights and the franchise. Freedom required "simply the right to enjoy as they [freedmen] choose the proceeds of their own labor." Yet Harlan's "simple right" appeared hardly simple at all to conservatives who looked backward to the days when blacks had "no rights which the white man was bound to respect." Harlan's "simple right" was nothing less than the foundation principle of American middle class society. Each person reaped the benefits of his own work. Harlan himself made clear the implications of his view when he criticized the fears of border state senators Saulsbury and Anthony Kennedy (D, Maryland). Instead of the race war they predicted after abolition, why should not the government protect the ex-slaves if in fact they were the weaker elements of society? Would not whites do as much for the weaker members of their own race, Harlan asked. Although Harlan did not specify whether the locus of protection might originate at the state or federal level, the idea of government intervention for the protection of blacks was novel, innovative, and, depending upon perspective, entirely hopeful or despairing. Republican moderates were open to the new situations the war created and their position allowed for movement toward a more radical vision. In attempting to delimit political freedom, Harlan endorsed an activist government role to protect the freedmen in their civil freedom. One can imagine border state and conservative fears when moderates like Harlan, in explaining their moderation, ended up being radical. But that was the nature of the war.[41]

To be sure, other Republicans expressed no sympathy with innovative concepts of freedom and refrained from seeing any wider implication for abolition in the nation. Yet all acknowledged S. No. 108's importance. While its provisions might not meet exact hopes and philosophies, it was acceptable to a broad antislavery coalition in Congress, No less a radical than Charles Sumner, a man who gloried in his own prophecy, saw the incremental nature of abolition in the District of Columbia. Sumner supported compensation for loyal masters not from any belief in the slaveholder's right to reimbursement, but from the knowledge that Congress must act "in the light of existing usages, and even existing prejudices, under which these odious relations [slavery] have assumed the force of law." Sumner's magnanimity doubtless resulted in part from confidence that the votes existed to abolish slavery in the federal district, and he was careful to distinguish compensation (which he supported) from ramson (which he opposed).

Once slavery was gone, Sumner believed, a fundamental change would occur in America. Society, courts, and laws would be refined, purified, and elevated. Like his Massachusetts colleague Henry Wilson, Sumner also envisioned the dawn of substantive freedom for blacks—marking them not as ex-slaves (freedmen), but as co-heirs with whites of the possibility of America—free men; "What God and Nature decree rebellion cannot arrest."[42]

The length and depth of feeling connected with the Senate's debate on abolition highlighted the bill's importance. the pro-colonization *National Intelligencer* noted that both supporters and foes of the measure saw it as something more than its specific provisions, either as an "entering wedge" for more radical projects, or a symbolic "ban of interdict" against the social system of the slaveholding states. The *National Intelligencer*, like other supporters of Lincoln's gradual, compensated, state-sponsored emancipation, did not question congressional power to abolish slavery in the District, only congressional wisdom. Noting that the District's Board of Aldermen opposed abolition and found the District "an asylum for free negroes, a population undesirable in every American community," the newspaper urged referral of any abolition bill to the people of the District for their concurrence. Although left unstated, such a move would have been the death of abolition, for the District's whites (the only qualified voters) would never approve the measure. When Senator Waitman T. Willey (Unionist, Virginia) proposed a District referendum on abolition, the Senate rejected the amendment convincingly.[43]

Various attempts were made to amend S. No. 108 while in Committee of the Whole. Originally, no provision was included for enforcement of freedom for the ex-slaves. The assumption that color was a sign of slave status would be abrogated in the District, and that would be enough. Nor was there provision for government intervention to secure freedmen's rights. abolition destroyed slavery, and with slavery gone, freedom and rights revived automatically. Blacks would then take care of themselves, so the thinking went. But gradually, this absolute laissez-faire attitude toward freedom was modified. The abolitionist concept of a bi-polar world of free or slave,without any room for areas of gray worked in theory (and certainly was the ideal of many in and out of Congress). But by their training as lawyers and their profession as legislators, congressmen were pre-disposed to establish some rules for protecting blacks in their newly won freedom. Therefore, amendments were added to S. No. 108 which secured freedmen the right to testify at compensation board hearings, thereby safeguarding their interest in freedom and providing a check against payment to disloyal slaveholders. Ex-slaves would receive certificates of freedom, not because they would be needed in the District, but in recognition of the continuing slave system of surrounding Maryland and loyal Virginia.[44]

On April 3, S. No. 108 came to the Senate proper from the Committee of the Whole. Just prior to passage, James Doolittle successfully attached his colonization amendment to the bill, authorizing $100,000 for the voluntary resettlement of the District's blacks. The amendment passed the Senate 27 to 10, all ten negative votes coming from Republicans. So, as S. No. 108 stood before the final vote, moderates had demanded and received two significant concessions. Loyal masters would be compensated for the loss of their slave property, and colonization of ex-slaves remained a possible solution to the question of their future. Radicals managed to retain only one part—though a key one—of the original proposal—abolition would be immediate.[45]

But these compromise were insufficient (nor were they ever really intended) to win over die-hard conservatives. Both Lazarus Powell and James Bayard (D, Delaware) made long anti-abolition speeches, despite the majority now solidified behind abolition. In his final effort to halt passage, Bayard called his colleagues back to a consideration of the founding principles of the republic. He did not suppose that Americans of 1862 were more moral, or wise, or understood constitutional law better than did their forefathers. Those past leaders wold not approve what was about to happen. They would not understand, as Bayard did not understand, a perspective oriented toward the new rather than the old, toward the possible and not the impossible, from the forefathers themselves to the present generation and its children. The past no longer exercised its iron rule upon the needs of the present. Bayard and his compatriots did not grasp the point, had in fact been caught up in history, and were not being left behind. But those with eyes had seen and with ears had heard; a majority of the Senate had seen and heard. On April 3, the Senate passed the bill abolishing slavery in the District of Columbia by a vote of 29 to 14. The New York *Tribune* put it squarely: "The world *does* move."[46]

The abolition bill went ot the House of Representatives amid conservatives' undying hopes that drastic alterations might yet be made, and amid radical trumpeting of the bill as a turning point in the fight against slavery.[47] The members of the House confronted novel and momentous questions and they would have to apply the Constitution to the "new condition of things." Representative Benjamin F. Thomas (R, Massachusetts) was content to allow the executive, acting through the war power, to attack slavery in the rebel states. Where Congress had power, as in the territories and the District, it should act. While supporting abolition, congressman John T. Nixon (R, New Jersey) preferred a gradual approach. Even so, Nixon warned, the slave power must not expect unlimited conciliation. The South had to be taught that the Union would be preserved. To accomplish that goal, every slave might be armed against his master, and every white driven from the Gulf Coast. The South would become a land of enfranchised Negroes. Of course, this was not Nixon's recommended policy. Rather, it was the limit to which he would go to save the nation. Rhetorically at least, it was far indeed.[48]

Francis P. Blair (R, Missouri), the first Republican congressman elected in a slave state, exhibited the racial tension that permeated segments of the northern alliance. Blair favored emancipation but only with colonization. The rebellion, Blair maintained, did not start over the slave question but over the racial issue of Negro equality. Southerners feared forced emancipation and subsequent amalgamation, and rebelled in order to preserve white superiority. Put that way, it was easier to understand the war that raged across the nation; it would have been a crime *not* to have rebelled if preservation of white superiority was the goal. Blair's own racial attitude was limiting that he, like other proponents of colonization, could not conceive of freedom for the ex-slave protected by law alone without the moral sense of the people backing equality. How long would the North support an army trying to make the races equal? Blair doubted the effectiveness of law or arms as means of maintaining the freedmen's liberty. Proponents of colonization observed and/or shared their countrymen's despair over coexistence between the races. Although supporting colonization, Blair assumed that there would be both government intervention by law to secure liberty and also efforts to create some type of equality between the races. He believed those efforts doomed to failure, but he did not argue against a non-existent alternative.[49]

John J. Crittenden, among others, opposed abolition, fearing alternately the effect it would have on white southerners, and on the slaves themselves. "Men cannot learn to be freemen while they are slaves," said Representative Edward H. Rollins (R, New Hampshire), putting aside the antislavery argument that freedom was natural and inherent, and that slavery was a condition learned only through positive law. Congress extended that positive law over the District early in the century. If Congress now abolished it, the natural condition of the person would be restored. The Constitution was a "new Magna Carta to mankind," according to Judiciary Committee chairman John Bingham. The original Magna Carta pertained to freemen only; the Constitution was broader and applied to all persons. Bingham believed "person" referred to slaves as well as free. Rights to life and liberty were held equally before the law, and the slave, who Bingham believed to be a natural born citizen, possessed those rights. Citizenship did not depend upon possession of the franchise or eligibility for office. These privileges might flow from citizenship, but could not define it. After all, women and children did not vote, yet they were undeniably citizens. The principles founded in the teachings of Jesus and the Declaration of Independence—that all are created equal—was also implicit in the Constitution, Bingham believed. Abolition would, according to like-minded congressman Samuel C. Fessenden (R, Maine), transform the slave whose rights were denied into a free man with rights "upon which none can trespass with impunity." Free people, black and white, would be secured in their freedom by the same shield of the "nation's majesty."[50]

James Ashley (R, Ohio), who had worked with Senator Morrill in framing the abolition bill, disliked some of the Senate's amendments, especially the colonization feature. Still, he urged the House and all friends of emancipation to support the bill. Resistance to abolition in the District was futile. "God is marching on," Ashley concluded, quoting from Julia Ward Howe's new poem, "Battle Hymn of the Republic." Owen Lovejoy, a staunch antislavery leader, voiced the emergent consensus against slavery, founded upon a shifting mixture of constitutionalism, law, and moral principle: "I am tired of all the twaddle about due process of law for the master when everybody knows that every slave in the District of Columbia and in the United States has been robbed of his freedom without due process of law." After only two days of debate on the House floor, the abolition bill passed 92 to 38. Negative votes came from Democrats and other conservatives who had unsuccessfully tried (as in the Senate) to kill the measure by adding on a mandatory referendum clause. Unyielding though they were, conservatives in the House could not change the inescapable fact that the war had significantly altered the realm of the possible, and had given those who were willing to act, the chance to act.[51]

"Let Ethiopia lift up her hands to God, for a great good is coming out of this war," exclaimed the black minister at Washington's Bethel Church. In the shadow of the Capitol, two to three hundred blacks gathered to give thanks for their liberation with such exuberance that one white man present called it "a spectacle for men and angels." Antislavery leaders shared a similar enthusiasm for the dawn of freedom, the new presumption of liberty rather than slavery. Confident of the President's approval of the bill despite its immediate rather than gradual approach, they believed that abolition in the District was the first profound result of the war. In the face of the suffering and misery already experienced and that yet to come, "I thanked God even for this war," wrote a correspondent to the New York *Tribune*. The continued suffering would, indeed, have its purpose, as the Washington columnist for the *National Anti-Slavery Standard* noted; abolition in the District of Columbia was only the first step of the government toward "universal emancipation."[52]

Conservatives accepted the abolition of slavery in the District with resignation and unceasing fear about the future. Both the Washington *National Intelligencer* and the New York *Times* had supported gradual rather than immediate abolition. Both now expected severe disruptions in District society. Slavery might well be doomed as an institution, but "turning loose" two thousand slaves unprepared for freedom, betrayed their fundamental views. They were afraid for white society and government. Members of the Unionist coalition who tolerated abolition as long as it took years for fulfillment or if it was coupled with colonization, shared the backward looking and essentially pessimistic psychology of pro-slavery advocates, at least to the extent that each group despaired over a future linked to abolition. Pro-slavery forces rejected emancipation and abolition outright; gradualists and colonizationists were forced to accept abolition, but did not like it. The interplay between these conservative elements of the northern coalition with the more moderate and radical members provides a key for understanding the Union's steady acceptance of emancipation, abolition, and freedom. As the North looked for more effective means to defeat the South, the Republican-abolitionist notion of the "slave power" suggested the area to strike.[53]

Yet the fears of the future illustrated the tension that existed not only within the political coalition ruling the North, but also within northern society. A correspondent of Treasury Secretary Salmon Chase, though favoring the District abolition bill, proposed that the new freedmen work as grave diggers at the plains of Manassas. This employment was "immediate and suitable" and allowed "judicious surveillance" of the freedmen as they prepared for citizenship. Some whites also saw justice in black men burying white soldiers as a form of repayment for their freedom. White ambivalence toward freedmen confined the great shouts of hallelujah to churches and private places. When two blacks serenaded Secretary Chase with a private concert, they apologized that it was not public and "more brilliant." They demurred because of the "present excited state of the public mind,"a sobering reminder of the reality of American society.[54]

Abolition in itself, as momentous as it was, existed in tension with the prevailing fears and prejudices of the time. The bestowal, or rather, reaffirmation of freedom for the black would gain meaning through experience and not solely by intention. The reality of freedom would be the conjoining experience and intention. Already in April of 1862 some Republicans had learned from their experience of southern and conservative fearfulness. There were members of the northern coalition who already realized there could be no limbo of neither slave nor free; "ex-slave" and "freedman" were inadequate substitutes for the status of free person and citizen. The accomplishment of the embodiment of freedom is the history of the war itself. Some Unionists realized early in the war that the freedom given blacks meant more than the mere absence of legal bondage. Rather, it embraced the possession of equal rights before the law. But a more general acceptance of this abolitionist vision of war possibilities would require far more time for fulfillment than abolition itself. Yet the two were linked from the beginning and remained so throughout the war era. As with abolition, the issue of qualitative freedom also first emerged in the District of Columbia. Begun during the debate on the abolition bill, it continued long after abolition's passage. "Of course" the District's black code must now be swept away, one abolitionist wrote. It was the only way blacks had a chance for survival.[55]

Lincoln's approval of the District abolition bill on April 16 set the compensation procedure in place, and the three commissioners he appointed began hearings late in the month.[56] Congressional attention did not focus on the mechanics of compensation (save for an explanatory bill passed in July),[57] but upon the questions arising as a consequence of abolition. During the debate on the abolition bill, Republican senator John Sherman had described the District as the place where prejudice against the black was least. Subsequently, he argued, it was a perfect place to experiment to see the highest possible degree of self-government blacks might attain. Sherman's view made sense, not because of any marked lack of prejudice, but because Congress possessed unquestionable power to experiment in the District. How to conceive the consequences of freedom proved more difficult, however, than recognizing that they were present.[58]

While abolitionists led the rest of the Unoinist coalition and Congress to abolition in the District, they did not have nearly so unified a viewpoint when it came to dealing with freedom's consequences. Gerrit Smith and Henry Cheever, among others, maintained that freedom was freedom, and if the Constitution was interpreted correctly, no special laws or constitutional amendments were necessary. So long as oppressive hands were kept off the former slaves, they might be left alone "where the rest of us are in the hand of God, and subject to the great law which feeds the industrious and sometimes lets the idle starve—." This passive, non-governmental approach to freedom was popular among religious-based, educational efforts, like those already begun at Fort Monroe and Port Royal.[59]

But the key condition necessary for the non-governmental approach to succeed was the absence of oppression. Even hesitant antislavery partners recognized the problems posed by oppressive, race-minded laws that existed in many northern states. In particular, the new constitution of Illinois drew wide ranging criticism for its exclusion of black immigration and suffrage. Horace Greeley's New York *Tribune* viewed the anti-black clauses with sadness, hoping their authors might yet live to be ashamed of their work. The Washington *National Intelligencer*, though hardly in favor of racial equality, suggested the tenor more radical coalitionists took when it remarked that the "barbarism of Illinois shall not long survive when the barbarism of South Carolina is no more."[60] Although preferring the Constitution and laws as they were (*if* correctly interpreted), Gerrit Smith was aware of the reality of oppression in race-centered laws that jeopardized the quality of newly won freedom. Believing that slavery once abolished would never return, Smith nevertheless reserved for the federal government the role of guarantor and shield for the rights of all. The guarantee of a republican form of government ruled out black laws like those of Illinois and other states. The citizenship rights of all must be preserved in spite of those laws. The *Dred Scott* decision was repealed, Smith explained, and qualifications for civil and political rights now must be the same for both races:

> Men will then buy and sell, and exercise all the rights of citizenship, not because of their complexion, but simply because they are men. . . . The denial to manhood of the rights of manhood will then be seen to be the guiltiest and meanest crime.[61]

Similarly, the New York *Times* recognized the need ot do something for the freed blacks and accepted the responsibility as a northern one. Putting aside for the moment the question of congressional authority, the *Times*' editor saw two alternatives. One, proposed by Charles Sumner, would consider rebel states as territories, giving Congress a plenitude of power to secure freedmen's rights. Yet this option would not please Lincoln, a cautious man and not one for constitutional "shell games." The editor dismissed that possibility. He also rejected out of hand an abandonment of the former slaves to their own devices, fearing southern intransigence would surface the moment the war ended. The editor worried that that resistance might go so far as southern judges declaring that the war had not abrogated the right to hold property in men. To prevent that calamity, the *Times*' editor suggested that freedmen be made wards of the federal government, removed from state court jurisdiction, and given protection through federal courts or special courts created for the purpose. The proposal, in many ways similar to the Freedmen's Bureau courts and access to federal courts guaranteed through the Fourteenth Amendment, illustrated how seriously some northerners took the question of blacks' future. Once the option of colonization was dismissed and the reality of an emergent bi-racial society acknowledged, the question of how to secure black rights became prominent. Congress addressed some of these issues rather quickly, again in the nation's laboratory, the District of Columbia.[62]

In May Congress reformed the law governing jurors in the District. Limited to white male citizens between 21 and 65, the reform aimed to prevent those who were known to hold rebel sympathies from serving on grand or petit juries. No debate centered on the racial aspect of white only jurors. Presumably the judicial process was to remain under absolute white control. Yet two months later, in the supplemental act to the abolition bill, [63] Sumner inserted an amendment that guaranteed participation of witnesses in all District judicial proceedings, without regard to color. The right to testify before compensation board meetings had been secured for blacks by the original abolition bill. Sumner's amendment guaranteed black testimony in all judicial hearings and trials, a small but important step toward the civil equality he and other abolitionists envisioned. Both houses adopted his proposal.[64]

Even before the abolition of slavery in the District, James Grimes had suggested the creation of an educational system for the District's blacks. The system was segregated and, though it was the first created to secure education for black children, its step toward equality would have been debatable at best had not Henry Wilson successfully attached an amendment to the measure. Retrieving a section from his bill to repeal the black code, Wilson's amendment struck down all District and city provisions that distinguished crimes and punishments on the basis of race. This clause, accepted without debate in both houses, marked the beginning of the legal presumption of freedom, so that color would no longer be a reason for crime or more severe punishment. If an act was criminal, it would be so for both races, and the penalty would be the same. In these tentative steps blacks began the long process toward achieving equality before the law.[65]

These steps were small, indeed, when judged against the standard of complete equality. And yet, small as they were, these steps were a startling advance over what was imaginable hardly a year before. By mid 1862, the contours of struggle were formed in surprising detail. Equality before the law, government power, and direct federal-individual relationships were all present as legitimate policy options for the consideration of policy makers. The government had only to assess their benefits in light of opportunities and necessities.

If there are such things as currents of history, unfolding struggles, or divine plans, if men and women do learn from experience, shaping and being shaped by it, then the opening of freedom may be easier to understand. Yet understood, it is no less profound. This was the first fruit of the lived experience of war—the evolving notion of what abolition must mean. No greater sign of the change in America could be found than the abolition of slavery at the seat of government, precisely one year after the firing at Charleston harbor.

NOTES FOR CHAPTER THREE

1. Edwin Stanton to General William Robinson, printed in the Washington *National Intelligencer*, January 21, 1862. For Confederate designs on Washington, see *OR*, Series I, part 2, 391.

2. E. B. Long, *The Civil War Day by Day: An Almanac* (Garden City, New York: Doubleday and Company, 1971), 123; Robert F. Engs, *Freedom's First Generation: Black Hampton, Virginia, 1861-1890* ([Philadelphia]: University of Pennsylvania Press, 1979), 29; *Dictionary of American Biography*, edited by Allen Johnson (New York: Charles Scribner's Sons, 1964), hereafter *DAB*.

3. Edward L. Pierce, *Enfranchisement and Citizenship: Addresses and Papers* (Boston: Roberts Brothers, 1896), 19, 22-23. Although published in November, 1861, Pierce wrote the article in August. A. W. Stevens, who edited *Enfranchisement and Citizenship* in 1896, noted that the essays therein covered the times when the nation "first groped and stumbled and then decisively acted" for the freedmen, ibid., iii-iv. In his original version to the President, Secretary of War Cameron contended that contraband slaves were entitled to "freedom and protection" by the federal government. This section of the report was suppressed in the final, official version. For questions over Cameron's antislavery motives, however, see *National Anti-Slavery Standard*, December, 7, 14, 1861.

4. Pierce, *Enfranchisement and Citizenship*, 24.

5. Ibid., 27, 28. On Frémont's "Missouri Emancipation," see Allan Nevins, *Frémont: Pathfinder of the West* (New York: Frederick Ungar Publishing Company, 1939, 1955, 1961 reprint), 2:499-507, and Lincoln, *Coll. Works*, 4:506-507, 517-18.

6. *National Anti-Slavery Standard*, November 30, 1861; Washington *National Intelligencer*, December 5, 1861, February 7, 1862. Herman Belz argues that the disposition of the freed slaves was a "great unresolved issue in 1862" noting that most comment focused on where freed slaves would reside, not in their status or rights, Belz, "Protection of Personal Liberty in Republican Emancipation Legislation of 1862," *Journal of Southern History* (1976) 42:398. This seems true enough for some Republicans of the Unionist coalition, but not all and certainly not for abolitionists. See below the sentiment expressed by Gerrit Smith in his letter to John A. Gurley in the *National Anti-Slavery Standard*, January 4, 1862.

7. Sumner quoted in *National Anti-Slavery Standard*, November 30, 1861; Pierce, *Enfranchisement and Citizenship*, 35. See also letter of Brigadier General Joseph K. F. Mansfield in the New York *Times*, March 1862.

8. Lincoln, *Coll. Works*, 4:267; Washington *National Intelligencer*, December 7, 1861, January 21, 1862. See also generally, Hyman, *More Perfect Union*, 3-16, for the idea of the Constitution shaping quarrels.

9. Phillips, *Speeches*, 440, speaking in December, 1861. For typical conservative nay-saying, see Hyman, *More Perfect Union*, chs. 3, 5, 7.

10. Phillips, as quoted in the New York *Tribune*, March 18, 1862.

11. Phillips, *Speeches*, 445; *National Anti-Slavery Standard*, December 7, 14, 1861.

12. Beecher's Thanksgiving sermon in *National Anti-Slavery Standard*, December 21, 1861.

13. Lincoln, *Coll. Works*, 4:168-69, 249-71. For Gerrit Smith's analysis of Lincoln's devotion to the Constitution, see Smith to Thaddeus Stevens, in

National Anti-Slavery Standard, December 21, 1861.

14. *National Anti-Slavery Standard*, December 14, 1861.

15. *Biographical Directory of the American Congress, 1774-1961* ([Washington]: Government Printing Office, 1961); *National Anti-Slavery Standard*, November 30, 1861; Cutler in ibid., January 11, 1862.

16. Ralph Waldo Emerson, *Journals of Ralph Waldo Emerson, with Annotations, edited by Edward Waldo Emerson and Waldo Emerson Forbes* (Boston and New York: Houghton Mifflin Company, 1913-1914), 9:448; *National Anti-Slavery Standard*, January 11, 1862; Washington *National Intelligencer*, March 21, 1862.

17. Constance Green, *The Secret City: A History of Race Relations in the Nation's Capital* (Princeton, New Jersey: Princeton University Press, 1967), 75-76, and ch. 4; Edward Ingle, *The Negro in the District of Columbia* (Baltimore: The Johns Hopkins Press, 1893), 65; Article I, section 8, clause 27, of the Constitution.

18. Ingle, *Negro in D. C.*, 11; *National Anti-Slavery Standard*, December 28, 1861, April 26, 1862; *Liberator*, April 11, 1862.

19. House *Journal*, 37:2, 33-34; *Cong. Globe*, 37:2, 10. Representative John Hutchins (R, Ohio), introduced a resolution similar to Wilson's in the House on December 4, listing the number of fugitives as 45, House *Journal*, 37:2, 32.

20. *National Anti-Slavery Standard*, December 7, 14, 1861. There was a report that an Arlington "madam" kept her Virginia slaves boarded in the District jail, having moved from Secessia to the District, ibid., December 7, 1861.

21. *Cong. Globe*, 37:2, 11-12, 26.

22. Ibid., 50, 55.

23. Smith to Gurley, *National Anti-Slavery Standard*, January 4, 1862.

24. Ibid., January 4, 11, 1862.

25. *Cong. Globe*, 37:2, 264, 310-14.

26. Ibid., 318-19, 321.

27. A resolution citing Marshal Lamon for contempt of Congress for refusing to allow senators to inspect the District jail passed without a division, ibid., 444. See also *National Anti-Slavery Standard*, January 18, 25, February 1, 1862.

28. *Cong. Globe*, 37:2, 16, 36, 89-90, 785; *National Anti-Slavery Standard*, December 21, 28, 1861.

29. *National Anti-Slavery Standard*, February 1, 8, 22, March 1, 1862; *Cong. Globe*, 37:2, 785. The House of Representatives was occupied with consideration of a tax bill, and Speaker Galusha Grow, when appointing committees in July, had placed too many conservatives on key panels, such as Judiciary and Territories, *National Anti-Slavery Standard*, March 8, 15, 1862.

30. *Cong. Globe*, 37:2, 89-90, 153, 995; *National Anti-Slavery Standard*, February 22, 1862.

31. *Cong. Globe*, 37:2, 917-18; National Archives, Record Group 46, Records of the Senate, 37A, B2 (hereafter, DNA, with RG number); *National Anti-Slavery Standard*, March 1, 1862.

32. Hans L. Trefousse, *The Radical Republicans: Lincoln's Vanguard for Racial Justice* (Baton Rouge: Louisiana State University Press, 1968), ch.6; *National Anti-Slavery Standard*, March 15, 29, 1862. See also Betty L.

Fladeland, "Compensated Emancipation: A Rejected Alternative," *Journal of Southern History* (1976) 42:170, for the view that any form of compensated emancipation was dead before the Civil War. For conservatives' fears, see Amos Kendall to Lincoln, in the Washington *National Intelligencer*, February 22, 1862. For conservative support of gradual emancipation, see the editorial in ibid., January 20, 1862, which observed that change must be gradual to be "beneficial and permanent," since this was the way of human progress. See also the *National Intelligencer* for March 11, 13, 1862 and the New York *Times* for other opinions of gradual emancipation current at the time. Lincoln's gradual, compensated emancipation plan passed, but almost all border state men voted against the proposal, another example of southern intransigence on the issue of slavery. The New York *Times* called that vote a "source of mortification," April 3, 1862; see also *Cong. Globe*, 37:1, 1589. One editor remarked that Lincoln's proposal opened up "a chapter of various possibilities," and warned slaveholders that this was their last chance for compensation. "To sell, or not to sell. That is the question!" Then, the editor made his point–if slaveholders accepted the proposal, it would give slavery a new lease on life due to the proposal's gradualism. If rejected, the emancipation of the slaves ought to be "proclaimed by the President, enacted by the Congress, and Enforced by our armies," *National Anti-Slavery Standard*, March 29, 1862.

33. New York *Times*, March 6, 7, 1862; *Liberator*, March 14, 1862. The phrase "omnipresent traitor" is Sumner's. Wilson termed slavery the "Great Criminal."

34. New York *Times*, March 7, 1862. Sumner's suggestion of extending the language of the 1787 Ordinance is significant, since the Thirteenth Amendment did just that. See Chapter V, below, for Sumner's own proposed constitutional amendment to abolish slavery.

35. *Cong. Globe*, 37:2, 1191. Representative James Ashley reported to the House on the same day a bill to abolish slavery in the District, but the measure was recommitted to committee. Demonstrating its conservative alignment, the House Judiciary Committee had decided that Congress held no power to abolish slavery in the states by legislation, and rejected all emancipation and confiscation bills, *Cong. Globe*, 37:2, 1192; *National Anti-Slavery Standard*, March 8, 1862. See also Curry, *Blueprint for Modern America*, 37-40.

36. *Cong. Globe*, 37:2, 1191.

37. Ibid., 1249, 1266-67, App., 83-85; *National Anti-Slavery Standard*, March 22, 1862.

38. *Cong. Globe*, 37:2, 1300-1301, 1333-34.

39. Ibid., 1338, 1356, 1379; *National Anti-Slavery Standard*, April 5, 1862. When Saulsbury's amendment came up for the vote, it lost 0 to 35. Even Saulsbury voted against it.

40. *Cong. Globe*, 37:2, 1350-53.

41. Ibid., 1357, 1359; *Dred Scott v. Sandford*, 19 Howard, 407.

42. *Cong. Globe*, 37:2, 1375, 1379, 1446, 1449-51; see also David Donald, *Charles Sumner and the Rights of Man* (New York: Alfred A. Knopf, 1970), 58. The New York *Times*, April 1, 1862, criticized Sumner for going too fast, not seeing the practical problems involved with District abolition, and suggested that the rapidity which radical brought up abolition in Washington betrayed their fear that the slave power would soon return. The *Times* urged gradual, compensated emancipation as the best "example to the slave states." See also *Cong. Globe*, 37:2, 1473. Fessenden confirmed the *Times*' observation

that the time for acting was now; no one knew what the future held.

43. *National Anti-Slavery Standard*, March 27, 1862; Washington *National Intelligencer*, March 27, April 3, 1862; *Cong. Globe*, 37:2, 1479, 1517-19.

44. *Cong. Globe*, 37:2, 1474, 1518, 1520, 1522.

45. Ibid., 1522-23.

46. Ibid., 1523-26; Washington *National Intelligencer*, April 12, 1862; New York *Tribune*, April 4, 1862. See also George S. Henry, "Radical Republican policy toward the Negro, 1862-1872," (unpublished thesis, Yale University, 1968), 33-38. Henry's conclusion that Senator Wilson differed significantly in his concept of freedom from that of Charles Sumner seems incorrect. While Wilson did vote for colonization and Sumner voted against the amendment, Wilson's bill to repeal the black code carries great weight in assessing his view of freedom. In regard to compensation, Sumner himself was not above political compromise, as pointed out above. A similar conclusion seems appropriate for Wilson and the colonization issue. Radical uneasiness with the colonization feature of S. No. 108 was nevertheless apparent. Some senators thought about removing the amendment before sending the bill on to the House, although nothing came of that speculation. Wilson received only praise for his role in abolishing slavery in the District, New York *Tribune*, April 7, 1862; *Liberator*, April 11, 1862.

47. New York *Times*, April 4, 1862; *National Anti-Slavery Standard*, April 12, 1862. The *Times* hoped that the House would make abolition in the District gradual rather than immediate.

48. *Cong. Globe*, 37:2, 1614-16, 1618, 1629-31.

49. Ibid., 1632-34. See also Winthrop Jordan, *White Over Black: American Attitudes Toward the Negro, 1550-1812* (Chapel Hill: University of North Carolina Press, 1968), for an exhaustive treatment of southern fears of amalgamation, and in the same view, George M. Fredrickson, *The Black Image in the White Mind: The Debate on Afro-American Character and Destiny, 1817-1914* (New York: Harper and Row, 1971).

50. *Cong. Globe*, Cong. Globe, 37:2, 1634-35, 1638-39, 1642-43, App., 91, 94, 101-103. Commenting on John J. Crittenden, the *National Anti-Slavery Standard*, April 19, 1862, remarked: " 'It seems as if God Almighty could not thunder his truth loud enough to break the old man's deafness!' "referring to Crittenden's political stance: the Kentuckian was loyal to the last, but also pro-slavery to the last.

51. *Cong. Globe*, 37:2, 1645, 1647-49, App., 101-103. James Ashley apparently suggested the use of the 1787 Ordinance's language in his consultation with Senator Morrill; Ashley's bill also lacked a compensation feature, Ashley, *Duplicate Copy of the Souvenir from the Afro-American League of Tennessee to Hon. James M. Ashley* (Philadelphia: A. M. E. Church Publishing House, 1894), 329; Robert F. Horowitz, *The Great Impeacher: A Political Biography of James M. Ashley* (New York : Brooklyn College Press, 1979), 75-76; DNA, RG233, Records of the House, 37:1.

52. New York *Tribune*, April 15, 16, 17, 1862; *National Anti-Slavery Standard*, April 19, 26, 1862; New York *Times*, April 15, 1862; Curry, *Blueprint for Modern America*, 43.

53. Washington *National Intelligencer*, April 12, 1862; New York *Times*, April 17, 1862. See also the opinion in Ingle, *Negro in D. C.*, 42: "A premature law, that is, a law forced upon a people instead of springing from them, may not always be pernicious in its effects, but it is a dangerous experiment."

54. Frederick Edge to Chase, April 18, 1862, Alexder [sic] and James W. Hays to Chase, April 19, 1862, Salmon P. Chase Papers, DLC.

55. *National Anti-Slavery Standard*, April 19, 1862. Herman Belz, writing generally of Republican attitudes toward emancipation, argues that they did not see emancipation as a matter of securing civil rights and personal liberty, but as a way of depriving the South of labor and aligning blacks with the Union, Belz, "Personal Liberty," *Journal of Southern History*, 42:396. By not considering the North as a coalition, Belz fails to point out the interplay and dynamism within the coalition. Isolated components, whether colonizationist, Republican, abolitionist, or pro-slavery, do not adequately represent the tension within northern ranks nor the value of experience as a teacher. Clearly, the military situation provided a major reason for abolition, but that does not necessarily speak to the meaning of abolition either in 1862 or in 1865.

56. *United States Statutes at Large* (Washington: various publishers and years), 12:376-78 (hereafter *SAL*); *National Anti-Slavery Standard*, May 3, 1862.

57. As he signed the abolition of slavery bill, Lincoln suggested a supplemental law that would cover certain "loopholes" he found in the original measure, primarily to prevent claims from being made after 90 days, and also a provision for slaveholders that might be absent from the District, minors, or the insane. The Senate waited two months before considering a supplemental bill (S. 351), and when it came before that body, the bill included other provisions explicitly declaring that labor within the District emancipated. Henry Wilson, who originally introduced the bill, had provided that slaves formerly resident in the District but who had been sent away to escape the effects of abolition, would be freed. District of Columbia Committee chairman James Grimes spoke against the provision, arguing that Congress could not reach within a slave state to work emancipation. The provision was struck out. The Senate passed the bill. All the "yeas" came from Republicans and one Unionist; all the "nays" from Democrats and one Unionist. James Ashley rushed the bill through the House, answering only one question during floor debate. Labor within the District now automatically freed a slave, but passage through the District on an errand did not. The bill passed the House 69 to 36, *Cong. Globe*, 37:2, 1680, 1686, 2674, 2879, 2933, 2992, 3136, 3138, 3215-16; *SAL*, 12:538-39.

58. *Cong. Globe*, 37:2, 1525; Washington *National Intelligencer*, April 4, 1862.

59. Cheever's speech before the 29th Annual meeting of the American Anti-Slavery Society, May 6, 1862, reprinted in the *National Anti-Slavery Standard*, May 10, 1862; Gerrit Smith to Montgomery Blair, April 5, 1862, in *Liberator*, April 18, 1862; Charles M. Storey to Wilson, April 26, 1862, Henry Wilson Papers, DLC; G. C. Vincent to Chase, March 11, 1862, Salmon P. Chase Papers, DLC; Engs, *Freedom's First*, ch.3; Willie Lee Rose, *Rehearsal for Reconstruction: The Port Royal Experiment* (Indianapolis: Bobbs-Merrill, 1964), ch. 5 and passim.

60. Washington *National Intelligencer*, March 7, April 5, 1862; New York *Tribune*, April 9, 1862. Illinois also ratified the Corwin Amendment during this period, pleading the inviolability of state slavery.

61. Smith to Blair, April 5, 1862, in *Liberator*, April 18, 1862.

62. New York *Times*, March 23, 1862.

63. See above, note 54.

64. *Cong. Globe*, 37:2, 2019-20, 2667-68, 3138, 3216.

65. Ibid., 1854, 2020, 2037, 2157; Ingle, *Negro in D. C.*, 24-25, 38-40. See also Wilhelmus B. Bryan, *A History of the National Capital; from its Foundation through the Period of the Adoption of the Organic Act* (New York: Macmillan Company, 1916), 2:513-28, for an unsympathetic treatment of the plight of the free blacks in the District.

IV

WE CANNOT ESCAPE HISTORY

In his annual message of 1862, Abraham Lincoln wrote: "Fellow citizens, we cannot escape history."

In December 1862 history included the 1861 Confiscation Act, the abolition of slavery in the District of Columbia and the territories, a second confiscation act, recognition of the black republics of Liberia and Haiti, and the preliminary Emancipation Proclamation.[1] These were facts, segments of the war's reality that highlighted the profound difference from antebellum America. Slavery had been attacked, even destroyed in places, and millions of black people were free by authority of the war power. Together with a myriad of other experiences, this was the history which Lincoln wrote about. "We cannot escape history" was descriptive.

Equally, the President's words suggested a future toward which events were pushing the country. The shared experience of war–history–propelled the nation along a road it could never otherwise have travelled. Lecture-like in its admonition, the President reminded his readers, and doubtless himself, that they could not escape the reality of fratricide. Continuing, Lincoln remarked:

> We of this Congress and this administration, will be remembered in spite of ourselves. . . . We—even we here—hold the power, and bear the responsibility.

More than merely observing the history that surrounded them, Lincoln believed Congress and his administration should act in a manner that accepted the reality created by civil war. And more than accept, the government ought to affirm and work within that new reality. "We cannot escape history" was also predictive.

The inescapable history of the civil war focused upon the slave. The President made that conclusion directly when he wrote: "In giving freedom to the slave, we assure freedom to the free—honorable alike in what we give, and what we preserve."[2] Revealingly, freedom for those already free—whites—loomed large in the President's thinking, somehow connected with freedom for the slave and yet, somehow separate.

Lincoln still wanted a form of compensation for loyal masters—only paragraphs before the words quoted, he proposed three constitutional amendments guaranteeing gradual abolition (by 1900), compensation, ex-slaves' freedom, and the possibility of colonization. The Emancipation Proclamation, issued September 22, was preliminary; repent, and return home before the Proclamation went into effect on January 1, 1863.[3] Border states had been noticeably lacking in enthusiasm for Lincoln's gradual, compensated emancipation scheme, first proposed March 6, 1862 and suggested again in July. The idea appeared again in Lincoln's message to Congress in December. Viewed from this perspective, the President's understanding seemed not to have grown since abolition in the District of Columbia.

Nevertheless, Lincoln did issue the Emancipation Proclamation with its promise, under certain conditions, that all person held as slaves in rebel areas would be "thenceforward, and forever free." Lincoln also pledged the executive branch of the federal government to "recognize and maintain" the former slaves' freedom.[4] This expansion in the universe of liberty occurred at the same time that the President espoused his essentially backward-looking proposals of gradual, compensated emancipation and colonization. Indeed, the Proclamation itself lost much of its luster when the limitations it contained were measured against its promise. Lincoln reserved some of his most stirring rhetoric to recommend his gradual compensation plan:

> The dogmas of the quiet past, are inadequate to the stormy present. The occasion is piled high with difficulty, and we must rise to the occasion. As our case is new, so we must think anew, and act anew. We must disenthrall ourselves, and then we shall save our country.[5]

The ambiguity in Lincoln's thought on slavery and race is puzzling. Certainly the nation's leader was torn by profound and powerful emotions. Certainly he possessed, as one contemporary remembered, "a marvelous blending of sunshine and shadow." Drawn to Shakespeare's tragedies, Lincoln identified with Claudius, usurper of the throne of Denmark by his brother's murder, and with Macbeth, slayer of his cousin King Duncan. The President's own election followed by the multiple brothers' deaths in the war pressed him down. With the death of his beloved son Willie in February 1862, a loss from which Lincoln never fully recovered, the President's quest for meaning in the engulfing tide of death led him on an ever intensifying search of himself and finally, of God. He was slow to understand the war as a working out of Divine Judgment, the great cathartic expiation for the sin of slavery. Lincoln was both willing and unwilling to see himself as that instrument for national salvation and spiritual cleansing. He struggled with the awful will of God as only those do who, recognizing the truth, struggle when they wish to turn away. Perhaps he did turn away in those moments when he despaired of a future for the co-existence of black and white in America on terms other than master and slave. Or perhaps he merely followed the light given to him, interspersed as it was in the darkness that colors all human perceptions. Lincoln's is a mixed, tortured legacy of doubt and affirmation. Contradictions existed in the President's policies and actions because they existed within the man.[7]

Lincoln's rhetoric showed clearly the contradictions between the Emancipation Proclamation and gradual, compensated emancipation. Abolitionists had urged that the Unionist coalition take up new thoughts and actions from the beginning of the war. The President's new thoughts and actions, however, were in support of the narrowest and least expansive antislavery changes then possible. Yet Lincoln had said that the people must "disenthrall" themselves to save the Union. Disenthrall—to free from bondage. The interplay of meanings of this word proved vital. Ideas freed from the bondage of form were not enough; men must also be free. This was the message of Lincoln's words, and yet, the tension within his policies and statements indicated that the President had not yet taken to heart the full meaning of his own words: "We cannot escape history."

The war went on. It went on molding reality and Americans' perceptions. By June 1862 it was, in Sidney George Fisher's words, "getting to be a fearful thing," as the future became more obscure and change more certain. Southern hatred for the North was more intense than ever, as was northern determination to conquer treason and subjugate rebellion. Fisher could not help but wonder about the fate of constitutional free government. Abolition of slavery in the District of Columbia was only a first step in the continuing assault of free institutions upon a slave government. There had been "too much state law, too much state rights, too much of State slavery," according to Sinclair Tousey, a Republican antislavery activist. The situation demanded "NATIONAL LAWS, NATIONAL INSTITUTIONS, NATION FREEDOM . . . THE NATION MUST BE SUPREME. The States must be subordinate."[8]

And so the frustrations of war worked upon the Unionist coalition, calling forward increasingly radical statements from some members. Leaders of the antislavery vanguard in Congress pressed for broader and deeper measures to secure the principle of national freedom, and a barely possible sectional slavery. Illinois Representative Owen Lovejoy's proposal for freedom in the territories emphasized that wherever the federal government exercised exclusive jurisdiction, freedom reigned. Charles Sumner's measure did the same, using the language of the venerable Northwest Ordinance. As a result of these proposals, the "rights" of states dimmed in comparison to pre-war claims of near omnipotence. The twin questions of what to do with freedmen and what to do with the South were seen as aspects of the same fundamental question, and the fear of experimentation began slowly to fade. Charles G. Leland, editor of the *Continental Monthly*, wrote of the need for "Union-izing" the South once the war was over. Colonization was the the key, but with a twist. Rather than deport blacks, Leland proposed to export northern whites to the South to take the freedmen under their tutelage and to counterbalance southern white treason.[9]

But the end of slavery in the federal district did not satisfy abolitionists. Throughout the months between that law's enactment in April and Lincoln's Emancipation Proclamation in September, radicals in and out of Congress pressed for greater efforts against slavery. Congressmen, geared to legalistic and practical efforts, focused attention on the banning of slavery from the territories and a better, more effective confiscation law. Radicals outside of government continued to influence opinion, driving the point home again and again—the fruit of war must be the death of slavery. That message made an impression. Men not known for abolitionist views observed the force of the radical analysis of the war, and found it at least partially persuasive. It convinced because it fit the new reality created by the war. The *North American Review* lectured "over-scrupulous moralists" squeamish about the "unchristian title of war." It was not war at all, the *Review* observed, but the self-defense of the nation "against anarchy."[10] William Whiting, shortly to be appointed by Lincoln as War Department Solicitor, wondered whether any right of property, or claim of local law, or construction of the Constitution, could be superior to the nation's survival. He answered his own question with a resounding, "no," making the connection abolitionists had suggested all along: "Slavery is no longer local or domestic after it has become an engine of war."[11]

To defend the nation, attack slavery. This was the simple message radicals preached to their countrymen. And yet, it was only a first level of meaning. To awaken the power of the government and direct it against the South and slavery even during war was no easy feat. The abolitionist program envisioned more than the end of slavery, but the inertia of history was something to be reckoned with seriously. "Seventy years has the Union postponed the negro," Wendell Phillips declared. "For seventy years has he been beguiled with the promises, as she erected one bulwark after another around slavery, that he should have the influence of our common institutions. I claim it to-day."[12] Common institutions; common, free institutions for men and women of both races, for both sections, in one nation. This was the essence of the radical platform, the positive side of the end of slavery. As the Constitution forbade states to confer titles of nobility, so too, should it forbid title to property in man. To achieve this goal, something more than a mere end of slavery was required.[13]

Phillips probably did not contemplate at this time an amendment to the Constitution as the vehicle for his vision. Interpreted correctly, he believed there was no need for an amendment. Interpreted in the light of America's truest principles, the Constitution would serve well. John S. Rock, a lawyer, abolitionist, and black man from Boston, had visited the District of Columbia shortly after abolition. While there he was spat upon, assaulted, and threatened with death. District law did not sanction these abuses; it positively forbade them. Abolitionist Rock soon learned that law without spirit had little meaning. The abolitionist program sought to animate the law with the spirit of liberty. As Rock said:

> The Abolitionists believe in the Declaration of Independence, It is our great charter; and we hope that, ere this closes, the whole nation will believe in it, and accept the great truths it teaches.[14]

Phillips hoped that the vast majority of southern whites who were not slaveholders would recognize in the North their true friend, and in the slaveholding class, their true enemy. With that awareness, the fate of freedmen might be happily secured. Without it, other abolitionists were less hopeful. Granting that prejudice against the black would exist as long as he was enslaved, one writer to the *Liberator* did not believe the prejudice would evaporate immediately upon freedom. When slavery was destroyed the political and social fabric of the South would need reconstruction in order to "secure and maintain [freedmen's] equal rights against the obstacles two centuries of enslavement had imbedded in the pathway of his progress." Liberty, albeit the natural state of men, could not exist without some aid in the southern soil so long contaminated by slavery. Just as Rock experienced law without spirit, so could spirit without law yield similar bitter fruit in a post-war South where slavery had ended, but freedom had not been born.[15]

And southern blacks would remain on southern soil. Gradually, even conservatives began to see the hopelessness of colonization as a solution to the question of "what to do with the freedmen." The impracticality of moving four million people seemed overwhelming, and was itself a convincing argument against the idea. Conservatives, of course despaired of the vision that abolitionists proposed. Instead, they offered an ameliorated or "regulated servitude" as an alternative to abolition. Something less than the harsh slave system, it hardly qualified as freedom in radicals' eyes. The President remained a devoted proponent of colonization, but neither his support for removal, nor conservative counter-proposals, deterred antislavery leaders from publicly proclaiming their vision of a bi-racial nation. Blacks were not inherently lazy and ill-prepared for freedom, stated Republican pamphleteer Lorenzo Sherwood. The public mood might yet for a time make anti-abolition sentiments fashionable. But a time was soon approaching, wrote Sherwood, for the white American to show his bravery and accept abolition. The American was not finished "with the business of disenthrallment. His language is the language of liberty." Sherwood allowed that colonization efforts might be made. Yet he called white America to something greater and ultimately more compelling:

> Every humane consideration clusters to the policy of disenthralling the colored man, and of making him a being of power. Nothing can oppose it but the pro-slavery spirit that seeks to enslave the American mind to barbarism and the colored millions and their increase to perpetual bondage.[16]

What of the pro-slavery spirit? What of those in the North who were bent upon reunion based upon an alliance of the white South and the northern Democracy? It was the fear of exactly this alliance that sparked many to advocate abolition, so that "the cause of the war may not become active again." To rally the nation to that standard, conservatives adopted for their motto the pithy expression that also was their platform—"the Union as it was, the Constitution as it is." Short and to the point, the conservative platform contained, on the other hand, no real program. It proposed instead a backward-looking embrace of all that was, raising nostalgia to the level of constitutional and libertarian principle.[17]

Cautious toward Republican innovations from the beginning, some Democrats held out the fond hope of a compromised settlement between North and South, wherein the South would give up its pretended independence, and the North its pretended power over slavery. The Union and only the Union was the acceptable goal for the war effort, according to this thinking. Anything else would drive the South to ever greater resistance (civil war evidently not being enough proof of southern resistance to reunion). Indeed, the war that began by the firing on Fort Sumter really was not caused by the South at all, but because northern "ultras" had prevailed. The only southern crime was not fighting the antislavery heresy within the Union. "The Union as it was, the Constitution as it is" was motto, platform, and ideal. It was a device of calculated effect, for who could argue with the sentiment. The war was for the Union and the maintenance of the Constitution. Wendell Phillips also called for the Constitution "as it was." But the phrase was not value-free, for each group brought to it its own definition of Union and Constitution. While conservatives lacked a program, they did possess a hidden agenda and a none too subtle message behind the motto. Once expressed, all else fell into place: "the Constitution as it is, the Union as it was, and the Negroes where they are."[18]

Conservatives were increasingly occupied with rejecting both Republican policy initiatives and antislavery policy options. Safeguarding a South-North alliance that many Republicans saw as the reason for the war, conservatives earned their reputation as "the ever-mischief-making, ever-meddling, and never-contented politicians (who continue to believe that the millenium would at once arrive were Emancipation only extinguished)." But Republicans and abolitionists were equally tenacious when declaring "never more will the South come back to be served and toadied to."[19] In truth, the Unionist coalition was breaking apart as conservatives increasingly rejected greater change. Not only did they negate policies, they seemed to negate reality itself by refusing to acknowledge what had already happened. With such an attitude, conservatives opened themselves to Phillips' devastating parody of their platform; " 'Lay the pieces carefully together in their places; put the gunpowder and the match in again, say the Constitution backwards instead of your prayers, and there will never be another rebellion!' "[20]

Republicans may have been harsh in judging conservatives. But though conservatives spoke from narrowness and ignorance, the breadth of their opposition was as great as the war itself. Circulation of paper "greenbacks," declarations of martial law, abolition in the federal district and the territories, even Lincoln's gradual, compensated emancipation plan—all were opposed by elements of the emergent border state conservative/Democratic alliance. What did they favor? Enforcement of the fugitive slave law, for if Republicans wished to exercise the Constitution's power, then they must also fulfill its duties. Therefore, conservatives urged the return of fugitive slaves to their loyal masters. Anything less was not merely unconstitutional, but a "fraud." Whatever changes might occur in the nation, conservatives reminded their countrymen that the Constitution and state laws would be the same as before the war. Only changes that the states agreed to would have any lasting effect. So not only were Republican antislavery policies wrongheaded, dangerous, heretical, or treasonable in themselves, they were irrelevant. Conservatives wanted state authority to reign triumphant before, during, and presumably after a war fought to establish the supremacy of the nation.[21]

Little wonder that the Unionist coalition fragmented along lines of perception and policy. The wonder was that coalition had existed at all. Republicans suspected that conservatives opposed something more than war measures—that some opposed the war itself. If Charles Ingersoll, a Philadelphia Democrat and cousin of Sidney George Fisher, supported the war, he would uphold paper currency and other measures. But Ingersoll opposed the war, and therefore, opposed measures designed to prosecute it. Republicans began to group together traitors and opponents of the Administration. While undoubtedly unfair to principled persons who opposed certain war policies, the grouping made sense. War shaped the Union and the Constitution in profound ways. Republicans and their abolitionist allies became colleagues in their acceptance of and openness to, that new reality. As the war continued the Unionist coalition shifted leftward. There was a growing awareness of the convergence between vision and reality. Those who did not share the vision, could not cope with the reality.[22]

The Unionist coalition fragmented during the summer and early fall of 1862. Until then the coalition seemed more like two polarized camps held together by ever loosening threads. The President was in the untenable middle, as he had been from the outset of the war. A moderate when moderation's virtue was losing its appeal, Lincoln clung to his perceptions, principles, and forebodings. Moderate conservatives believed that he was amenable to their arguments. Democratic party chairman August Belmont urged the President to "equally crush the secessionists of the South and the fanatical disorganizers of the North, who [were] both equally dangerous to the country and its institutions."[23]

Belmont's plea had a chance of success. A moderate leaning to conservatism might hope to find common ground with a moderate leaning to antislavery. A *modus vivendi* for the sake of the Union was not unreasonable. Lincoln gave indications of his displeasure with radical solutions for the war's problems and the reluctance with which he "accepted this issue of battle forced upon me." In May 1862 Lincoln responded to General David Hunter's order freeing slaves in Georgia, Florida, and South Carolina, by letting it be known that no general could take such an action without his approval and support. Lincoln gave Hunter neither, and revoked the order. The President held firm to his action despite loud protests from abolitionists.[24]

Lincoln was unwilling to abandon his plan for gradual, compensated emancipation or to abandon hope for colonization; positions that were themselves radical for a more peaceful time. Antebellum southerners did not separate colonizationists from abolitionists, since both wanted emancipation. The key, however, lay in the fact that the times were not peaceful and that solutions that had been radical in peacetime, paled in war's light.

Abolitionists at home and abroad viewed Lincoln with mixed emotions. While his heart was clearly in the right place, his policies seemed anachronistic. Gradual, compensated emancipation might be tolerable as a first step—but only just so. Yet abolitionists were growing impatient with Lincoln's persistent attachment to the least radical option. In June Lincoln's friend Charles Sumner defended the President and recommended a review of what already had been accomplished with the President's approval. Abolition in the District of Columbia, and recognition of Liberia and Haiti were important signs of the President's commitment to antislavery. Beyond Sumner's defense, perhaps a greater source of hope for abolitionists was Lincoln's explicit determination to win the war, or die: "I expect to maintain this contest until successful, or till I die, or am conquered, or my term expires, or Congress or the Country forsakes me."[25]

Yet the President was very reluctant to accept the burden that abolitionists and other radicals demanded he carry. When a group of Quakers from Pennsylvania petitioned him to emancipate slaves, Lincoln balked. Arguing against resolutions drafted with the aid of William Lloyd Garrison, Lincoln told the Friends that a decree of emancipation could not abolish slavery. If it could, then John Brown would have done so long ago. The South refused to accept the Constitution, how could anyone expect it to heed an emancipation proclamation? The President assured his guests that he was aware of the magnitude of the tasks before him, that he might in fact be God's instrument in accomplishing "a great work." But he was not sure that God's way was necessarily their way. And so he hesitated.

In rebuttal, abolitionists pointed out the difference between John Brown and Abraham Lincoln. The former was one, brave, martyred soul. The latter was President of the United States. Brown's power to enforce freedom extended only so far as the range of his guns as Harpers Ferry. Lincoln's jurisdiction, however, "buttressed by law, duty and necessity . . . reaches further than his armies." As commander-in-chief of the military, Lincoln's "fiat [was] irrevocable unless the whole nation perishes with him." Brown's decree was abnormal and revolutionary. Lincoln's would be normal and lawful because his position and power were of a different order.[26]

Lincoln was not convinced. Only July 12, 1862, he appealed once again to the border states, hoping to secure support for gradual, compensated, state-sponsored emancipation. The President understood the military importance of the border states and was, himself, a son of Kentucky. Those facts convinced Lincoln that he understood the country's peril all the more clearly. Addressing congressmen from the border, he observed that they held "more power for good than any other equal number of members." If they had all voted for his gradual emancipation plan in March, the war might very well have been finished, or at least, "substantially ended." He warned them that "the incidents of war" could not be avoided forever. If the war continued, slavery would be abolished "by mere friction and abrasion." Compensated emancipation was the best solution open to the border states, and therefore, to the country. He wanted these congressmen to understand him: he did not "speak for emancipation *at once*, but of a *decision* at once to emancipation *gradually*." Lincoln was close to embracing the old abolitionist slogan of "immediate emancipation, gradually accomplished." Yet he was still not an abolitionist. Lincoln realized that he had given "dissatisfaction, if not offense" to radicals by his repudiation of General Hunter's emancipation order. Those offended were also important members of the Unionist coalition. Conservatives must realize that he did not want to alienate radicals any more than he wanted to alienate them. Congressmen from the border region could relieve much radical pressure on him if they only agreed to his proposals—now, without delay.[27]

They did not. A clear majority refused to endorse the President's plan. Embodied in H. R. 576, Lincoln's gradual, compensated emancipation scheme died from lack of congressional interest.[28]

Was Lincoln out of touch with reality; had his mistakened caution for leadership? Wendell Phillips thought so. Phillips admitted that the President was an honest man who tried to do his duty. "But Mr. Lincoln is not a genius; he is not a leader." As servant of the people, Lincoln looked for the political trend, and did not lead the nation in new directions. As the country was not ready for emancipation, so neither was Lincoln. Abolitionists believed Lincoln went against his own beliefs, that he knew slavery lay at the bottom of the rebellion, and yet, that he refused to take the opportunity to strike at the war's cause. Lincoln was not an abolitionist; that much was clear. But by his constant refrain of colonization, the President was not a mere cipher in the struggle for liberty, but a positive force for evil, or so the abolitionist critique went. He recognized and encouraged white racism every time he endorsed colonization.[29]

This abolitionist view, a harsh and biased assessment, was only one possible reading of Lincoln the man and the President. But it was a disturbing reading. Prudence is not a fault in character or in leadership, and certainly Lincoln was prudent. Was he too prudent, too concerned with border state sensibilities, too aware of political balances? He was of the border, and yet, he hated slavery. He possessed greater power than any other President, yet he failed to strike at what he hated. He loved the Constitution, fought to defend it, and grieved over the death his decisions caused. Abolitionists, Democrats, border state men, Republicans—all doubted his leadership, if not his ability to lead. But despite disagreement over policy, over constitutional views and philosophy, the truly disturbing fact may have lain elsewhere.

When his allies looked beyond Lincoln the President to Lincoln the man, they were not sure what they say, but they were all too sure of what they did *not* see. Abraham Lincoln had no vision, no great hope for black and white, no great dream for what America might be. He fought only to save a hollow shell called Union. During the summer of 1862, Lincoln struggled with himself, his God, and his country, to find a vision, a liberating justification for fighting and death. He progressed and retreated, stood still and moved forward. Finally, caught up by events and his own personal search, the President of the United States learned that he, too, could not escape history.[30]

The second confiscation act's passage on July 17, 1862 was an important event for Lincoln and the nation. The first confiscation law treated slave property gingerly, declaring only those slaves used for insurrectionary purposes to be confiscable. The narrowness of that law's scope was clear from the outset, and its author, Lyman Trumbull, moved quickly to remedy the legal situation. When Congress reconvened in December 1861, he introduced another confiscation bill, much broader than the first. The bill languished in committee for months before Congress turned its attention to it. In the interim the national legislature abolished slavery in the federal district and the territories, recognized Haiti and Liberia, and prohibited army officers from returning fugitive slaves. Lack of immediate congressional attention in confiscation, therefore, did not signify lack of antislavery interest in Congress or the country at large. But the issue was so controversial in 1862, the House Judiciary Committee decided not to consider any bill touching upon confiscation or slave liberation.[31]

Nevertheless, public debate about confiscation continued, and the need for a decision about massive confiscation did not recede. And massive confiscation was precisely what Trumbull had proposed. The Philadelphia *Press* correctly observed that the time to accept or reject confiscation had arrived, and that "in the way we signify either our acceptance or rejection, we shape the policy of this war." The *Press* went on, linking the power to confiscate with the ability to wage war, for "if confiscation is wrong in theory, then the war is wrong." Every power must be used to defeat the South, and common sense indicated that rebels' slaves should be released from service to treason. Anything less indirectly sustained the rebellion.[32]

Not everyone agreed. Opponents of confiscation anchored their argument on two foundations. Many pointed to the Constitution's strict definition of treason, the punishments it allowed, and its prohibitions against bills of attainder, *ex post facto* laws, corruption of blood, and forfeitures of property beyond the life of the convicted. Confiscation of traitors' property might be allowable, but the accused had first to be convicted of treason. Yet the essence of the rebellion lay precisely in the regional suspension of United States law and authority. No courts could function in the South, and no one could be convicted of treason or any other crime because treason was so massive. To that extent, the rebellion's aim, to revoke the Constitution's authority over the South, was successful. Nevertheless, some northerners wanted to bind the government by constitutional safeguards, the net effect of which protected the rights of people who no longer claimed rights, immunities, or protections under the Constitution.[33]

Opponents of confiscation also grounded their arguments in distinctions between belligerent and municipal powers available to the government. Southerners in rebellion might be viewed either as traitors or as enemy aliens. The Constitution, narrowly conceived, severely limited what the government could do to traitors. Confiscation as a penal statute involved the question of citizens' constitutional rights. But massive confiscation, a measure "absolutely novel in our legislation," might be justified as a use of the war power—a belligerent right against a *de facto* enemy.[34]

Some opponents emphasized restraints the Constitution placed upon Congress, pointing especially to the prohibitions on property forfeiture beyond the natural life of the convict. For Congress to punish an act more severely by not calling it treason, thereby skirting constitutional limitations, would "degrade [those prohibitions] into a mere quibble about the nomenclature of criminal law." Congress could punish treason by death, but the traitor's estate was safe. But Congress did not exercise authority over the South, and therefore, could not justly require individual's allegiance. Precedent seemed clear. The British had occupied American territory during the War of 1812. American courts had subsequently held that the allegiance of affected Americans was temporarily suspended. The government could not protect them and the citizens' duties were thereby absolved. Viewed from that perspective, Congress could not punish treason with confiscation because there was no treason.[35]

If sovereign, municipal power did not justify confiscation, did the war power? To rely on belligerent rights under the law of nations, required the assumption of the rules of civilized warfare. These rules, as they had evolved, distinguished between public and private property. The former was subject to confiscation. The United States, however, had always maintained that the private property of enemy aliens was exempt. Again the War of 1812 offered precedent. Americans (especially Secretary of State John Quincy Adams) had argued then that British decrees of emancipation based upon the war power were illegal and did not free American slaves, because slaves were private, and not public, property.[36]

If the United States repudiated this doctrine, conservatives argued, and chose to confiscate private property, another distinction would arise. The title to real property did not pass to another through mere occupation, or holding of the property—only the right to *use* the property. Once the rebellion ended and the usurped power of the federal government was restored, the captured property reverted to its titular owner. The other type of private property, personal, included chattel slaves. In that case, title could be transferred, but only through actual possession and physical removal to a place of safety. Hence, mere decrees did not affect slaves' status. The only sure way to possess and remove slaves was through the army. Therefore, personal property might be confiscated only through the war power of the President, manifested in the army.[37]

Other opponents believed that the federal government possessed both municipal and belligerent powers in fighting the rebellion. But could Congress treat southerners as both citizens and enemy aliens simultaneously? Put another way, was it possible to confiscate treason? Two answers were given—an abrupt "no," and a problematic, "yes, but—."

Pamphleteer Anna Ella Carroll denied that Congress could exercise the war power over southern property. To do so, to treat rebels as enemy aliens, would be an admission and recognition of the Confederacy, the rejection of which was the point of the war. Legally, Carroll believed that Congress could not "war" with its own citizens. As Union armies captured southern property, the Constitution's authority was immediately restored. The ancient right of *postliminium*, whereby property and people returned to their former status upon recapture, nullified attempted changes in property status. Carroll warned that unless "wise counsels shall prevail, or unless restrained by the President, Congress 'unchained by the Constitution,' will move its armies swiftly over the liberties of the country, both South and North."[38] The upshot was that Congress could not confiscate property; the President might, but only under very specific circumstances.

Proponents of confiscation were hard-pressed to rebut conservatives' strict construction. The letter of the Constitution seemed clear and unmistakable. Massive treason would go unpunished if the Constitution were perceived as an obstacle.

The fundamental error opponents of confiscation made, advocates argued, was ignoring the context in which the nation found itself. Confusing the law of peace and the law of war deprived the government of any chance at all to vindicate its existence. Self-preservation, "must override all those laws and constitutional provisions which regulate the exercise, in peace, of its dormant, undisputed authority."[39] Regular constitutional obligations and rights, the *jus paci*, were suspended until the *status pacis* returned. The Constitution forbade the common law practice of attainder, not necessarily legislative enactments. Neither did the Constitution limit Congress' ability to design punishments for treason. And there was treason. Under the circumstances, confiscating slaves was a legitimate punishment. After all, state law defined property, and by that reckoning, slaves were property. Justice sanctioned the ironic twisting of slave laws against slave society. By that approach confiscation and/or military emancipation were tools for carrying out the war's goal—preservation of the Union.[40]

William Whiting presented the best case for congressional power to confiscate. Whiting began with the useful distinction of emancipation through confiscation, and abolition. The former affected individual slaves; the latter would operate "on all citizens residing [in slave states], and effects a change of local law." Congress might confiscate private property—even slave property—if the public necessity warranted it. Congress might even abolish slavery by law if it became more than a domestic institution and intruded upon the nation's "rights, interest, duties or obligations," or impeded the execution of the laws or infringed on the rights of United States citizens.[41] After such a sweeping claim of power, actual confiscation seemed restrained. Whiting's diligent justification of the power to confiscate reenforces the view that Americans were wedded to the form and substance of law as the defining language of political life.

Whiting found the power of eminent domain a useful source for constitutionally authorized confiscation. Property could be appropriated, and the only requirement needed was public use, and an indemnity to the owner. Legal title to the taken property would be transferred. Significantly, Whiting defined public use as any seizure for the benefit of the United States. Benefit did not necessarily imply use, for the taken property could be "*disused, removed*, or *destroyed*." Nor were there any restrictions upon the kind of property Congress might seize—slaves included. Pointing also to Congress' charter to promote the common defense, Whiting argued that masters might not be entitled to compensation if Congress decided to draft slaves into the army and, incidentally, altered their property status. Slaves, like other residents, were subjects of the United States, owing allegiance and service.[42]

The fate of slaves captured through military engagements should be determined by Congress, Whiting argued, and the President should execute the laws. There was no conflict between presidential and congressional powers, because Congress and the executive both possessed war powers. While the President through the army might emancipate, the war power also authorized congressional confiscation. Whiting maintained that there was a difference between confiscation as punishment for a crime during peace time, and confiscation as a tool to suppress the rebellion. The *fact* of civil war allowed Congress to exercise belligerent rights against its own citizens. Whiting reasoned that traitors were those who levied war against the United States. War legally existed, and therefore, the rebels were traitors. At war, the United States possessed all belligerent powers plus the sovereign powers it held over all its subjects. War freed the President and Congress from having to see rebels only as subjects and not also as enemies. By the rebels' actions, northerners and southerners were co-belligerents. Yet the law of nations that governed how belligerents might act toward one another, did not limit the United States in how it treated subject traitors. Belligerent rights allowed the United States to take enemy property, and title transferred *ipso facto*. Whiting's theory provided the best of both worlds–southerners were traitors *and* belligerents. What could not be done to one, could be done to the other. As Whiting declared, "The rights of war and the rights of peace cannot coexist. One must yield to another." Citizens might be protected by the Constitution during war and peace, but the rights protected differed according to the circumstance.[43]

Congress possessed "plenary authority" to pass confiscation laws against belligerent enemies for the public good. When used in tandem with the President's war power, it made property lost by rebels during the war, lost for good. Even individual loyal citizens living in the Confederacy might have to yield their property because the national safety superseded individual rights. Acknowledging the distinction in that confiscation and/or emancipation was not abolition, Whiting nevertheless sketched an expansive and forceful view of government power.[44]

Commentators differed on the long-term effects of military-sponsored emancipation. Without the intervention of federal power, a contributor to the *North American Review* noted, freedmen might revert to slave status if they were claimed by their former masters because there was "no right to freedom . . . under the laws of the United States." On the other hand, a writer for the *Monthly Law Reporter* maintained that military emancipation did not transfer title but destroyed the property altogether. Once destroyed, like a ship sunk during battle, the property could not impede the army, could not be resurrected, and could not be returned, nor restitution made. The status would be destroyed, though the person would remain. This might obtain for military emancipation, complementary to but distinct from confiscation. The latter required legislation. On the chance that the more cautious opinion might prove correct (or might win out in the debate), that military emancipation would not destroy property but only hold title in abeyance during the army's presence, proponents believed that confiscation was a necessary legal remedy. Yet it was difficult for proponents not to feel some measure of guilt for the war, difficult not to believe the rebellion was the "wrath from an offended God for our treading the negro in the dust in contradiction of our Declaration of Independence."[45] Southerners might have to pay the price by the loss of their property, but the nation as a whole also shared in the responsibility for massive confiscation.

The second confiscation law, first proposed in December 1861, took seven months to enact, and during that interim, other issues gained temporary preeminence. Both houses of Congress referred the controversial confiscation issue to special committees for careful consideration. Republicans differed on the focus, and ultimate purpose of the bill. Some looked for the substantive change in southern society that would follow massive confiscation and property redistribution. The South would be fundamentally changed, the slaveholder aristocracy displaced, and the Union restored not as it was, but as it ought to be. Other Republicans, more moderate, saw confiscation as a means to punish rebellion but, therefore, insisted upon judicial proceedings to determine individual guilt.

Both houses of Congress considered various confiscation proposals until May 1862, when the Senate postponed the matter indefinitely and took up other business. Thereupon the House passed its confiscation bill, sending it to the Senate. The upper chamber took up the bill in late June, substituted a more conservative measure in its stead, and returned the matter to the House for concurrence. Almost immediately, the House refused, and sent the confiscation proposal back to the Senate. In order to end the deadlock, on July 8 each house appointed three members to a conference committee. Resisting radical efforts for a more sweeping bill, one without judicial proceedings for seized property, the conferees reported a compromise measure on July 11. Omitting two-thirds of the Senate version, the compromise contained provisions for confiscation as punishment for treason and inciting insurrection, prohibited the return of fugitive slaves except to loyal masters, provided for the enlistment of blacks into the army, and left open the question of the colonization of freed blacks. *In rem* judicial proceedings (in which the seized property itself, and not the owner, would be "put in trial") were adopted as the normal method of confiscation. This allowed confiscation to proceed even if the owner of the property did not attend the court hearing, a likely occurrence since rebels would hardly appear before federal authorities. And the conference committee included a new section in the bill emancipating slaves owned by persons engaged in or aiding the rebellion.[46]

The constitutional prohibition against corruption of blood and forfeiture beyond the life of the person convicted weighed heavily upon the minds of conservative members of Congress, as well as President Lincoln. So, too, did the resort to the unusual *in rem* proceedings, more often associated with admiralty law. Indeed, Lincoln had a veto message prepared for the confiscation act. He objected to a phrase that suggested that conviction of treason or incitement to treason actually freed rebels' slaves. He preferred to argue that the title to the slaves would first pass to the nation. The government then might dispose of the title as it saw fit. Additionally, Lincoln wished an explicit method outlined in the bill for determining whether slaves seized met the conditions for freedom specified in the act. Most worrisome for the President, however, were the possible corruption of blood and *ex post facto* features of the act. Aware of his displeasure, Congress passed an extraordinary explanatory resolution to the effect that no forfeiture of property would go beyond the life of the offender. Satisfied, Lincoln signed the confiscation bill on July 17.[47]

Conservatives continued to stress the constitutional limits of confiscation. They emphasized the necessity of convicting the accused person of treason before confiscating his property. This argument, of course, missed the mark as the genius of *in rem* proceedings obviated the requirement of trail and conviction of a person for treason. The cautious cared little for supposed abolitionists goals ("philanthropy or treason, call it what you please"), so long as the Constitution was violated. Some were so snesitive about white civil liberties that one writer for the *North American Review* would have preferred arming the slaves and inviting a slave revolt, rather than violate any constitutional right of whites.[48]

William Whiting made an extensive defense of the Second Confiscation Act in an appendix of his *The War Powers of the President and Legislative Powers of Congress*. After a detailed examination of the English common law meaning of bill of attainder, Whiting concluded that a congressional statute had to contain four provisions before it became an attainder and, therefore, unconstitutional: 1) the death penalty (or banishment); 2) punishment *ex post facto*; 3) guilt determined by legislative act; and 4) the penalty had to work corruption of blood and forfeiture beyond life estate. Whiting carefully distinguished between punishment for treason and the effects that an attainder of treason had had in English common law. The former, he maintained, was not limited. Only the manner of punishment, the legal mechanism employed, was controlled by the Constitution. Accepting the conservative claim that confiscation was limited by the treason clauses of Article III, section 3 of the Constitution, (and ignoring the defense that *in rem* proceedings affected property, not persons), Whiting concluded that the Second Confiscation Act was constitutional and a suitable weapon for the suppression of the rebellion.[49]

By making all rebel property liable to confiscation, the scope of the 1862 law was broad, indeed. Whiting was justified in claiming the law as "one of the most important penal acts ever passed by the Congress of the United States." But at least in one of its particulars, the act hit a very sensitive nerve. Slaves owned by rebels were freed, not in *in rem* proceedings, but by military action as they came behind Union lines. Congress did not sanction slave confiscation so much as slave emancipation.

The President of the United States brooded about slavery. On June 18 he confided to Vice-President Hannibal Hamlin his tentative decision to free the slaves. On July 12, with the confiscation bill and is emancipation clause nearing passage, Lincoln appealed to border state congressmen to agree to his plan for federally supported, state-sponsored, gradual, compensated emancipation. "Friction and abrasion" alone, Lincoln warned, would destroy slavery no matter what border residents—or he—wanted.

Even before the men from Kentucky, Missouri, Maryland, and Delaware rejected his offer, Lincoln began the process by which he personally would ratify what had thus far been achieved during the war. The slave and his relation to the Union was the inescapable fact the President had to face. Torn between his hatred of slavery and his constitutional caution, Lincoln confronted the question that Wendell

Phillips put so forcefully:

> Hitherto the negro has been a hated question. The Union moved majestic on its path, and shut him out, eclipsing him from the sun of equality and happiness. He has changed his position to-day. He now stands between us and the sun of our safety and prosperity.[50]

Returning on July 13 from the funeral of Secretary of War Edwin Stanton's infant son, the President occupied a carriage with Secretary of State William Seward and Navy Secretary Gideon Welles. Unexpectedly, the President remarked that he had about concluded that emancipation of rebel slaves was a military necessity.

Surprised, because Lincoln had previously opposed emancipation by the federal executive, Seward and Welles readily agreed with the President, saying that emancipation was "justifiable . . . expedient and necessary." The President requested the secretaries' opinions since his proposal to border state men (made only the day before) was still outstanding. Any notice of emancipation in rebel sates might severely harm chances for the border state proposal. Still wedded to gradualism as the best method for emancipation, Lincoln's "native sagacity and power of thought" now drew him to a more radical conclusion, at least concerning the rebel states.

The next day, July 14, Lincoln's friend Illinois senator Orville Browning brought the President a copy of the confiscation law just enacted by Congress. Browning urged the President's veto of the measure, believing that it was much too radical. Lincoln disclosed nothing of his own struggle with the question of emancipation, but signed the confiscation law after Congress passed its explanatory resolution.[51]

On Monday, July 21, the Cabinet assembled at 10:00 a.m. For the first time, Lincoln gave general expression to his new thoughts about slavery, speaking of his determination to take "some definitive steps" on the subject. He outlined several proposals, including the use of black laborers on military works, and an "effective" colonization program. At that time he opposed using blacks in the armed forces, despite General David Hunter's request for that authorization. The Cabinet meeting ended, but reconvened the next day to continue the discussion.

The Cabinet dropped the colonization plan and, despite Secretary Chase's strong advocacy, the President still opposed arming freedmen. The recently passed Confiscation Act loomed large in Lincoln's thinking, and he then proposed to issue a proclamation of emancipation based on that law. The act's sixth section declared that after sixty days from the President's promulgation, the property of southerners still in rebellion against the Union would be subject to confiscation. Lincoln told his Cabinet that he intended in his December annual message to Congress to renew his plan for gradual, compensated emancipation in the border states. He would include any repentant rebel states, also. In any event the President intended that slaves held by rebels would, on January 1, 1863, "thenceforward, and forever, be free."

Reaction in the Cabinet to Lincoln's proposal was mixed. Chase thought that there should be no compensation for loyal masters. Instead, he suggested emancipation through a relatively quiet, piecemeal approach, allowing each commanding general to free slaves in his military department. The proclamation Lincoln proposed might cause severe financial instability. Seward, too, surprised the President with his strong argument against the proclamation of freedom at that time. Without a Union victory upon which to base the edict, Seward thought that Lincoln's measure might seem to Europe like the last gasp of a failing government. To avoid the semblance of desperation, Seward urged forbearance. Postmaster General Montgomery Blair also echoed Seward's concern about foreign reaction. Blair further suggested that there was no need for a proclamation, that even the most radical Republicans did not then demand emancipation. Playing upon the President's sensitivity to the border states, Blair argued that emancipation of rebels' slaves was tantamount to universal emancipation. Almost everyone agreed that slavery could not exist in the border states alone. To keep the border loyal, Blair maintained, Lincoln must forbear.

The President reluctantly agreed, leaving emancipation for "further consideration." He hardly seemed to be the tortured, self-doubting Lincoln searching for a solution to slavery and the war. With reluctance, the President held emancipation in abeyance. His reasoning had gone to freedom and the use of black recruits for the war effort. The Union's chronic need for manpower was an ever-pressing concern, and the President could justify taking and using black laborers in most instances. Nevertheless, Lincoln still opposed the use of black troops, rejecting in August two black regiments raised in Indiana.[53]

The enigma of thwarted emancipation grew. The Confiscation Act's sixth section, under which Lincoln first proposed to issue a proclamation of freedom, required the President's public promulgation to include a sixty day warning period before the proclamation went into effect. Lincoln issued that proclamation on July 25, eight days after he signed the Confiscation Act and three days after postponing emancipation. Yet Lincoln took the text of his July 25 proclamation from the first draft of his proposed (and postponed) emancipation order. Lincoln only omitted the final paragraph emancipating slaves.

The proclamation as issued set a sixty day period after which rebel slaves (and other property) could be seized and forfeited. Yet the confiscation and emancipation features of the 1862 confiscation law were distinct; slaves were specifically declared *free*, not just confiscable. Lincoln's emancipation proposal continued in the tradition of the first, 1861, confiscation act. He wanted to maintain the useful legal fiction that slaves were property (state law defined property), applying congressional war power to this property. In tandem with congressional authority, Lincoln would also have used his authority as commander-in-chief to free all persons held as slaves in rebel areas. Since the President would have relied partially on the "slaves as property" argument, his July 25 proclamation can be seen as an emancipation edict or sorts. In sixty days slave property in rebel areas would be subject to seizure and forfeiture.[54]

But it was not seen as emancipation.[55] The President was criticized by antislavery men as little more than a tool of the border states or, at least, as a captive of his own fears about their alienation. Lincoln, however, was rapidly losing patience with the border position and professed friends from the region who "hold my hands while my enemies stab me." Their appeals had "paralyzed me more in this struggle than any other thing." Lincoln let Reverdy Johnson, former attorney general and special State Department agent to New Orleans, know that he would not lose the war "leaving any available card unplayed." On the other hand, Lincoln's own misgivings about emancipation were clear when he wrote a New Orleans resident on July 28: "I shall do nothing in malice. What I deal with is too vast for malicious dealing." With such warnings issuing from Lincoln and others, word leaked out that a change in policy was in the offing.

Writing to New Orleans commanding general Benjamin Butler, Secretary Chase detailed his own views of emancipation, characterizing the President's compensation proposal as a dying idea. Chase upheld the freedmen's rights to "life, liberty and the pursuit of happiness by the same laws which protect[ed]" him. Recognizing that many in the North disagreed with him, however, Chase suggested that the South be made the area of black settlement, so that the blacks already in the North would "slide southward" and leave behind no questions for whites to quarrel about. Chase went on to tell Butler that the nullification of General Hunter's emancipation order in May had been a mistake that would not now be repeated. "The truth is, my dear General," the Secretary wrote, "that there has been a great change in the public mind within the last few weeks." Was the change in the public mind, or in Lincoln's? Chase had an intimate knowledge of the President's thinking. Clearly, he meant to prepare Butler for a dramatic alteration of Administration policy.[56]

But the change did not come. Seward's prerequisite of a Union military victory proved to be a formidable requirement. Given the time to ponder and brood over the question, Lincoln began to sound less like a would-be emancipator and more life a man looking for an escape. Chase followed up his letter to Butler by pressing Lincoln for emancipation and the use of black troops. On August 3 Lincoln told the Cabinet that the was "pretty well cured of objections to any measure except want of adaptedness to put down the rebellion. . . ." Military necessity remained the key that would unlock the presidential war power, the power by which persons who were slaves would become free.

The President had few kind words for the candidates for freedom. Addressing a delegation of free blacks on August 14, Lincoln painted perhaps his grimmest picture of America. Each race suffered by the presence of the other, and the future offered little more than the past or the present:

> even when you cease to be slaves, you are yet far removed from being placed on an equality with the white race. You are cut off from many of the advantages which the other race enjoy. The aspiration of men is to enjoy equality with the best when free, but on this broad continent, not a single man of your race is made the equal of a single man of ours. . . . I do not propose to discuss this, but to present it as a fact with which we have to deal. I cannot alter it if I would. . . . See our present condition—the country engaged in war!—our white men cutting one another's throats, none knowing how far it will extend; and then consider what we know to be the truth. But for your race among us there could not be war, although many men engaged on either side do not care for you one way or the other. Nevertheless, I repeat, without the institution of Slavery and the colored race as a basis, the war could not have an existence.
>
> It is better for us both, therefore, to be separated.[57]

Lincoln's remarks shocked abolitionists. In the President's view, the black did not fit into the scheme of America and was, indeed, the cause of the present blood-letting. Disturbingly, the President's repulsion lay with "white men cutting one another's throats," not with the suffering slaves had endured for decades. The *Liberator* bluntly denounced Lincoln's address as a "tissue of absurdities and false assumptions." A meeting of New York blacks gave the lie to the assumptions. Blacks were not "a different race of people," they maintained. They were Americans. The United States was their native country. There was no reason they should leave the land they loved. Despite its faults, despite the racism and slavery and discrimination, America was their home as much as the white man's. If they were to be "colonized" anywhere, it would have to be in a South free of slavery.

What was the President's attitude toward slavery, the black, and the war? Responding to Horace Greeley's "Prayer of Twenty Millions," Lincoln gave the best statement of his pragmatic Unionism. Whatever was necessary to restore the Union, he would do. Freeing all, or none, or a part of southern slaves—those were all clear options for the President. Or at least he wished the public to believe so. Exactly a month before Lincoln had told his Cabinet of his disposition to free the slaves in order to win the war. In the interim he proposed colonization in his most forceful statement yet on the subject, and at least publicly kept open the option of continued bondage for some (if not all) southern slaves. Was the President maneuvering for political room, putting pro-slavery elements off-guard by appearing to side with their own anti-black prejudices?[58]

Abolitionists and radical Republicans were dismayed at Lincoln's words, if not despairing. William Lloyd Garrison grew skeptical about the President's honesty, suggesting his control by the "satanic democracy of the North, and the traitorous 'loyalty' of the Border States." The situation appeared on the surface much as the *North American Review* described it: rebel states would resume all their rights once the war ended. Only continued tenacious rebellion could possibly play into the abolitionists' hands.[59]

Tenacious rebellion—this was the key, not only to the war's incredible length, but also to Lincoln's thinking. The military victory long sought as Seward's *sine qua non* for emancipation still eluded. No—it did not even approach. Second Bull Run was yet another Union disaster, not so much in abject defeat (though there was that, too) as in lack of victory. Numerous reasons were cited for the galling fact—poor generalship, congressional interference with the army, insufficient troop strength. To Lincoln and undoubtedly to many others it seemed, perhaps, a sign of Divine displeasure. In the aftermath of Second Bull Run, in the bitterness and creeping fear that join with confusion, Lincoln looked for the reason—the one reason—to explain all the war, death, suffering, and agony that the nation had endured, and to explain his own agony:

> The will of God prevails. In great contests each party claims to act in accordance with the will of God. Both *may* be, and one *must* be wrong. God can not be *for*, and *against* the same thing at the same time. In the present civil war it is quite possible that God's purpose is something different from the purpose of either party—and yet the human instrumentalities, working just as they do, are of the best adaptation to effect His purpose. I am almost ready to say this is probably true—that God wills this contest, and wills that it shall not end yet. By his mere quiet power, on the minds

of the now contestants, He could have either *saved* or *destroyed* the Union without a human contest. Yet the contest began. And having begun He could give final victory to either side any day. Yet the contest proceeds.

The will of God prevails—God wills this contest—yet it proceeds. Lincoln's crisis of faith did not center upon the Divine Will, for he followed a familiar affirmation, confusion, resignation, and acceptance pattern. Lincoln's crisis centered upon his will—what *he* would do. It is not entirely unfair to ask who Lincoln competed with more in the "great contest"—the South, or himself. In the end, Lincoln quit the contest, and gave the decision over to God.[60]

"No tongue can tell, no mind conceive, no pen portray the horrible sights I witnessed this morning. God grant that these things may soon end," wrote a soldier after viewing Antietam battlefield.

"Eye hath not seen, nor ear heard, neither have entered into the heart of man, the things which God hath prepared for them that love him." (1 Cor. 2:9).

Two statements, striking in their difference, yet parallel in sentiment. The first written after a great battle; the second a vision of heaven. The first a plea for God's intervention; the second a promise of comfort. The first a soldier's reaction to the field at Antietam. The second an apostle's view of the peaceable kingdom. For Lincoln the two became one—Antietam was the sign of election and favor and, indeed, what God had prepared. By the outcome of that battle, it was clear that "God had decided the question in favor of the slaves." Therefore, Lincoln was convinced that his proclamation of freedom would not be papal bull against a comet.[61]

On September 22 Lincoln issued the momentous deed of freedom. Based upon his war power as commander-in-chief, Lincoln declared that on January 1, 1863 all slaves held in areas still in rebellion would be "thenceforward, and forever free." The executive would "recognize and maintain" ex-slaves' freedom.[62] It was "an exercise of extraordinary power," in Gideon Welles' phrase—a measure too profound to be based "on mere humanitarian principles." Justification lay rather in the proclamation's true purpose—preservation of the Union. Indeed, emancipation was to be a punishment for continued rebellion and its threat an inducement to lay down southern arms. True, certain military benefits might accrue to the Union if it tapped the vast manpower potential of southern slaves. The great military benefit, however, and Lincoln's ultimate purpose, was to end the war. The humanitarian aspect of emancipation was secondary. God may have decided the issue of freedom and slavery, but as for future race relations, the Almighty apparently remained mute. The quality of freedom Lincoln pledged to recognize and maintain was an open question. The very next day, September 23, the President resumed his efforts to colonize American blacks. Although Lincoln would not tolerate compulsion or deportation, neither did he believe four million blacks could be Americans.[63]

Whatever Lincoln's personal view of emancipation and its aftermath, the Proclamation had great effect. If nothing more, it was a tremendous claim for the President's authority. Because the Constitution authorized the war power, emancipation by the President (or by Congress as in sections nine and ten of the 1862 Confiscation Act) was a striking new link between the federal government and individuals. Circumstances allowed and required state governments to be bypassed, though not ignored. The meaning of the war became clear with emancipation, despite the Proclamation's drawbacks and limitations. State law defined property, but freedom was national in scope. Freedom was the nation's business, and any institution that attempted to destroy the nation or the nation's business, must itself be destroyed. If malignant slavery did not end, the nation, the nation's government, and the nation's liberty would. Because the Constitution belonged to the people of 1862 and not to those of 1787, emancipation was necessary to secure everyone's freedom. The war had changed and was changing reality. "Let it search," Ralph Waldo Emerson wrote, "let it grind, let it overturn, and like the fire when it finds no more fuel, it burns out." Events took on a life of their own, demanding new responses. For all its deficiencies, the Emancipation Proclamation was such a response.[64]

Abolitionists divided sharply in their views of the document. Garrison granted that it was a cause for rejoicing "as far as it goes," but his concern centered on slavery's continued existence. Congressman James Ashley criticized the one hundred day interim before emancipation took effect, saying it was like apologizing beforehand. (Lincoln recognized the truth of the remark, responding, "Ashley, that's a center shot.") Writing in the *New Englander*, the Reverend N. H. Eggleston also faulted the Proclamation for its delayed effect, saying that without the delay it would have been "more just, more dignified, more manly, and more Christian. As a war measure, it would have been more effective." Still, it was better than nothing, much better than nothing in Gerrit Smith's view. Wendell Phillips summed up the viewpoint: "How decent Abe grows."[65]

Republican governors meeting in Altoona, Pennsylvania, supported Lincoln's decision, calling the Proclamation "a measure of justice and sound policy." In general, the Republican press fell into line behind the decree. The Emancipation Proclamation was a "decree of fate rather than the utterance of any man," according to the Philadelphia *American*. The Chicago *Tribune* declared "so splendid a vision has hardly shone upon the world since the day of the Messiah." More radical Republican pressmen, however, emphasized the Proclamation as a beginning rather than a conclusion. The weight of the federal government had been removed from the backs of the slaves, but they could not yet fight for themselves. The Proclamation was "rather innocent and harmless," observed the Perry (Pennsylvania) *Freeman*; force was still the chief means to conquer the rebellion—"by powder and balls, by bombs and bayonets, by sword and by fire." The Springfield (Massachusetts) *Republican* summed up the radical position concisely in its statement. Years of struggle were still ahead, "not all of it bloody, but all of it bitter":

> The destruction of slavery involves the reconstruction of states and State constitutions. The liberated men are to have rights before the law—laws made for the regulation of their relations to each other and to the white proprietors of the soil.[66]

In radical eyes the best thing about the Proclamation was its existence. No longer could northern politicians avoid the issue of slavery and freedom, for the Proclamation worked its effect while men slept, armies rested, and generals waited. In a sense, the battle shifted from Richmond to Boston: "For there can be no durable peace, no sound Constitution, until we have fought this battle.... It were to patch a peace to cry Peace whilst this vital difference exists."[67] Men who for years had feared the appellation "abolitionist" because of its political opprobrium were freed along with the slaves. Secretary Chase and friends sat together one evening and merrily called one another abolitionists, reveling in the "novel sensation of appropriating that horrible name." As the *Liberator* noted, emancipation brought out the tendencies on the other sides, too, turning "every pseudo-loyal toad . . . into a semi-rebellious devil without disguise." So border state men, once allies in the war effort, might well become opponents.[68]

Conservatives were skeptical about Lincoln's "new policy," openly questioning its worth. The Proclamation's one hundred day delay convinced some that the measure was a sop to radicals. At least this was the hope, for if the emancipation measure was more than placating move, it raised issues "too tremendous, and . . . fraught with consequences . . . to admit to calculation or forecast." Democratic newspapers, however, were quick to forecast a future of "darkness and blood," in the words of the New York *Journal of Commerce*. The Proclamation was illegal and unconstitutional, for it confiscated slave property without conviction for treason, suspended state laws, and invited slave insurrection. Most conservatives felt betrayed by Lincoln's new policy. The Philadelphia *Journal* described the decree as a thunderbolt to conservatives, and a joy only to a set of "insane fanatics." To comfort its readers, the St. Lawrence (New York) *Advance* assured that the Proclamation "will prove to be a dead letter and an abortion," serving only to intensify southern resistance and making reunion all the more difficult. Hence, emancipation was wrong on legal, constitutional, political, and military grounds. Emancipation, along with previous antislavery measures, only confirmed the Democratic view that abolition had raised its "hydra-head."[69]

Democrats and conservatives in general continued to call for "the Union as it was, the Constitution as it is," hoping that through this device the South could be restored to the Union with her rights (that is, slavery) intact. Once restored, there might be a need for constitutional revision, Democratic party chairman August Belmont suggested. But revisions would seek better definition of the limits of federal and state power, and be aimed against the "ultra and arbitrary spirit" of the present Administration. Many conservatives who had given Lincoln the benefit of the doubt, now spoke in opposition. In the congressional elections of October and November, 1862, Democrats made their best showing in years, adding thirty-five seats in the House of Representatives. Allies of the Administration attempted to counter conservative attacks by re-emphasizing the connection between the rebellion and slavery. How did they want to fight the war, "what do the anti-energy, anti-action, anti-contraband-digging, anti every thing and go-ahead in the war gentlemen propose?" In the end all antislavery men could hope for was education. Just as the war had impressed them with the necessity of ending slavery, so might northern Democrats and other conservatives learn to let go of slavery, to let go of attachment to a system they sometimes held more dear than slaveholders. The devotion to slavery was passing away and had been ever since "Saint Sumter's Day." Republicans, radicals, abolitionists, Lincoln—all waited for history to make the inescapable indisputable.[70]

More disturbing was former Supreme Court Justice Benjamin R. Curtis' opposition to the Emancipation Proclamation. Curtis, one of two justices to dissent from the *Dred Scott* decision in 1857, embodied the conservative principles of constitutional construction dear to the hearts of many Americans. Although he supported the war, Curtis' narrow legalism would make effective prosecution of that war difficult, and certainly ruled out the Proclamation. Curtis asserted that the Emancipation Proclamation repealed and annulled state laws, thereby failing to distinguish between emancipation and abolition. That the Proclamation did not abolish slavery was a key point in Whiting's argument, and a reason Garrison was so disappointed with the decree. Substantially, Curtis dismissed the notion that there was anything like a "war power" under the Constitution, fearing that if it were once invoked, the "gigantic shadow" of presidential war powers might blot out northern as well as southern constitutional rights.[71]

Another constitutional conservative also had misgivings about the Proclamation, although his reactions assumed the color of his recent thinking. Lincoln's first public response to emancipation was, "I can only trust in God I have made no mistake." Lincoln remained unsure of his decision. Unless the North responded properly, not with "breath alone [that] kills no rebels," but with troops to crush out the rebellion, Lincoln feared his Proclamation would be a failure. He continued to push for colonization ventures to Central America and Haiti, for colonization like every other action, like emancipation itself, aimed toward restoring the Union—nothing more, nothing less. And while there was much support for the Proclamation and the Proclamation's President:

> Now who has done the greatest deed Which History has ever known, And who, in Freedom's direst need, Became her bravest champion? Who a whole continent set free? Who killed the curse and broke the ban Which made a lie of liberty? You—Father Abraham—you're the man![72]

yet Lincoln's own words seem truer to the mark, and a more fitting summation of the enigma of emancipation:

> If I had had my way, this war would never have commenced; If I had been allowed my way this war would have ended before this, but we find it still continues; and we must believe that He permits it for some wise purpose of his own, mysterious and unknown to us.[73]

Some wise purpose. The months of July through November were times of discovery for the government—Congress and President. The Second Confiscation Act accepted the idea of massive seizure and redistribution of property as a punishment for rebellion and a means to reconstruct the South. Emancipation fostered by that law was a significant step forward, yet suffered from the same war circumstance that made it possible. Confusion about slaves' status—whether person to be set free from treasonable bonds, or property to be seized and adjudicated—lessened the visionary quality of this approach to emancipation. The President's Proclamation also allowed an ambiguous interpretation. Although persons by Lincoln's reckoning, slaves were not so clearly Americans. To be sure, each measure, proclamation, and statute, were necessary, incremental steps toward freedom, and each step was beyond anything that might have been imagined a mere two years before. Blacks might be free, but they were not yet part of America, the special status of "freedmen" marking a subtle yet profound difference from average "freemen." To have meaning, freedom had to exist within a context, in connection with a place, society, and culture. This was the component missing from confiscation and emancipation; this was the part of the abolitionist ideal not yet implemented. And for this, there was a hollowness to emancipation, a certain lack. As there was no vision, so there was no joy.

What to do with the blacks now that they were free? A constant question after 1862. Americans fought a war, enacted laws, concocted schemes, but all failed to answer that question.

> Truly may it be said that Africa has invaded and conquered our country, and though we may call the negro a slave, he is the master of our destiny.[74]

We cannot escape history.

NOTES FOR CHAPTER FOUR

1. On June 5, 1862, Congress granted diplomatic recognition to Haiti and Liberia. Slavery was abolished in the territories of the United States on June 19, 1862, *SAL*, 12:421, 432.

2. Lincoln, *Coll. Works*, 5:537. I have eliminated the emphasis in the original.

3. Ibid., 5:530-36.

4. Ibid., 5:434, 530-36. Secretary of State William H. Seward suggested the phrase "to maintain" freedmen's liberty, David Donald, *Inside Lincoln's Cabinet: The Civil War Diaries of Salmon P. Chase* (New York: Longsmans, Green and Company, 1954), 151.

5. Lincoln, *Coll. Works*, 5:537.

6. Don E. Fehrenbacher notes that "if the United States had a patron saint, it would no doubt be Abraham Lincoln." Stephen B. Oates, Lincoln's most recent biographer, observes the tendency to characterize Lincoln either as the "Great Emancipator" or as the "great ancestor" of racist white citizens' councils and the Ku Klux Klan. Resolution into neat and overprecise "either/or" categories drains meaning from ambiguity. Lincoln was neither incarnate racist nor noble equalitarian; he was both. Fehrenbacher, "Only His Step-Children," *Civil War History* (1974) 20:292; Oates, "The Man of Our Redemption: Abraham Lincoln and the Emancipation of the Slave," *Presidential Studies Quarterly* (1979) 9:15. See also the entire issue of the *Papers of the Abraham Lincoln Association*, volume 2 (1980), dealing with the topic of Lincoln and race; Benjamin Quarles, *Lincoln and the Negro* (New York: Oxford University, 1962), especially chs. 5 and 6.

7. My treatment of Lincoln is based upon George Forgie, *Patricide in the House Divided: A Psychological Interpretation of Lincoln and His Age* (New York: Norton, 1979), 243-93; Stephen B. Oates, *With Malice Toward None: The Life of Abraham Lincoln* (New York: Harper and Row, 1977), 287-93, and generally; Rheinhold Niebuhr, "The Religion of Lincoln," in Allan Nevins, ed., *Lincoln and the Gettysburg Address* (Urbana, Illinois: University of Illinois Press, 1964), 72-87; "Meditation on the Divine Will," in Lincoln, *Coll. Works*, 5:403-404. Quotation, James Ashley, *Duplicate Souvenir*, 755. See also Harriet F. Durham, "Lincoln's Sons and the Murfan Syndrome," *Lincoln Herald* (1977), 67-71, for a possible link between Lincoln's melancholia and the genetic disorder Murfan Syndrome.

8. Fisher, *Diary*, 429; Tousey, "State Rights," in *Continental Monthly* (May 1862) 1:541; *DAB*; William Whiting, *The War Powers of the President and the Legislative Powers of Congress in relation to Rebellion, Treason, and Slavery* (Boston: J. L. Shorey, 1863), 4th ed., vi.

9. *Cong. Globe*, 37:2, 2030; DNA, RG46, Records of the Senate, 37A, B2, S. 331; Leland, "Desperation and Colonization," in *Continental Monthly* (June 1862) 1:660; N. H. Eggleston, "Emancipation," in *New Englander* (October 1862) 21:786, noted that the question of slavery and rebellion "came up side by side."

10. *Liberator*, July 11, 1862; *North American Review* (January 1862) 94:158.

11. Whiting, *War Power*, iv.

12. Wendell Phillips, "The War for the Union; A Lecture," in Frank M. Freidel, comp., *Union Pamphlets of the Civil War, 1861-1865* (Cambridge:

Belknap Press of the Harvard University Press, 1967), 1:315.

13. Ibid., 313.

14. *Liberator*, June 20, quotation, July 18, 1862.

15. Phillips, "War," in Freidel, *Union Pamphlets*, 1:319; *Liberator*, June 20, 1862.

16. Emma Willard, "Via Media: A Peaceful and Permanent Settlement of the Slavery Question," in Freidel, *Union Pamphlets*, 1:348-50; Sherwood, "Slavery and Nobility v. Democracy," in *Continental Monthly* (July 1862) 2:103-105; New York *Times*, May 13, 1862. See also Belz, "Personal Liberty," *Journal of Southern History*, 42:388-91.

17. Quotation, Fisher, *Diary*, 424; Sidney George Fisher, *The Trial of the Constitution* (New York: Da Capo, 1972), 287-88; Anonymous, "Facts for the People!," in Freidel, *Union Pamphlets*, 1:437; Joel H. Silbey, *A Respectable Minority: The Democratic Party in the Civil War Era, 1860-1868* (New York: Norton, 1977), 49-51.

18. Belmont, *Letters*, 79-84; "Facts," in Freidel, *Union Pamphlets*, 1:415; motto as quoted in Silbey, *Respectable Minority*, 51.

19. Leland, "Desperation and Colonization," in *Continental Monthly* (June 1862) 1:659.

20. Phillips, "War," in Freidel, *Union Pamphlets*, 1:306.

21. Fisher, *Diary*, 430-31; Edward Ingersoll, "Personal Liberty and Martial Law: A Review of Some Pamphlets of the Day," in Freidel, *Union Pamphlets*, 1:292; Fisher, *Trial of the Constitution*, 298-99; *North American Review* (April 1862) 94:446, 453-57.

22. Fisher, *Diary*, 430-31; Whiting, *War Power*, 129.

23. Belmont, *Letters*, 84.

24. Lincoln, *Coll. Works*, 5:212, 219, 225; *OR*, Series I, 14:341; *Liberator*, May 23, 30, 1862.

25. British and Foreign Antislavery Society, *Anti-Slavery Reporter*, 10:84-85; Sumner letter in ibid., 10:162; Lincoln, *Coll. Works*, 5:292.

26. William Lloyd Garrison, *The Letters of William Lloyd Garrison, edited by Walter M. Merrill* (Cambridge: The Belknap Press of Harvard University Press, 1979), 5:97-98; Lincoln, *Coll. Works*, 5:278-79; *Liberator*, July 4, 1862.

27. Lincoln, *Coll. Works*, 5:317-19; Gilbert H. Barnes, *The Antislavery Impulse, 1830-1844* (New York: D. Appleton-Century Company, 1933), 48-49.

28. Lincoln, *Coll. Works*, 5:324-25; New York *Tribune*, July 19, 1862; Cain, *Bates*, 216-18. See also Edward C. Smith, *The Borderland in the Civil War* (New York: AMS Press, 1970 reprint, c1927), 376-78.

29. *Liberator*, July 4, 11, 1862.

30. James G. Randall, *Lincoln and the South* (Baton Rouge: Louisiana State University Press, 1946), 1-4, 48, and passim; Oates, *With Malice Toward None*, 263-67, 283; Fisher, *Diary*, 443; and note Henry Ward Beecher's lament that "Richmond determines, Washington reasons. Richmond is inflexible, Washington vacillates," in *Liberator*, September 19, 1862. For a differing view of the value of the Union, see Herman Belz, *Emancipation and Equal Rights: Politics and Constitutionalism in the Civil War Era* (New York: Norton, 1978), 30-33.

31. *SAL*, 12:319; DNA, RG233, House Judiciary Committee minutes, 37:1, 211.

32. Philadelphia *Press* reprinted in *Liberator*, May 9, 1862.
33. Anna Ella Carroll, "The Relation of the National Government to Revolted Citizens Defined...," in Freidel, *Union Pamphlets*, 1:357-61; Hyman, *More Perfect Union*, 95-97.
34. "The Rightful Power of Congress to Confiscate and Emancipate," *Monthly Law Reporter* (June 1862) 469.
35. Ibid., 471-79.
36. Ibid., 480-86.
37. Ibid., 486-93.
38. Ibid., 469-70; Carroll, "Relation," in Freidel, *Union Pamphlets*, 1:365-66, 373-75, 380; for rebuttal see Grosvenor P. Lowrey, "The Commander-in-Chief; A Defence upon Legal Grounds of the Proclamation of Emancipation," in ibid., 492-94.
39. Hyman, *More Perfect Union*, 97; *Monthly Law Reporter* (September 1862) 645-46, quotation, 646.
40. Carroll, "Relation," in Freidel, *Union Pamphlets*, 1:365-66, 373-75, 380.
41. Whiting, *War Power*, i-ii, iv-v.
42. Ibid., 17-24.
43. Ibid., 29-30, 37-49, quotation, 51.
44. Ibid., 52-54, 56-59, quotation, 54. On the adequacy of the Constitution in general, see Hyman, *More Perfect Union*, ch. 8, and for a similar view, though contemporary, see Leonard Bacon, "Reply to Professor [Joel] Parker," in *New Englander* (April 1863) 22:191-258.
45. *North American Review* (April 1862) 94:452; *Monthly Law Reporter* (September 1862) 653-55.
46. Curry, *Blueprint for Modern America*, 70, 78-94; Belz, *Emancipation and Equal Rights*, 33-38; Syrett, "Confiscation Acts," 24-25, and generally chs. 2 and 3; Lucie, "Confiscation," *Civil War History* (1977) 23:311-13. Lucie suggests that the emancipation clauses of the Second Confiscation Act provided slaves with possible avenues for securing their freedom through United States courts by habeas corpus proceedings. This possibility was soon superseded, in Lucie's judgment, by the Emancipation Proclamation, ibid., 316-20; Donald, *Sumner and the Rights of Man*, 60-67. On the emancipation bill lost in the Senate, see Herman Belz, *A New Birth of Freedom* (Westport, Connecticut: Greenwood Press, 1976), 7-9.
47. Lucie, "Confiscation," *Civil War History* (1977) 23:308; Belz, *Emancipation and Equal Rights*, 37; Lincoln, *Coll Works*, 5:326, 328-31; *SAL*, 12:589-92; Trefousse, *Radical Republicans*, 216-22.
48. *North American Review* (October 1862) 95:522-33; Lucie, "Confiscation," *Civil War History* (1977) 23:312. See the *Liberator*, September 26, 1862, for the observation that the Second Confiscation Act was "substantial emancipation."
49. Whiting, *War Power*, i, 86-89, 91-92, 97-106, 109, 113-14. Although Whiting predicted that *in rem* proceedings would be an effective means of enforcement (ibid., 124-28), the Second Confiscation Act, like its predecessor, was not vigorously enforced. Lyman Trumbull remarked in March 1864 during debate on the Thirteenth Amendment, that he did not know of one slave freed by the first confiscation act, and the second law was not enforced for a long time after its passasge. The United States attorney for Kentucky had not received instructions from the Attorney General on procedures under the 1862 law by January 1863, despite eagerness on his part to begin confiscation

of rebel property, *Cong. Globe*, 38:1, 1313; DNA, RG60, Letters Received, Kentucky, U. S. Attorney, 1841-1866, and Letters Received, Private Citizens, 1840-1866; Eric Foner, *Politics and Ideology in the Age of the Civil War* (New York: Oxford University Press, 1980), 131-32. See also "State Rights," in *New Englander* (October 1862) 21:715-18.

50. Whiting, *War Power*, 113; Lucie, "Confiscation," *Civil War History* (1977) 23:319; Oates, *With Malice Toward None*, 307-308; Phillips, "War," in Freidel, *Union Pamphlets*, 1:318; Hamlin, *Hamlin*, 428-29. For a concise analysis of Lincoln's options, see Hans L. Trefousse, *Lincoln's Decision for Emancipation* (Philadelphia: J. B. Lippincott Company, 1975), 7-9.

51. Gideon Welles, *Diary, edited by Howard K. Beale* (New York: W. W. Norton, 1960), 1:70-71; Oates, *With Malice Toward None*, 308-10; Fisher, *Diary*, 443; Lincoln, *Coll. Works*, 5:328.

52. Donald, *Inside Lincoln's Cabinet*, 95-96, 98-99; Lincoln, *Coll. Works*, 5:336-38; *SAL*, 12:590; Belz, *Reconstructing the Union*, 103. Interestingly, Lincoln's proposal for emancipation rested upon the Confiscation Act (and therefore the Congress' war power) together with his own power as commander-in-chief.

53. Donald, *Inside Lincoln's Cabinet*, 99; Oates, *With Malice Toward None*, 310-12, 331; Montgomery Blair opinion dated July 23, 1862, in Salmon P. Chase Papers, DLC; Lincoln, *Coll. Works*, 5:338, 356-57. The only circumstances Lincoln found completely objectionable was the taking of slaves not capable of work, from loyal masters, without their consent.

54. Lincoln, *Coll. Works*, 5:336-37, 341-42; *SAL*, 12:589-92; Lucie, "Confiscation," *Civil War History* (1977) 23:319.

55. A few saw irony in the timing of Lincoln's emancipation edict. The sixty days of warning established in the July 25 proclamation of the Second Confiscation Act would expire in three days, September 25, making all rebel-owned slaves (if property) subject to confiscation/emancipation. Some believed that Lincoln's Emancipation Proclamation gave the rebellious South until January 1, 1863, before freeing the slaves–one hundred more days–because the President chose to assert the presidential war power and regard slaves as persons, *Liberator*, September 26, 1862. The *Liberator* apparently was confused; the Second Confiscation Act did not confiscate slaves, so much as free them. The abolitionist point remained, however: Lincoln's interposition of executive power delayed freedom of rebel-owned slaves for another one hundred days.

56. Joseph Geiyer to Chase, July 26, 1862, Salmon P. Chase Papers, DLC; Lincoln, *Coll. Works*, 5:343, 346; Oates, *With Malice Toward None*, 311; Chase to Butler, July 31, 1862, in Butler, *Correspondence*, 2:132-34.

57. Donald, *Inside Lincoln's Cabinet*, 105-106; Lincoln, *Coll. Works*, 5:370-75, quotation, 372.

58. *Liberator*, August 29, 1862, September 12, 1862; New York *Tribune*, August 20, 1862; Lincoln, *Coll. Works*, 5:388; Oates, *With Malice Toward None*, 312-13. See also British and Foreign Antislavery Society, *Anti-Slavery Reporter*, 10:263; James M. McPherson, *The Struggle for Equality: Abolitionists and the Negro in the Civil War and Reconstruction* (Princeton, New Jersey: Princeton University Press, 1964), 116-17; Trefousse, *Radical Republicans*, 224-26.

59. Garrison, *Letters*, 5:112; *North American Review* (October 1862) 95:517. For Lincoln and the border, see also Donald, *Inside Lincoln's Cabinet*,

105, 136; Randall, *Lincoln and the South*, ch. 2.

60. Quotation in Lincoln, *Coll. Works*, 5:403-404; Oates, *With Malice Toward None*, 314-17; *North American Review* (October 1862) 95:519-21; Donald, *Inside Lincoln's Cabinet*, 150; Welles, *Diary*, 1:143. See Niebuhr, in Nevins, ed., *Lincoln and the Gettysburg Address*, 75: "Lincoln . . . put the whole tragic drama of the Civil War in a religio-dramatic setting."

61. Antietam quotation, in E. B. Long, *The Civil War Day by Day*, 268; Welles, *Diary*, 1:143; Lincoln, *Coll. Works*, 5:420.

62. Lincoln, *Coll. Works*, 5:433-36. Seward's suggestion was the phrase that the government ought not only to recognize but "maintain" freedmen's liberty, Donald, *Inside Lincoln's Cabinet*, 151-52; Welles, *Diary*, 1:143.

63. Welles, *Dairy*, 1:144, 152; Donald, *Inside Lincoln's Cabinet*, 147, 149-52, 156. Lincoln's efforts to secure by treaty land for black colonization in Central America failed, British and Foreign Antislavery Society, *Anti-Slavery Reporter*, 10:263; Oates, *With Malice Toward None*, 330. Seward also insisted that colonization be voluntary. Bates and Blair disagreed, but the President sided with Seward on this issue also. On September 23, Blair asked that papers with his disagreement over the timing of the Proclamation not be filed, Blair to Lincoln, Abraham Lincoln Papers, DLC. See also George M. Fredrickson, *The Black Image in the White Mind: The Debate on Afro-American Character and Destiny, 1817-1914* (New York: Harper and Row, 1971), 153, 155-57, 159-64, for abolitionists who also viewed America as a white man's country.

64. Lincoln, *Coll. Works*, 5:435; *SAL*, 12:591-92; Fisher, *Trial of the Constitution*, 90, 96, 187; Whiting, *War Power*, 6-7; Emerson, *Journals*, 9:462; F. P. Stanton, "The Freedmen of the South," in *Continental Monthly* (December 1862) 2:730. For an extended defense of the President's war power to emancipate, see Whiting, *War Power*, 60, 67-82, and for an historian's contrary view, see Clarence A. Berdahl, *War Powers of the Executive of the United States* ([Urbana, Illinois:] University of Illinois Studies in Social Science, volume IX, Nos. 1 and 2, c1921, 1970 reprint), 268. Note the following from N. H. Eggleston: "New convictions have seized the public mind and have been wrought into it with wonderful rapidity and force, " Eggleston, "Emancipation," in *New Englander* (October 1862) 21:786.

65. Trefousse, *Radical Republicans*, 228-34; McPherson, *Struggle for Equality*, 118-19; Garrison, *Letters*, 5:114-15; *Liberator*, September 26, 1862; Mabee, *Black Freedom*, 335-39; Ashley, *Duplicate Souvenir*, 260, 760; N. H. Eggleston, "Emancipation," in *New Englander* (October 1862), 21:818; George M. Fredrickson, *The Inner Civil War: Northern Intellectuals and the Crisis of the Union* (New York: Harper Torchbook edition, 1968), ch. 8.

66. Washington *National Intelligencer*, September 27, 1862; Philadelphia *American*, September 24, 1862; Chicago *Tribune*, Cincinnati *Commercial*, Perry (Pennsylvania) *Freeman*, and Springfield (Massachusetts) *Republican*, reprinted without date in Washington *National Intelligencer*, October 7, 1862; Welles, *Diary*, 1:144-45.

67. Emerson, *Journals*, 9:452.

68. Rutherford B. Hayes, *Diary and Letters of Rutherford Birchard Hayes* ([n. p.]: Ohio State Archaeology and History Society, 1924), 50; *Liberator*, October 3, 1862; Welles, *Diary*, 1:158-60. See also Fisher, *Trial of the Constitution*, 283-84, 289-93, 306-10, and the appendix Fisher attached to Lincoln's Proclamation. Before the Proclamation was issued, Fisher suggested gradual emancipation along the lines of the schemes northern states adopted

in the late eighteenth century, freeing children born after a date certain.

69. Washington, *National Intelligencer*, September 23, 26, 27, 1862; New York *Journal of Commerce*, New York *World* (Independent), Providence *Post*, Buffalo *Courier*, Philadelphia *Journal*, St. Lawrence (New York) *Advance*, reprinted without date in Washington *National Intelligencer*, October 8, 1862; Anonymous, "Facts," in Freidel, *Union Pamphlets*, 1:420-21. See also Forrest G. Wood, *Black Scare: The Racist Response to Emancipation and Reconstruction* (Berkeley and Los Angeles: University of California Press, 1968), 20-33.

70. Belmont, *Letters*, 85, 137-39; Silbey, *Respectable Minority*, 51, 66-70; Charles G. Leland, "Up and Act, " in *Continental Monthly* (September 1862) 2:316; C. S. Henry, "The Constitution as it is,–the Union as it was," ibid., (October 1862) 2:383; Donald, *Inside Lincoln's Cabinet*, 137. For General George B. McClellan's reaction to the Emancipation Proclamation, see Edward McPherson, *The Political History of the United States of America During the Great Rebellion, 1860-1865* (New York: Da Capo Press, 1972), 227n.

71. Benjamin R. Curtis, *Executive Power* (Boston: Little, Brown and Company, 1862), 9-10, 12-15, 17, 21, 31; Whiting, *War Power*, ii; Garrison, *Letters*, 5:114-15. See also for rebuttal to Curtis, Lowrey, "Commander in Chief," in Freidel, *Union Pamphlets*, 1:490-91. And for the belief that abolition would follow emancipation, see N. H. Eggleston, "Emancipation," in *New Englander* (October 1862) 21:783-84.

72. Lincoln, *Coll. Works*, 5:438, 444; Bates, *Dairy*, 268; poem, Anonymous, "The Proclamation," in *Continental Monthly* (November 1862) 2:603.

73. Lincoln, *Coll. Works*, 5:478. See also Niebuhr's statement: "In short, [Lincoln] exhibited not his own ambiguity, but the moral ambiguity of the political order," in Nevins, ed., *Lincoln and the Gettysburg Address*, 82.

74. Fisher, *Trial of the Constitution*, 299.

V

WE ARE MAKING HISTORY

Five weeks after Lincoln issued the Emancipation Proclamation, a month before it became effective, Attorney General Edward Bates delivered an opinion to Secretary of the Treasury Salmon P. Chase. He stated that free blacks born in the United States were citizens of the United States, and of the states where they resided.[1] Little noted at the time, Bates' opinion provided a key, incremental step in the fulfillment of freedom for blacks in America.

It is characteristic of the advance in thinking brought about by the war that Bates' decision caused little immediate stir. Yet before the war, the question of black citizenship had prompted intermittent discussion and some controversy. In 1790 Congress limited naturalization to whites only, and in 1813 distinguished United States citizens as a class from free blacks by requiring that seamen on American vessels be United States citizens *or* free person of color born in the United States.[2] Missouri's admission to the Union in 1821 was the occasion for debate because the new state's constitution prohibited the immigration of free blacks into its territory. Congressmen from states where free blacks were citizens objected to the apparent violation of the Constitution's guarantee of the privileges and immunities of United States citizens in the several states. The discussion pointed up the confusion about black citizenship and also the precise nature of the privileges and immunities of United States citizens–a confusion that continued through the 1860s. Did possession of rights determine status, that is, citizenship, or did status determine rights? Did birth determine status? In 1821 Congress did not answer these question, admitted Missouri, and passed a "Pontius Pilate" resolution disclaiming responsibility for violations of the United States Constitution. In 1821 Attorney General William Wirt confirmed the argument that status flowed from rights. In an opinion concerning Virginia free blacks, Wirt observed that they had discernably fewer rights than white residents. Therefore, blacks were not citizens of Virginia, and therefore, not citizens of the United States. Because United States citizenship would imply eligibility for federal office, Wirt also found this a compelling reason to deny blacks national citizenship.[3]

Wirt's opinion remained the official government view through the intervening years down to the Civil War. It was formidably supported in the *Dred Scott* decision of 1857, particularly by Chief Justice Roger B. Taney. Taney's reasoning was, at best, complex. Although he seemingly denied the "status follows rights" argument, Taney did believe that discriminatory legislation in the states proved that blacks were not intended to be citizens of the United States. Therefore, blacks were not persons in the meaning of the Constitution, and they had no rights that white men were bound to respect.

Reaction to the *Dred Scott* decision brought divergent northern and southern views into focus. The southern view of the question triumphed in Taney's opinion, although many southerners thought Taney had not gone far enough. Northern opinion had found expression even before the *Dred Scott* decision, primarily in personal liberty laws (really anti-fugitive slave laws) designed to protect northern states' own black citizens. Before 1857, free blacks might hope for passports and federal pre-emption lands in the West. After 1857 the Executive branch of the federal government more consistently denied all privileges of United States citizenship to blacks. Republicans, on the whole, believed the *Dred Scott* ruling on black citizenship and the unconstitutionality of the Missouri Compromise were mere *obiter dicta*–opinion only–and not binding constitutional interpretation. They had little choice. If accepted, the *Dred Scott* opinion undercut the entire basis of Republican pre-war constitutional ideology, that is, Congress' power to prevent the extension of slavery in the territories. If Congress did not possess that power, Republican politics would be irrelevant.[4]

Because reaction to the *Dred Scott* decision was so mixed, white Americans were confused about the status and rights of free blacks in the several states. Ohio, New York, and Massachusetts allowed blacks to vote in the 1860 presidential election. One northerner thereupon declared Lincoln's election invalid, because blacks, a people who "are not and cannot be" citizens, had voted. But the logic of the claim was flawed, betraying a misunderstanding of the connection between citizenship and suffrage. As Attorney General Bates later stated, the two were not necessarily connected at all. Indeed, Wisconsin, Indiana, Minnesota, and Oregon all allowed aliens to vote in their state elections.[5]

The status of free blacks remained a question throughout the first year and a half of the war, and with the Emancipation Proclamation the question became much more important. On January 1, 1862, millions of southern slaves would become freedmen. Would they also become citizens? On November 29, 1862, Bates answered Treasury Secretary

Chase's inquiry about the legality of a black man commanding an intra-coastal ship. The law required the position of captain to be filled by a United States citizen. Thus two elements of an important question came together: were blacks citizens of the United States; indeed, could they be? Shortly before Bates delivered his opinion, William Whiting, War Department Solicitor, concluded that blacks had *always* been citizens of some of the states and had enjoyed the rights of citizenship. Whiting accepted the general view that states created citizens and that state citizenship determined national status. Nothing, therefore, barred blacks as a class from United States citizenship. But he came very close to endorsing the view that the possession of rights determined citizenship.

The key to Bates' 1862 opinion, however, lay in the division of status from rights. Finding no "clear and satisfactory definition of the phrase citizen of the United States" in law books or court records, Bates gave his own definition. Privileges or rights were not useful characteristics in defining status, since some rights might be exercised by non-citizens (aliens could be elected to office, for example) and many citizens (women and children) did not have the right to vote. Because of the lack of correlation between rights and status, Bates concluded that the Constitution's use of the word citizen referred only to the individual's relationship to the nation. A citizen was "neither more not less than a member of the nation," and within that status, all were equally citizens. Every citizen of a state was a citizen of the United States, and every United States citizen was a citizen of the state where he lived. The Attorney General broke the dependence of United States citizenship upon state citizenship, finding instead a primacy for the nation. Membership in the nation derived from birth in the United States. The Constitution said "not one word, and furnish[ed] not one hint, in relation to the color, or to the ancestral race, of the natural-born citizens."[6]

Secretary Chase had not asked whether a slave was a citizen of the United States, so Bates skirted that issue. Yet the Attorney General observed that the Constitution placed no color bar on citizenship. To say it did was a "naked assumption" not warranted by the Constitution's language. Bates appeared to accept much of the abolitionist view of the issue. Blacks, if born free in the United States, were citizens of the United States. But what did that mean? What rights and privileges were thereby secured? Concerning these questions, Bates' conservatism came to the fore.

Referring specifically to William Wirt's 1821 opinion, Bates dismissed the view that blacks were not citizens of the United States because they did not share full rights and privileges with white

Virginians. State law discriminations concerning rights and privileges did not affect status and could not affect the right to national citizenship. But this did not mean that all United States citizens possessed the same rights. Bates distinguished between certain unspecified political rights all citizens had, and those political powers held only by some, the franchise and eligibility for office as examples. The Attorney General did not specify what the privileges and immunities of United States citizens were, although he again stressed that possession of rights did not affect status. In the end, Bates dismissed the *Dred Scott* decision, finding nothing in it to bar free blacks from national citizenship.[7]

In a sense, Bates defined away much of the crucial nature of the question. Free blacks might well be citizens of the United States, whatever that meant. The exact nature of the rights that adhered to the status remained ambiguous. The Attorney General chose not to cite the small body of precedent that listed rights of United States citizens, a list most explicitly developed in Justice Bushrod Washington's circuit court opinion in the case of *Corfield* v. *Coryell* (1823). Among the rights that Washington included were protection by the government, acquisition of property, enjoyment of life and liberty, transit and resettlement, writ of habeas corpus, and access to the judicial system. This listing was similar to the rights abolitionists envisioned for the freedman, although abolitionists more often referred generally to human rights. Yet Bates by-passed the question of rights, and the immediate reaction to his opinion suggested that the practical benefit for blacks would be "small at most."[8]

Nonetheless, Bates' opinion was important. His conservatism led him to side-step the critical issue of rights, but his conservatism found no problem declaring free blacks to be citizens of the United States. Bates' opinion ratified what had occurred during the first year and a half of the war, and acknowledged the citizenship of free blacks for the first time. Still, there were corollary questions. Did slaves, once emancipated, become natural, free-born men and, therefore, citizens? If they did not, must Congress naturalize ex-slaves by statute? These were important questions, but abolitionists were not without hope. They believed that the war would solve this problem, too.[9]

"Progress! Ordinarily we must take some microscope to watch it." Wendell Phillips marveled at the changes that had occurred in America since the war began. "What vast progress in these two years," he continued, "what immense progress! And all of it the PEOPLE'S progress." Confiscation of rebels' property, abolition of slavery in the federal district and the territories, black citizenship, and the final

Emancipation Proclamation of January 1, 1863–all had occurred in just two years. What progress, indeed. Coupled with Lincoln's decision to enroll black soldiers in the federal army, each innovation had changed the condition of blacks. Each change tended to alter their legal and moral status. Abolitionists had long maintained that there was no limbo between slavery and freedom. Bates' opinion on citizenship supported their view. American law made no provision for "denizens," inhabitants who were neither citizens nor aliens. Slaves were not aliens, and Bates declined to say whether they were citizens. But ex-slaves were another matter altogether. Given the choice of two categories, alien or citizen, freed blacks had to be citizens. But this conclusion did not occur immediately. The progress of war called forth this answer, but like so many others, only gradually. The pilgrimage from bondage to liberty could not occur overnight.[10]

The final decree of emancipation on January 1, 1863, marked a decisive change in the war's object. After the hundred day grace period announced the previous September 22, Lincoln decided that "broken eggs can not be mended. I have issued the emancipation proclamation, and I can not retract it." The President had struggled nearly a year and a half to fight the war without touching the institution of slavery. Now that necessity had brought him to emancipation, he would not turn back.[11] Edward Everett Hale summed up well when he wrote, "there is no more Egypt for us, even if we wanted it. We are asked, simply, whether we will go *now* into the promised land, by one vigorous effort." America's exodus from slavery to the promised land of equal opportunity–Hale's vision–was still too radical for many northerners, including Lincoln. The President proclaimed the finality of emancipation and in the next thought conjured up a "system of apprenticeship for the colored people." Gideon Welles awaited the results of events "deep as they may plough their furrows in our once happy land." The war tore the civil fabric, subduing the errors "which no trivial measure could [have] eradicate[d]." A land of freedom did not yet exist, only a promised possibility of good and evil: "The seed which is being sown will germinate and bear fruit, and tares and weeds will also spring up under the new dispensation."[12]

The fruits and weeds of emancipation were readily apparent to Americans, but whether freedom was fruit or weed depended upon one's point of view. South Carolina blacks behind Union lines welcomed freedom with a rendition of "My Country 'tis of Thee," a song never quite appropriate until emancipation. The spirit with which they sang did not guarantee their future happiness or security. For that, government intervention would be needed. And for that, the Constitution must be seen, in Congressman James Ashley's words, as a "charter of national liberty." Interpreted in that way, there was no need for a constitutional amendment to abolish slavery. With the power war provided, slavery could be destroyed. But the present generation would have to make that decision.

And so would Lincoln. The President gained respect from abolitionists immediately after January 1, 1862, that " bright and brilliant day." Henry W. Bellows, Unitarian clergyman and president of the United States Sanitary Commission, reminded his countrymen of Isaiah's prophecy: "and the government shall be upon his shoulders." While that prophecy was usually applied to the Messiah, Bellows suggested its appropriateness for Lincoln and urged Americans to support the President in bearing his burden. Sidney George Fisher, though no abolitionist, thought Lincoln "the only man of confidence in the government." Abused as Lincoln was by Democrats (and later by disillusioned abolitionists), Fisher believed that all eventually would be forced to recognize the President's leadership.[13]

Supporters defended Lincoln's use of extraordinary power. In an anecdote worthy of Lincoln himself, New York lawyer Grosvenor P. Lowery made the point:

> "I guess this is the law," said an indiscreet practitioner, before the chief-magistrate of a western village. "I guess it ain't," said the irate dignitary, "and I have the last *guess*." The Commander-in-chief who must bear the final responsibility, and is clothed for the occasion with all the discretion of the nation, has exercised it finally.[14]

In a direct attack on Benjamin Curtis' pamphlet, *Executive Power*, Lowery insisted that "*rebels in arms against the Constitution, must not be spoken of as men having constitutional rights*." "Ordinarily," Lowery explained, "the mind stops at the Constitution, the Alpha and Omega of American liberty. . . . " Yet these were not ordinary times, and the mind sought the higher law behind the Constitution "which shall sustain and be in agreement with it." The President had reached beyond the usual limits of power to meet a completely novel situation. The Emancipation Proclamation was the result, and the duty of citizens was to accept it. This was the essence of loyalty, as Horace Bushnell described it:

> No real statesman will undertake to be a mere lawyer, standing fast in the letter, when eternal doom has pushed it by. Every man can see that, under the doom of war, we were bound to [reach] just the crisis we have reached, proclamation or no proclamation. It was right, for a time, to say "the Constitution as it is," but it could not always be. . . . When affairs move rapidly, the real statseman keeps up with affairs. Nothing is now left us . . . from the first nothing was finally to be left us, but to champion the

> liberty of the slave.... These throes of civil disorder are but the schooling of our loyalty.... What loyalty was we did not even know before.[15]

The changes were dramatic not solely in attitude but in categories of meaning. Toward the end of 1863 Sidney George Fisher noted how many people, once indifferent to antislavery, now favored emancipation: "the term 'abolitionist' has ceased to be one of reproach."[16]

Not so with conservatives. Just as the war ought not liberate slaves, so the war did not free some lawyers from their dependence on literalism. George Ticknor Curtis, brother of Benjamin Curtis, a counsel for Dred Scott, and a leading lawyer of the day, scoffed at the "war measure heresy" that treated the Constitution as "a thing made of India-rubber, to be stretched in one direction in time of peace and in another direction in time of war."[17] The *Monthly Law Reporter* featured a lengthy article in January 1863 attacking the war powers doctrine of William Whiting. Point by point the claim of national power to confiscate and emancipation was denied or tempered in such a way as to leave the government little room to maneuver. The Constitution guaranteed compensation for seizure and reserved power to the states. Belligerent rights were circumscribed by civilization's rules, and the government had no business trying to foment slave insurrection southward, the article maintained. The Emancipation Proclamation, in the anonymous writer's opinion, was problematic. If illegal, it was of no consequence. And to determine its legality, one should search the precedents, studying the past for a guide to the future. The past–the law–ruled the present.[18]

This begged the question. The matter at issue was deciding what the law actually was. To invoke the standard of "this is a government of laws and not of men," as the *Monthly Law Reporter* writer did, failed to solve the problem. Similarly, conservatives' quibbles over the Proclamation demonstrated legalism at its worst. Because Lincoln referred to himself as the "executive" rather than the "commander-in-chief," the Washington *National Intelligencer* suggested the possible invalidity of the Proclamation. Samuel F. B. Morse, on the other hand, rejected the emancipation outright. He believed that the Proclamation did not attack the cornerstone of the Confederacy because slavery was not the key. Rather, Morse believed that the foundation of both northern and southern societies was the inequality of the races. Lincoln himself had said as much, Morse pointed out, in his address to free blacks in August 1862. No government policy could change the biological superiority of whites. With that in mind, Morse believed that the war might be ended when both sides recognized their ultimate agreement in racial principle, left slavery and race relations alone, and avoided the "irritating busybodism" of emancipation.[19]

Despite pleas for unity from Administration supporters, Democrats and other conservatives increased their vocal opposition to the war's "sudden" turn. James Ashley misread the situation when he termed conservatives an "unnatural coalition" of pro-slavery and timid men. Nothing was more natural than the coalition of genuine pro-slavery advocates and those afraid of the black. Fears of black insurrection were fears of slavery and not of emancipation, the Reverend N. H. Eggleston noted in reference to the race uprising at Santo Domingo. But Americans, fearful of the shadow blacks cast upon their land, could not make the distinction. Fear was an easy sentiment to cultivate, nurture, and attempt to build into a consensus. Democrats counted on growing opposition to Republican-abolitionist policies–a strategy already proved by the dramatic gains made in the 1862 elections. So fearful was Ohio state senator Isaac Welch, that he suggested Lincoln call a special session of Congress. If Democrats could form a working majority, then Republicans ought to let them run the war. With their hands full, coping with reality rather than sitting on the sidelines, the Democrats themselves would "ultimately make a good enough war party."[20]

But Democrats as a whole were not in power and even those few who held high office displayed none of the elasticity that characterized Republicans. Andrew Johnson, military governor of occupied Tennessee, set the tone of racial hostility for those who supported the war effort. He was, first, for the government with slavery under the Constitution as it was; second, Johnson favored the government without blacks and with the Constitution as it was. "If as the car of state move along, the negroes get in the way," he remarked, "let them be crushed. If they keep out of the way, let them remain where they are." With sentiments like these issuing from a Unionist, presidentially appointed military governor of conquered Tennessee, there can be little wonder at the depth of racial antagonism within the northern coalition. Such sentiments could not help but encourage less loyal men in their opposition to war policy. This type of encouragement was the "meanest kind of disloyalty," in Horace Bushnell's phrase, the disloyalty that "keeps just within the law . . . which takes on airs of patriotic concern for the Constitution, when it really has none for all the wrong that can be done by enemies openly fighting against it."

By mid-1863 the resurgence of the Democratic party was remarkable, especially in the wake of the Union victories at Vicksburg and Gettysburg. More disturbing was the New York City anti-draft, anti-black riot of that same July, 1863. As if in answer to the nation's situation, the Democrats presented their platform without a program in the same week that rioting shook New York:

> The country we so dearly love, which love shall still remain, To warm the hearts of Democrats, and make it one again; The Nation cries aloud on those Who ask for honest laws, The Constitution as it is, The Union as it was.
>
> The North and South have acted wrong, And wrong they will remain Till honest old-line Democrats Will make them right again A million voices then will shout Amid the world's applause The Constitution as it is, The Union as it was.

And lest antislavery advocates miss the point, one particularly blunt correspondent wrote Ohio's Ben Wade: "It is your purpose to instruct your sucking blood abolitionists to destroy the Union with slavery. Well you will be responsible for a severe penalty by death when the old Union is restored but not by your party."[21]

Supporters of the war countered with renewed visions of a new Union of "hearts, no less than interest," that might transcend the catchwords Democrats proposed. The Union as it was appealed "only to the ignorant and unthinking." Unfortunately, many were just as happy for not thinking about issues the war raised. Their opposition to the war and antislavery-related measures frustrated antislavery men. As on chaplain prayed, "Overturn all their wicked and treasonable de[s]igns, and in brief, play hell with them generally."[22]

Republicans aided the Almighty in playing hell with conservatives' attitudes about the black. Lincoln's decision to enlist blacks into the federal army was an important step toward functional and psychological equality with whites. Although the enlistment of blacks was prompted by the great need for troops, the effect of blacks fighting with whites demonstrated that blacks were neither incapable of winning their freedom, nor uninterested in the war's outcome. Opposition to black troops remained, especially when abolitionists made explicit the claim for equality based upon black participation in the war. Nevertheless, northern whites learned that black troops were effective and discovered that the stereotype of black behavior was incorrect. That true, white attitudes and behavior began to change.[23]

Perhaps most significant was a little noticed law passed by Congress on March 3, 1863. As early as May 13 the previous year, Congress had considered a bill to extend the charter of the Washington-Alexandria Railroad Company, allowing it to cross the District of Columbia and connect in Maryland. The bill had no trouble passing in the House, but bogged down in the Senate. Laid over until the third session of Congress that began December 1, 1862, the Senate adopted several unimportant amendments before Senator John C. Ten Eyck objected.

The legislation would extend a Virginia charter company through the District, and Ten Eyck doubted Congress' power to authorize the extension. Lot M. Morrill (R, Maine), the bill's sponsor, countered, and Ten Eyck dropped his opposition. In the wake of this brief debate, Charles Sumner offered a momentous amendment. Reacting to a rumored statement from a member of the House, Sumner denounced the racial discrimination that occurred on the District tram lines. An aged black person reportedly had been dropped off one of the tram cars into the snow and mud. As Congress considered the extension of the Washington-Alexandria Railroad, Sumner argued it should also intervene and end the discrimination.

Timothy Howe of Wisconsin suggested that the law already made a rail company liable if it refused service to anyone with the proper fare. Sumner's proposed amendment, "that no person shall be excluded from the cars on account of color," was unnecessary in Howe's opinion. Up to a point, Sumner agreed that the law did make the company liable. But the Massachusetts senator went on to declare:

> [T]hat liability is not recognized here; and the Senator knows very well that whenever slavery is in question, human rights are constantly disregarded–these principles of law which he recognizes are constantly set aside; and therefore it becomes the duty of Congress to interfere, and specially declare them.

Without further debate the Senate adopted Sumner's amendment, 19 to 18. No Democrat or Unionist voted for the measure. Every border state senator voted against it, along with northern Democrats and four Republicans. The bill passed the Senate the same day, and the House subsequently agreed to the Senate's changes. Discrimination on the Washington-Alexandria Railroad line became illegal on March 3, 1863.[24]

Sumner's remarks offer a key to understanding the abolitionists' perception of reality. When addressing the issue of discrimination in the District, he spoke of slavery in the present tense. But the status of "slave" had been abolished almost a year before. The discrimination Sumner protested remained essentially slavery, however, because discrimination, like slavery itself, denied human rights. Slavery was the denial of rights. When the law was silent or when men chose to ignore its force, then Congress must declare that human rights belonged to all free persons. Even some who held the black as "degraded" recognized him as a person with certain fundamental rights that should be guarded against the "almost universal" popular prejudice. Just as ex-slaves should not be left to the "tender mercies" of former masters, so freedmen should not be abandoned to prejudice. With the slave institution dying the "almost universal" prejudice against blacks loomed ever larger as a problem. But prejudice was no discrete phenomenon, no creature without a history. Slavery itself bred prejudice, and in a sense, lived on through it. William Lloyd Garrison phrased the idea precisely: "Slavery has done a deadly and most atheistical work in engendering this spirit. It is to the soul as leprosy to the body." It was the spirit of selfishness and fear, of men who worried about their own liberties and simultaneously fastened upon blacks the shackles of bondage. It was the spirit of self-destruction for southern society. It was the spirit of slavery, and it was precisely the point that Sumner made: to end slavery, form and spirit both must be abolished. Salmon Chase summed up the opportunity the war presented and the meaning radicals drew from it: "this war came upon us in order that the nation might be born again into a new life, ennobled and made glorious by justice and freedom."[25]

By the end of 1863 there had been an important change in attitude toward the black. Fighting for their freedom, blacks increasingly won the respect if not the admiration of whites. The vicious New York City draft/race riot of July notwithstanding, a kind of "revolution" had occurred. It was a revolution that assumed, for the first time, a permanent place for large numbers of free blacks in the United States, and a growing acceptance of civil equality, protection of personal liberty, and the rights of citizenship for both races.[26]

"The trial of the Constitution has been in progress ever since it was adopted," wrote a reviewer of Sidney George Fisher's *The Trial of the Constitution*. During the Civil War the Constitution was evolving "more rapidly and more beneficially" than at any other time in the nation's history, according to the *North American Review*. That often unfortunate history had witnessed states exercising much power, "*reserving* to the United States" only the extra powers state could not execute separately. That division of power, the *Review* noted, was exactly the opposite of the Framers' intentions. But war changed that, redirecting attention toward the federal government and the powers it possessed. Fisher, as usual, put it best. The Constitution "was obliged to yield to necessity." But contrary to conservative arguments, the Constitution was not overthrown and in that sense, did not actually "yield" to necessity. Rather, interpretations of limits and powers gave way to the imperative of survival and, more gradually, to the imperative of freedom.[27]

By December 1863 Congress and the President had taken large steps to ensure the survival of the nation and the triumph of freedom. But were these measures constitutional? This was not the same question that might have been asked in 1860. Then, if unconstitutional, an action could not be done. Yet in 1863 confiscation, emancipation, abolition–all were done or being done at some place in the Union. To ask if actions were constitutional now meant, would they *still* be done, would their effects continue on after the war ended.

Emancipation was constitutional; commentators said so and, more important, Lincoln believed so. But the question became how to ensure it, to make it work; in short, how to enforce emancipation? There would be, no doubt, "an unprecedented crop" of lawsuits questioning the Proclamation, seeking the Supreme Court's declaration on its effect. How would the Court decide, even granting likely changes in its membership? More generally, what was the most effective means to make emancipation, confiscation, territorial abolition, anti-discrimination, constitutional, that is, permanent? Would the means be, as Chase suggested, to send loyal southerners, converted to antislavery by the war, back home to amend slave state constitutions into free ones? What then of federal efforts for the black and federal enforcement of emancipation? Concerned, Henry Wilson pointed to congressional actions to ensure "equal and impartial liberty"–abolition in the District, repeal of its black code, allowance of black testimony in its courts. Were these experiments to be abandoned, never to be made national? What, in sum, of the national commitment to freedom? There had to be a symbol of the government's, and therefore of the nation's, conversion from slavery to freedom. Abolition of slavery "in solemn form, would unquestionably be decisive against all attempts to nullify the Proclamation through new compromises, or to perpetuate a remnant of the slave system," Garrison wrote to Gerrit Smith. "I fear nothing for the cause of the slave while war last; only when peace is won, and political intrigue shall begin its desperate work." As the nation's most solemn expression of principle was the Constitution, so the most solemn lessons of war–survival and freedom–required constitutional expression.[28]

Constitutional expression demanded congressional involvement and action. A government dedicated to freedom must actively discourage slavery. To do nothing would favor the institution, and favoring slavery would "impair and destroy the freedom of all."[29] The war impressed this lesson upon congressmen as they assembled for the first session of the Thirty-Eighth Congress in December, 1863.[30] Secession, based upon slavery, had attempted the nation's overthrow. The slave power's long history of denying civil rights to antislavery northerners confirmed the conclusion. Suppression of free antislavery speech in the South, censorship of the mails, mob violence against antislavery advocates, and finally the war itself, proved that slavery and freedom were incompatible. The Republican platform of 1860 cited Bill of

Rights grievances against the South and slavery. By December 1863 the realization had grown that slavery violated not only the rights of white northerners, but also of black southerners. The war was making freedom universal. As Emerson noted, "a civil war sweeps away all the false issues on which it began, and arrives presently at real and lasting questions."[31]

Eight months earlier the *North American Review* had suggested the need to advance "to the very outmost limit of power." Congressmen assembled in December took that advice, and began reshaping the nation's fundamental charter to reflect the newer reality. A constitutional amendment to abolish slavery throughout the United States would complete what the war had begun.[32]

Relatively few amendments had been proposed since the Constitution went into effect in 1789. During the secession winter, congressmen made two hundred and twenty-seven attempts to alter the fundamental charter. After Sumter through 1863, however, Congress considered only eighteen amendments; none was seriously debated. But on December 14, 1863, three significant proposal came before the House of Representatives. Ohio congressman James Ashley proposed the first constitutional amendment to abolish slavery throughout the United States. Following the pattern established in his proposal for abolition in the District of Columbia in 1862, Ashley used the language of the Northwest Ordinance. Within minutes of Ashley's action, James Wilson, Republican from Iowa, also submitted a constitutional amendment abolishing slavery throughout the country. Noting that slavery was "incompatible with a free government," Wilson's measure abolished slavery and included a second section giving Congress "power to enforce the [abolition of slavery] by appropriate legislation."

In the short interim between Ashley's and Wilson's proposals, Illinois Republican Owen Lovejoy had introduced a bill. Although not presented as a constitutional amendment, Lovejoy's bill would "give effect" to the Declaration of Independence and certain provisions of the Constitution, so that all slaves would be freed and protected "as all other citizens" from unreasonable search and seizure, and given standing in judicial proceedings. In his attempt to "constitutionalize" the Declaration of Independence, Lovejoy reflected his radical principles. Ashley's and Wilson's constitutional amendments were less explicit about the status of former slaves. Yet Lovejoy's bill and another concerning freedmen's rights introduced by Massachusetts Republican Thomas D. Elliot, demonstrated congressional concern about the freedmen's condition.[33]

No abolition amendment appeared in the Senate until a month

later, in January 1864. On the eleventh, Missouri Unionist John Henderson introduced a constitutional amendment that employed the Northwest Ordinance formula, which was sent to the Senate Judiciary Committee. The respective judiciary committees of the two houses considered the issue and, after a month with no report, Charles Sumner introduced yet another abolition amendment. Sumner's language, however, differed markedly from the Northwest Ordinance model. Instead, Sumner's amendment declared that "all persons are equal before the law, so that no person can hold another as a slave." The proposed amendment would apply to state law as well as federal law. Like Lovejoy's earlier measure, Sumner's amendment was grounded in his abolitionist belief that slavery and freedom were incompatible and that all men were meant to be free and equal before the law. The words he chose expressed that belief. Yet they were unfamiliar words, and because of that, proved suspicious. Attorney General Bates wondered just what "equality before the law" was, and questioned Sumner's conclusion that equality would *ipso facto* prohibit slavery. Citing the Northwest Ordinance itself, Bates pointed to servitude as punishment for crime, an exception that the other proposed constitutional amendments retained.

Bates had hit upon the key sticking point that had prompted Sumner's language in the first place. There was not total incompatibility between freedom and slavery in the Northwest Ordinance. Nor did it assume freedom as the natural condition of men, thereby making slavery impossible. In the states first affected by the Ordinance, slavery had continued on for a time.[34]

The contest for the amendment's language was important as a vehicle of interpretation. Sumner's proposal went to the Senate Judiciary Committee where other proposals were already under discussion. Ironically, an earlier proposed thirteenth amendment was still before the states, offered as the last gasp of the secession crisis Congress. That amendment would do exactly the opposite of these new proposals, that is, guarantee forever the existence of slavery in the states. Senator Henry B. Anthony suggested withdrawing the former proposition, noting the dramatic reversal in the nation's thinking during the past two years. "What the Republican party could not do," Anthony stated, "what no election could do, what no peaceable movement would have been able to accomplish in many years, slavery has done of itself. It has sealed its own doom. . . . It has committed suicide." The former amendment was not withdrawn, however, due to Attorney General Bates' belief that a once-proffered constitutional change could not be recalled. There were certain rules that had to be followed in altering the nation's charter, and they would be followed carefully.

Speculation about freedmen's rights, always part of the abolitionist vision, had spread into the popular press and, to a lesser degree, into the halls of Congress. Sumner's and Lovejoy's bills reflected their concern with post-war freedmen's condition. The discussion was necessary and inevitable as the Congress began serious consideration of the abolition amendment. Although the consensus in Congress and country for abolition grew throughout the last year and a half of the war, the required two-thirds majority of both houses to pass a constitutional amendment took a full year to achieve. Of more importance than the decision for abolition, however, was the new question of the meaning of abolition. The ensuing history of the Thirteenth Amendment, like the history of the war to that time, was a contest for meaning beyond form.

Conservative commentators, even those who supported the war, worried over what they perceived as a tendency to ignore the rights a post-war South might still enjoy. The continuing preoccupation with white civil liberties played nicely into the hands of the extreme anti-war, anti-freedom elements of the North, exemplified by Samuel F. B. Morse. It was Morse who reversed the moral of the war experience that had led so many others to choose abolition. "It is not slavery," he said, "it is Abolitionism, that is our national sin."[36]

But it was slavery that continued to eat away at the war effort despite confiscation and emancipation. Kentucky treated freedmen as runaways, specifically flouting the Emancipation Proclamation. Behind Union lines in Arkansas, A. C. Rogers, an applicant for the post of military governor, spoke against the changed circumstances that allowed freedmen to defend themselves by arms against their former masters. Duly reporting this to Senate Judiciary Committee chairman Lyman Trumbull, G. T. Allen asked how such a man could be made governor of a state "striving to pass the chrysalis from slavery to freedom? We must blot out slavery or perish as a nation," Trumbull's frequent correspondent concluded.[37]

Abolitionism had grown in stature and in power, at least to the extent that more and more Americans concluded that slavery must be destroyed, that "the rights of human nature are unitary, that oppression is of one hue the world over, no matter what the color of the oppressed." Contrary to Morse's view, the war was not an assault of northern fanatics against southern institutions, but "between downright slavery and upright freedom, between despotism and democracy, between the Old World and the New." In that context, as *Continental Monthly* editor Charles Henry put it, conservatism "means nothing but the saving of slavery."[38]

Some political commentators began seriously to consider the question of freedmen's rights. Two articles appeared in January 1864 that distinguished between civil (or natural) rights belonging to all citizens, and political rights. Orestes Brownson concluded that rebels might retain their civil rights, yet forfeit political participation as a penalty for the war. Brownson explicitly left the way open for this formula to be applied to freedmen. Yale professor George P. Fisher made a more detailed treatment of the question of freedmen's rights. Arguing that natural rights were separate from political rights, Fisher listed those natural rights that freedmen were entitled to: justice, liberty, the fruit of labor, family, and education, among others. The right to participate in the community's or the nation's political life was not a natural right, in Fisher's opinion. Yet the professor remarked that there must be some legal guarantee that natural rights not be violated. That guarantee might even be in the form of conferred political participation, so that an oppressed group could maintain its natural rights. Curiously, Fisher suggested that each community be allowed to decide whether freedmen would have political rights, reminding his readers that "to vote is to rule." Fisher was firm, however, in stating that there could be no option regarding blacks' natural rights.[39]

The Senate Judiciary Committee considered John Henderson's proposed constitutional amendment (S. No. 16) for a month before reporting it back to the Senate on February 11. Reaction in the capital was low-key, several days passing before the conservative Washington *National Intelligencer* or the pro-Administration Washington *Daily Morning Chronicle* noted either S. No. 16 or Sumner's alternate proposal. The *Intelligencer*'s editor preferred a constitutional convention after the war if the Constitution had to be amended. In that manner, he argued, "one-sided amendments" would be avoided. All states (including southern slave states) would have their voices heard. An amendment to the Constitution ought to be the last step of "regeneration and reconstruction," not the first. The war must first end; for Congress to propose an amendment abolishing slavery without the South's participation would be a "solecism and an anachronism in American politics," the *Intelligencer* concluded.[40]

Although staunchly antislavery, the *Chronicle* at first doubted the desirability of a constitutional amendment abolishing slavery. Alternately, it favored separate slave state action whereby reconstructing rebel states would individually abolish slavery. The *Chronicle* maintained that if slavery died (as was certain) the part of the Constitution relating to slavery would simply lose its relevance. When the Senate Judiciary Committee reported S. No. 16, however, the newspaper accepted the measure immediately, noting its excellent chances of passage in the Senate, and its less excellent prospects in the House. Like the *Intelligencer*, the *Chronicle* called for a constitutional convention, though the *Chronicle*'s editor did not intend the convention to be a delaying tactic. Instead, he wanted the convention assembled quickly, wasting no time to complete "this important reform."[41]

Both newspapers favored constitutional conventions, but for opposite reasons. The *Intelligencer* feared congressional action; the *Chronicle* feared there would be none. The *Intelligencer* ultimately revealed its conservatism, noting that the true conservative "must resist any such encroachment in the organic law of the land" when radicals proposed to strike at slavery "through the vitals of the Constitution." The *Chronicle*'s lack of faith in congressional action is more difficult to explain, particularly in light of its words of assurance to readers about the issues brought about by the war:

> Let us be patient–doing our whole duty in our time according to the lights of history, reason and intuition. That is all that is required of us. That is all we *can do*.[42]

After the committee's initial report, the Senate waited another month and a half before beginning debate on S. No. 16.[43] The amendment reported by the committee differed from Henderson's original text in that it now had two sections. The first section contained the actual abolition and prohibition of slavery, following the formula of the Northwest Ordinance. Apparently borrowing from the proposal made in the House by James Wilson, S. No. 16's second section gave Congress the power to enforce the abolition of slavery by "appropriate legislation." The amendment to the Constitution read as follows:

> Neither slavery nor involuntary servitude, except as punishment for crime, whereof the party shall have been duly convicted, shall exist within the United States, or any place subject to their jurisdiction.
>
> Congress shall have power to enforce this article by appropriate legislation.[44]

In his initial speech favoring the proposed amendment, judiciary committee chairman Lyman Trumbull reiterated the fundamental lesson of the war–slavery itself caused the antagonism between North and South. The final result of that antagonism was the existing war. Congress and President had attempted early in the war to attack slavery. Yet each measure, the two confiscation acts, and Lincoln's Emancipation Proclamation, had serious deficiencies, in Trumbull's view. Confiscation had proved ineffective and even in theory only released slaves of disloyal masters. Confiscation alone would not "extirpate" slavery from the country. Similarly, the Emancipation

Proclamation left portions of slavery behind Union lines untouched. Trumbull's purpose was the complete eradication of the system–the cause of the war and the nation's long history of political troubles. What he now sought was a "more efficient" means for accomplishing his goal. The effect would be to "take this question entirely away from the politics of the country. We relieve Congress of sectional strife" and restore freedom to an entire race. Trumbull believed a constitutional amendment was the only way to ensure that slavery would not be resurrected, and that conquered slave states could be readmitted to the Union more easily once they were free. The amendment would "secure to us further peace."[45]

Most other Republican senators supported Trumbull's analysis. Henry Wilson, more radical than his Illinois colleague, echoed the refrain that slavery was responsible for America's struggle with rebellion. The constitutional amendment would "obliterate the last vestiges of slavery in America," prohibiting it the refuge that it then enjoyed in places like Kentucky. New Hampshire's Daniel Clark pinpointed the cause of the war as the 1787 constitutional convention, when the Founders made the great mistake of admitting into the "bond of Union . . . antagonistic forces which have well nigh rent the Union asunder." Americans were now repaying the results of that initial error. Through previous antislavery measures Congress and President had freed individual slaves, but they had not overturned the rotten system itself. The proposed constitutional amendment, on the other hand, was "of wider scope and more searching operation. It goes deep into the soil, and upturns the roots of this poisonous plant to die and wither."[46]

Clark's point raised the question of the amendment's scope and purpose. Trumbull had spoken in terms that suggested the amendment would enforce itself, that once ratified, slavery would cease to exist. The Illinois senator mentioned the enforcement clause only in passing as he explained the amendment's language. He never expounded on the new grant of power given to Congress in the amendment's second section. Clark's remarks, however, suggested a more activist approach to abolition, conditioned by the realization that slavery was deep-rooted, indeed.[47]

The Senate was aware that the constitutional amendment involved something more than technical status (free of or slave). It also addressed the question of qualitative freedom for the prospective ex-slaves. In his remarks Wilson explicitly recognized free blacks as citizens of the United States, citing Bates' November, 1862 opinion. Combating that opinion, Kentucky's Unionist senator Garret Davis submitted an amendment specifically barring blacks from citizenship and office holding. His attempt was overwhelmingly defeated 5 to

32, showing that the Senate implicitly admitted Wilson's main argument that freedom conferred citizenship.[48] A constitutional amendment securing freedom for all blacks would also secure citizenship.

Reverdy Johnson, a former attorney general and presently senator from Maryland, supported that interpretation by inference. During the time S. No. 16 was before the Senate, that body also considered a bill to organize the Montana territory. Minnesota senator Morton Wilkinson proposed an amendment to the territorial bill granting the vote to "every free male citizen of the United States" over 21 years of age. Johnson opposed the amendment precisely on the grounds that by excluding the word "white," and in light of previous congressional acts, presidential proclamations, and the proposed constitutional amendment, the vote would thereby be given to any black who might journey to Montana. Willard Saulsbury of Delaware opposed the entire Montana bill because blacks were already citizens according to those now in charge of the government. Wilkinson's amendment was adopted 22 to 17, and Johnson immediately tried to retreat, arguing then that blacks could not be citizens of the United States because of the *Dred Scott* decision. Charles Sumner dismissed that argument forthrightly: "God forbid that Congress should consent to wear the strait-jacket of the Dred Scott decision!"[49]

Border state residents attempted to maintain the old dichotomy between freedom and civil equality. Reverdy Johnson opposed black citizenship, yet favored abolition by constitutional amendment. West Virginia senator Peter Van Winkle spoke against the "direct and indirect" efforts to raise the black to citizenship, but also supported the abolition of slavery. Republican Timothy Howe of Wisconsin, on the other hand, did not believe the amendment went far enough in specifying freedmen's rights.[50] Republicans in general, however, no longer accepted the divergence of freedom from rights, and border state men's attempts to divide the two were unsuccessful.

Opponents of the constitutional amendment centered their arguments on the proposed breach of traditional barriers between the federal government and individuals. Saulsbury commented that if relations between master and slave could be regulated (abolished), so might that of parent and child, or husband and wife. Hyperbole aside, Saulsbury's emphasis on the essentially radical character of the amendment was correct. Through the proposed constitutional change, the federal government would by-pass state governments and state laws in order to declare that property held in persons was no longer possible in the United States. For good measure, Congress would have *new* power to enforce the new relationships freedom would bring about. To abolish slavery and prevent its reestablishment was, in

Lyman Trumbull's words, "*the* great question." In answer, Kentucky's two senators, Davis and Lazarus Powell, proposed amendment after amendment in dilatory efforts to block a vote on abolition. California Democrat John McDougall opposed the constitutional amendment because it detracted, in his opinion, from the main object of defeating the South. The opponents rejected the main lesson of the war as they continued to spin fine, legalistic distinctions between expressed and reserved powers, spheres of sovereignty, and the means of conquering treason.[51]

The Senate disposed of Davis' and Powell's amendments and, in Committee of the Whole, reported the constitutional amendment to the floor on April 6, 1864. The following day Democratic senator Thomas Hendricks of Indiana made the key argument, as yet unstated, against the abolition amendment and its philosophy. Countering the joy of New Hampshire's John Hale over the prospect of abolition, Hendricks lamented the death and destruction that war had visited upon white Americans. Freedom for four million slaves did not seem worth the price, nor was freedom to be so broadly conceived as abolitionists envisioned:

> [equality] may be preached; it may be legislated for; may be prayed for; but there is that difference between the two races that renders it impossible. If they are among us as a free people, they are among us as an inferior people.[52]

The chronic and acute racism of many if not most white Americans, North and South, was the fundamental fact at variance with abolitionist hopes. Even those who were willing to grant blacks their freedom, like the amendment's original sponsor John Henderson, still assumed and believed in white supremacy. With charity added in equal portion to racism, a *laissez-faire* attitude might emerge, holding that blacks were free and that there should be no obstacles in their path. But neither ought there be positive federal aid. Only as charity exceeded racism and united with government action could freedom for the black be seen in qualitative terms rather than as status.[53]

That approach appeared most clearly in Sumner's substitute amendment, which declared that "all persons are equal before the law," prohibited slavery, and gave Congress power to make "all laws necessary and proper to carry this declaration into effect." Sumner preferred his language, copied from the French Declaration of the Rights of Man, over the committee's echo of the Northwest Ordinance because the former was more sweeping and the latter more legalistic. Trumbull noted the disagreements in the Judiciary Committee over the amendment's language, suggesting the present text was a compromise. (The Senate committee had dropped Henderson's original motion and fused the texts of the House members James Ashley and James Wilson.) Trumbull maintained, however, that rather than a liability, the committee's allusion to the Northwest Ordinance (and, therefore, to the Wilmot Proviso) fixed the constitutional amendment firmly in American tradition and history. Sumner's reference to the French Declaration of Rights had little relevance to American experience and legal tradition, Jacob Howard commented, and Trumbull concluded the rebuttal by noting that the language adopted byu the committee "will accomplish the object."

None of Sumner's objections nor Trumbull's or Howard's defenses of the committee text centered on substantive issues. Each thought the other's language inappropriate, but they agreed upon the goal. Freedom must transcend slavery and become the nation's law. When Sumner acquiesced to the committee's language, he did not consider his action a defeat of principle, but only of form.[54] "Nothing against slavery is unconstitutional," Sumner declared. "It is only hesitation which is unconstitutional."[55]

Kentucky's two stalwart pro-slavery senators made final attempts to stop the amendment, as did California's McDougall, who characterized proponents as men "maddened with a present sense of power" trying to "accomplish to-day what they fear may not be within their grasp tomorrow." Thereupon the Senate, the traditional fortress of southern opposition to antislavery agitation, voted 38 to 6 in favor of the abolition of slavery throughout the United States.[56]

Abolitionists might rightly take a measure of credit for pioneering the philosophy that validated the view that "the North must abolish slavery and slave labor, or the South will abolish freedom and free labor." The Washington *Daily Morning Chronicle* explicitly recognized William Lloyd Garrison and Wendell Phillips for lighting the "signal fires of freedom in the teeth of intolerance, nay, murderous public opinion." Orestes Brownson commended the abolitionists who had dared hold out the prophetic call of antislavery and urged his readers to accept the implication of freedom–civil equality between the races. The government had gone so far in the equal treatment of the races in the army, Brownson suggested, that "the wisest and safest plan" would be the abolition of all distinctions based on color in the areas subject to federal jurisdiction. Although opposed to a constitutional amendment only "for the negro," Brownson argued that all persons were equal before the law. Similarly, the *North American Review* urged a minimum of guardianship for the freedmen so long as they were protected from injustice and abuse.[57]

Moderate and some conservative elements of the Union coalition acknowledged what abolitionists had earlier proclaimed–slavery and freedom were antithetical and could not exist together. Moreover, the implicit issue of the quality of freedom blacks might experience had become explicit. In March 1864 Lincoln wrote to Louisiana governor Michael Hahn suggesting political rights for blacks as the logical extension of civil equality. To be sure, the President suggested that only some blacks–"the very intelligent, and especially those who have fought gallantly in our ranks"–be allowed to vote. Nevertheless, it was a significant step forward, made more so by Lincoln's heretofore stubborn moderation. Lincoln's own view of the war's progress indicates authoritatively his changing perception:

> I claim not to have controlled events, but confess plainly that events have controlled me. Now, at the end of three years struggle the nation's condition is not what either party, or any man devised, or expected. God alone now wills the removal of a great wrong, and wills also that we of the North as well as you of the South, shall pay fairly for our complicity in that wrong, impartial history will find therein new cause to attest and revere the justice and goodness of God.[58]

As the Senate approved the constitutional amendment, as the President spoke of limited black suffrage, as the Women's National League circulated 15,000 petitions favoring abolition, the focus shifted to the House of Representatives. There, Democratic gains in the 1862 elections assured a closer contest and made victory uncertain.[59]

The House began its consideration of S. No. 16 on May 31. Republican Judiciary Committee member Daniel Morris made the opening address. Morris acknowledged the divergence of view on the amendment, even within his own party. Despite differences over how to achieve the end, the essential point was clear–slavery had to be destroyed to save the nation. Because James Buchanan had been "an Executive steeped in slavery and doomed to eternal infamy," and had allowed the slave power an unchecked reign during his term as President, the United States found itself engulfed in a civil war. Abolition would prevent such a catastrophe from ever happening again.[60] Still, abolitionists had a sense of gratitude for the sin–the happy fault and necessary evil–for without the treason of slavery, absolution by abolition would not have been possible.[61]

New York Democrat Anson Herrick answered with the familiar conservative litany. The Constitution was something to "reverence as a masterpiece of wisdom in statesmanship." Scorning an appeal to put slavery's "putrescent carcass out of sight," Herrick argued that altering the terms of the Constitution would "absolutely upset" the social organization of the slave states, disturb property rights, and prolong rather than subdue the rebellion. The Constitution ought to shape rather than be shaped by events that surrounded it. Republicans countered that Congress was the "ultimate tribunal" to discern whether states were following constitutional requirements–appealing to the guarantee of republican government clause. The ideological limits were set for the debate, and perception conditioned the Constitution's nature and function–reverenced and closed, or adaptable and open. Republicans scheduled the debate on the amendment to being on June 14.[62]

On that day each side reiterated its basic view and argument. Ezra Wheeler, Republican of Wisconsin, noted that war had given the nation a new manifest destiny, which was freedom for the slave and the power to enforce the prohibition of slavery in the states.[63] Michigan's Francis Kellogg emphasized the tradition of the Declaration of Independence, its link with the Constitution through the latter's preamble, and abolition as the means to establish a more perfect union of freedom.[64]

It was clear that Democrats and other conservatives saw the proposed constitutional amendment as a significant, and therefore dangerous, change in the American social system. William Holman of Indiana was especially forceful in his statement. Beginning with homage to the Constitution as it was, "the serene light of the past, with all of the sacred memories of the past ages clustering around it, sanctified by tradition and history," Holman explained in detail what he believed the proposed Thirteenth Amendment was really about and what effect it would have upon the country and its citizens:

> But, sir, the amendment goes further. It confers on Congress the power to invade any State to enforce freedom of the African in war or peace. What is the meaning of all that? Is freedom the simple exemption from personal servitude? No, sir; in the language of America it means to participate in government, the freedom for which our fathers resisted the British empire. Mere exemption from servitude is a miserable idea of freedom. A pariah in the State, a subject, but more a citizen holding any right at the will of the government power. What is this but slavery? It exists in my own noble State. Then, sir, this amendment has some significance. Your policy, directed in its main purpose to the enfranchisement of a people who have looked with indifference on your struggle, who have given their strength to you enemies, and then the constitutional power to force them into freedom, to citizenship. If such be your purpose, why deceive a noble and confiding people? Your purpose in this amendment is not to increase the efficiency of your Army or to diminish the power of your enemies. No, sir, you diminish the one and increase the other. You run the hazard of all that to gratify your visionary fanaticism, the elevation of the African to the august rights of

> citizenship. The Federal power to invade the States for this purpose, as proposed by this amendment, strike down the cornerstone of the Republic, the local sovereignty of the States. . . . Policy and prudence condemn it, and if it were possible, sir, the very ashes of the Revolution would cry out against this subordination of the States in domestic affairs to the Federal power.[65]

Holman was right, incredibly right, notwithstanding the Republicans' lack of explicit theorizing about the amendment's effects. Much that Holman feared, much that he predicted as the future consequence of the abolition amendment, was already before Congress, and in a matter of weeks, became the law of the land. The previous day, June 13, the House had passed the army appropriation bill that equalized the pay of black and white soldiers. Between June 28 and July 2 Congress repealed the 1850 Fugitive Slave Act, the 1813 Seaman Act (which distinguished between blacks and United States citizens, used by Taney in his *Dred Scott* opinion), incorporated the Metropolitan Railroad Company for the District of Columbia with an anti-discrimination clause, and prohibited discrimination against black testimony in federal courts.[66]

Earlier, Wendell Phillips had made the point exactly:

> If I were a negro, I should pray God that this war might last twenty years. . . . I should dread every victory on the part of the North; for I believe that this war, while it last . . . is taking the rivets out of society; it is crumbling up the whole civil and social life into its original elements and when that work is completely done, no matter what may be the form of government that follows, the negro is always free.[67]

Both Phillips and Holman recognized the war for what it was, a revolutionary force in American history. Both saw the war and its consequences as decisive for the fate of freedmen. Congressional actions and, most forcefully, the constitutional amendment confirmed the direction the country was moving. The ideology of the viewer shaped the evaluation.

The House of Representatives could still succumb to racist impulses and the fear of change, despite attacks on slavery and its incidents, and despite Republican assertions that the manhood of blacks had already been manifested and that the "America of the past is gone forever." The vision of "a new nation . . . born from the agony through which the people are now passing," a nation meant to be "wholly free" with "liberty, equality before the law" as its great cornerstone, was still just a vision. On June 15 the House rejected the constitutional amendment abolishing slavery. Congressmen turned away from the capstone, the act of consolidation that would give constitutional expression to the supreme lesson of the war. Although a clear majority of 93 members favored the measure, and only 65 opposed it, two-thirds of the members voting, or 106 congressmen, were necessary for approval. Recognizing that they could not find enough additional affirmative votes, floor manager James Ashley announced on June 28 that the Republicans would not call up S. No. 16 for reconsideration until after the presidential election in November. By its action at the polls, the nation would signal its decision on the amendment of freedom.[68] The reelection of Abraham Lincoln would be a referendum on the war's progress and on the nation's policy toward blacks.

Earlier, in June, the Union National Convention (composed of Republicans and war Democrats) had endorsed the antislavery amendment and made its adoption part of their platform. No sooner was Lincoln renominated than his pocket-veto of the Wade-Davis bill sparked a great furor about his antislavery commitment.

The product of Senator Benjamin Wade and Representative Henry Winter Davis, the Wade-Davis bill would have made slavery illegal rather than rely on an abolition amendment. Both men were noted for the radical views on slavery and on the plenitude and priority of congressional authority in reconstruction. Davis' reliance on and trust of congressional power was so great that he suggested to Wade the irrelevance of the Thirteenth Amendment: "The constitutional amendment is dead–as I always knew & said it was; and never could do any political good." Davis preferred the approach followed throughout the war of specific, incremental steps against slavery and the Confederacy. Hence, additional clauses of the Wade-Davis bill secured congressional control of reconstruction and modified Lincoln's own ten percent formula for allowing conquered southern states to begin reconstruction. Just as disagreement on means, rather than ends, prompted Davis' denigration of the constitutional amendment, so disagreement on means sparked Lincoln's pocket-veto of the Wade-Davis bill.[69]

Davis' insistence upon congressional action to enforce the war's end–reconstruction–might be readily subsumed under the constitutional amendment's second section with its grant of new power to Congress. But Davis preferred reliance on the war power that existed rather than wait upon new constitutional power. The war power may have been sufficient for congressional control of reconstruction while war lasted. But it was the time after the war that the constitutional amendment was aimed towards. Without the amendment, when the war power faded, Congress' authority over southern reconstruction would also fade. Davis evidently did not envision the war power disappearing in the near future. Others questioned the wisdom of altering the Constitution. The *Monthly Law Reporter* followed Davis' reliance on congressional authority and the war power as adequate means to abolish slavery and maintain the Constitution "as it is."[70] Yet other commentators argued that the war had freed the Constitution from many antebellum constraints. The *North American Review* observed that the time had come to dispense with excessive reverence for the document or "Constitution-worship." It was time to recognize the error the Founders made when incorporating a compromise with slavery into the national charter. What the Founders "saw in a glass darkly, we see face to face," the *Review*'s writer noted. Henry E. Russell, in the *Continental Monthly*, observed both the Thirteenth Amendment's defeat in the House and the Democratic party's continuing attachment to the slaveholding interest. Slavery, therefore, posed an enduring fundamental flaw in the Constitution. Both journals concluded that the Thirteenth Amendment was a necessary and proper consequence of treason.[71]

The amendment was necessary for two reasons. Throughout its ascendance in pre-war America, the slave power had infringed upon the rights of white citizens; its suppression of free speech, free press, and free use of the mails was widely recognized. The Confederacy, avowedly based on slavery, was the ultimate infringement upon white citizens' rights because it took life in attempting to destroy the nation. To protect white citizens, slavery and the slave power had to be destroyed, never to return to life. The constitutional amendment would settle the question of reconstruction by securing the emancipation of slaves as firmly as possible. As Henry Russell put it, "to supplement and complete the work of reconstruction, we need to make impossible the presence of a power anywhere within the domain of the United States to hold a person in bondage." The Bill of Rights, formerly a mockery in the South, would become a "living power" to secure white rights and black freedom.[72]

The *North American Review* also favored a constitutional safeguard for black freedom and rights, noting that the benefits of the Emancipation Proclamation depended upon the willingness of the Executive to enforce its provisions. This, in truth, depended upon the character of the President. It was by no means certain that Lincoln would continue to oversee emancipation. Moreover, once the war was over, the *Review* doubted the North's willingness to resume military action against southerners solely to defend freedmen's liberty. The writer concluded that the nation must have the power to protect all its citizens, white and black. Liberty was not threatened by the national government, but by the states. As slavery was the cause, so state rights had been the expression of southern discontent and ultimately of secession. State-inspired, the war was the greatest threat to liberty in the American experience. The abolition of the root problem and the maintenance of freedmen's liberty by the national government were the best means to ensure the liberty of all and the triumph of nation over section.[73]

The freedmen's fate attracted more interest during the summer and fall of 1864. Joel Prentiss Bishop, a noted legal commentator, saw the newly freed southern slave as the only possible base for the reconstruction of southern states. Although Bishop believed that the Constitution was originally intended as a white man's document, he concluded that the North must turn to blacks in order to preserve representative government: "For the benefit of whites, then [blacks] may spring up as freemen in the seceded states, and hold these states against the waves of treason."[74] Bishop proposed as yet another lesson of the war that, in the face of massive treason, an original preference for whites must yield to bi-racial democracy. The Emancipation Proclamation was a promise of democracy to southern blacks. If the North repudiated the promise, Bishop contended, then blacks ought to take arms against both South and North, for each then would be "alike barbarians."[75]

Similarly, Ralph Waldo Emerson and Henry Russell saw the dawn of bi-racial democracy based primarily upon the war experience of white Americans. Calling the war the "second American revolution," Russell noted that it presented the "vexed question of the negro, what should be done with him, or for him, or to him." Russell and Emerson agreed that the new basis for American government was equality of all before the law. Their invocation of Charles Sumner's failed alternate language for the Thirteenth Amendment together with their support for the amendment as finally written, suggested the compatibility of the two approaches. It also suggested the essential identity of Sumner's language and the Amendment's text; freedom was more than the absence of slavery.[76]

Sumner's Massachusetts colleague Henry Wilson illustrated the point when explaining why he had compiled his *History of the Antislavery Measures of the 37th and 38th Congress*. By documenting the attacks upon slavery and its incidents, Wilson wrote historian Benjamin Lossing, he hoped to show "our friends . . . how much had been done, and I wish to encourage them to further efforts for the final extinction of slavery."[77] The extinction of slavery, status and incidental effects, lay behind the step-by-step approach pursued throughout the war.

This approach had achieved much during Lincoln's Administration. Yet Lincoln received little credit from the more radical members of the Union coalition. Orestes Brownson attacked the Emancipation

Proclamation, perhaps Lincoln's most important single gesture, as a "fritter[ing] away of the war power." Brownson doubted that any slave could plead the Proclamation before a court and secure his freedom. Not only were Lincoln's policies criticized and his commitment to antislavery openly questioned, Lincoln's character was often assailed. His leadership was criticized as being too weak, except when it was too strong.[78] Wendell Phillips epitomized the ambivalence that many felt toward Lincoln the President:

> As a citizen, therefore, I refuse to commit my future to the pleasant words of Abraham Lincoln. I rate him at the exact value of his *acts*–nothing more. I am willing to give him credit what has been done, in the exact degree in which I think *he* has done it. When he has done anything only on compulsion, at the last moment, bayonetted up to it by public opinion, I give him no credit–none at all. . . . But credit or not, his credit is the question; his laurels are not in question. The question is, what does he mean to do in the future?[79]

While Lincoln was not adored by radicals, their criticism of him paled into insignificance when compared to the vitriol heaped upon him by others. Democrats tirelessly tied Lincoln and "the negro" together in rhetoric that evoked the fear, frustration, and racism that possessed many northerners during the summer of 1864. Lincoln was referred to as the man who made the Constitution obsolete–Abraham Africanus I–a general agent for Negroes, a man who gave the word patriot a new meaning as one "who loves his country less, and the negro more." In their attempt to degrade Lincoln, Democrats resorted to parody, producing a new great commandment: "Thou shalt have no other God but the negro." At their hands, the Lord's Prayer took on a partisan hue:

> Father Abram, who art in Washington, of glorious memory–since the date of thy proclamation to free negroes, Thy kingdom come, and overthrow the republic; they will be done, and the laws perish. Give us this day our daily supply of greenbacks. Forgive us our plunders, but destroy the Copperheads. Lead us into fat pastures; but deliver us from the eye of detectives; and make us the equal of the negro; such shall be our kingdom, and the glory of thy administration.[80]

Democrats and conservatives were correct in their fears. The old Constitution, the constricting Constitution was already changed. The Thirteenth Amendment would make those changes permanent. More than simple words would change with ratification. A new Union, alive with power and possibilities, was emerging as the necessary and proper effect of civil war. The Constitution would, through the Thirteenth Amendment, incorporate the new past and the experience of war. It was exactly this change that conservatives feared and hated. If antislavery men welcomed and blessed a reborn nation, conservatives viewed the rebirth as a degeneration into "*Rouge et Noir*–blood and negroes." They made the point starkly. Republicans would rename the United States "New Africa," recognizing only "abolitionists, mesmerisers, spiritual mediums, free-lovers and negroes" as its citizenry.[81]

Republican propagandists were not silent during the barrage and squarely faced the slur of Lincoln the "gorilla." Noting the ominous circumstances when he entered office, Lincoln's supporters emphasized the lessons that the entire country had learned during the interim. The Union could not "fight with gloves" because slavery was the cause and the strength of the rebellion. Lincoln learned these lessons, Republicans argued, but had waited for the country to learn them also before he acted. As a man of the people, Lincoln kept to the delicate balance between overbearing leadership and overcaution.[82]

The argument was convincing. Lincoln's reelection had been a matter of grave doubt in the summer of 1864, yet his candidacy resulted in a surprisingly wide victory in November. Lincoln received 55 percent of the popular vote and a massive 212 to 21 electoral vote margin. The Republican-dominated Union party dramatically increased its strength in the House of Representatives from 102 to 149 seats, while the Democrats and allies declined from 75 to 42. As James Ashley had said the previous June, the fall elections were a referendum of sorts. The people chose continuation rather than abrupt reversal. At the very least, they registered their toleration of the emancipation-abolition sword. Even defeated presidential candidate George B. McClellan acknowledged that the people had chosen their course "with their eyes wide open."[83]

Conservatives and radicals viewed the future with open eyes. Sidney George Fisher had been strongly antislavery to this time, chiefly as a war matter. Now, however, he saw danger from directions other than southward. "Excessive and extreme ideas & measures" and the "fanaticism of the abolitionists" loomed on the horizon, and Fisher feared their takeover of moderate Republican government.[84]

At the same time, however, Lyman Trumbull received information of unrepentant treason in the supposedly loyal state of Kentucky, treason so great that "no union man's life would be safe in a court of any kind" there. If white men could not be sure of their rights in the "loyal" South, how much less had blacks to expect, and how much more to fear? These reasons, among others, prompted Henry Wilson's support of Salmon Chase as a replacement for the late Chief Justice Roger Taney. Adding "some great lawyer of Anti-Slavery sentiment, and deep convictions as Attorney General, and Congress true," Wilson wrote Lincoln, "we shall soon have no State *out* of the Union and no Slave *in* the Union."[85] With eyes open to the future and an appreciation of what had already happened, antislavery spokesmen adopted a new creed: "We believe that God Almighty is shaping a free and exalted nation out of this republic, by a law of progress which we did not make and cannot repeal."[86]

The second session of the 38th Congress convened on December 5, 1864. The same House members who had rejected the Thirteenth Amendment in June would have a second chance to endorse the measure during this session. A difference lay in the session's "lame duck" status which might relieve political burdens that had borne down too heavily the previous summer. Individual members lost their seats in the fall elections, the Republican-Union party increased its strength in the new Congress, and the presidential election had been a referendum on the cause of the war. The constitutional amendment abolishing slavery was an integral part of the balloters' choice. The Administration was confident with its victory and could be expected to back strongly the amendment during the House debate.

The amendment's floor manager, Ohio Republican James Ashley, gave notice on December 15 that he would call for reconsideration of the measure on January 9, 1865. Because the amendment had failed to receive the requisite two-thirds majority, the House had first to agree to reconsider. But the decision to again take up the measure required only a simple majority vote. This outcome was never in doubt. Still, reconsideration would be of little use if Ashley and the Administration could not find enough congressmen to form the needed two-thirds margin. It was absolutely imperative that every member who favored the amendment the previous summer be present when the vote came. To this end Ashley sent out a confidential circular, giving the estimated backers of the amendment as 108. With the expected whole number voting, however, this was still one vote short of the needed majority. Penning a note to the circular for Lincoln's attention, Ashley wrote: "*You* must help us *one* vote. Don't you know a sinner in the opposition who is on praying ground?"[87]

Intense lobbying occurred between December 15 and the expected vote in January. The President especially concentrated on border state men, where his contacts made him most effective. Greatest credit, after Ashley himself, however, went to Secretary of State William Seward, whose work with New York Democrats proved decisive. In a surprising turn of events, New York Democratic Governor Horatio Seymour refused to make the vote on the constitutional amendment a matter of party discipline, allowing each member the freedom to make his own choice.[88]

While lobbying continued behind the scenes, congressmen received messages from the "free" South, message that told how much southerners had still to learn about the rights of former slaves. These messages reminded northerners how much the Union needed free, loyal, rights-endowed blacks.[89] In the opinion of William M. Grosvenor, editor of the New Haven *Journal Courier*, the nation had passed through two crises. The first occurred in July, 1863 and was military–the battles of Vicksburg and Gettysburg. The second crisis was political and had occurred with the presidential election in November 1864. But in January 1865, the crisis became the effort to make a nation, to create one people. For that the "white-hot crucible" of civil war had been necessary. Now constitutional reform must follow and be a part of the changed reality. As a colonel of a regiment of Louisiana blacks, Grosvenor no doubt agreed with Yale professor Alexander Twining that emancipation, even universal liberation, did not alter state laws and, in that sense, did not change anything. Achieving the "essential purpose," the alteration of substance, required a constitutional amendment.[90]

On January 6, three days earlier than scheduled, Ashley asked for reconsideration of the Thirteenth Amendment. In doing so the Ohioan maintained his firm belief that the Constitution, correctly interpreted, did not allow slavery in the first place. Ashley believed there was a fundamental link between the ideas expressed in the Declaration of Independence and the Constitution of 1787. The theory of state sovereignty had become the tool of the slave power, however, and this "fatal heresy" had lured otherwise good men into treason and war. The Thirteenth Amendment was necessary, therefore, to uphold the twin, fundamental principles of freedom and national supremacy.

Ashley's Republican colleague Godlove S. Orth spoke immediately afterwards and reaffirmed Ashley's views. The constitutional amendment would prevent reenslavement and was the "practical application" of the truth that "all men are created equal." The Thirteenth Amendment assured that Congress' responsibility "to see that the name and spirit of human bondage shall be erased from every state constitution, and personal liberty without distinction assured to everyone of their citizens," would be met. "Equal protection under the law" was the means to fulfill that responsibility, the call to "carry up higher and higher the work of the fathers." In this way America would survive the war and be re-born.[91]

Debate on the amendment continued for a week. In answer to the proponents, Democrats focused their opposition to two main areas–the increase of federal power, and race. New Jersey Democrat Andrew

Rogers worried that if the federal government could touch slavery by constitutional amendment, it could also affect family relationships, marriage, private contracts, and state electoral laws. Rogers believed that Republicans would make the reserved powers of the states too fragile. Ohio's S. S. Cox feared federal intrusion in state affairs, wondering if it would end with nullification of all state discrimination against blacks. Cox's Democratic colleague Chilton White assured the House that blacks could never remain in the South without continuing federal military intervention. Blacks "will be free," said White, "just as long as the soldier sets his bayonet between the slave and the maser, and no longer."[92]

This was precisely why freedmen had to have civil rights. While Republicans accepted and expected an indeterminate period of occupation in the South, no one seriously looked to an indefinite federal military presence. New York Democrat Elijah Ward grasped the fact when he characterized the constitutional amendent as a measure making "all persons . . . equal under the law, without regard to color, and so that no person shall hereafter be held in bondage."[93] In that interpretation was correct, a long military occupation of the South would be unnecessary.

Objections to lengthy military occupation of the South and to abolition and freedmen's rights as means to lessen the need for such an unwelcome military venture, illustrates the deep connection between the constitutional conservatism expressed in the House debate, and racist suppositions about blacks and whites. The divine sanction of negro inferiority and white superiority were common arguments against mortal intervention into the realm of race relations.[94]

Most Democrats and conservatives were no longer pro-slavery in the sense of favoring the continuation of the formal status of "slave" and "master." But the racism that nurtured their previous defense of the slave status, remained and infused their opposition to changes. The system of slavery might be disposed of, although they believed a constitutional amendment the wrong method to achieve that end. Once the status of slave was destroyed, conservatives like Kentucky's George Yeaman hoped the other "dangerous schemes" of radicals including citizenship and political rights for blacks "associated . . . in the public mind as incident or necessary to [abolition's] accomplishment" would lose support. According to Daniel Voorhees of Indiana, the real issue was no longer abolition of status, but what civil and political rights freedmen would have. Recognizing that the tide was against the institution of slavery, conservatives attempted to preserve as much of the racial basis of slavery as possible by introducing the novel notion that freedom in America was nothing more than the absence of slavery.

Status and condition would have no intrinsic bond.[95]

Republicans answered the argument by pointing out that the great centralizing force had not been emancipation, but slavery itself. The Supreme Court decisions in *Dred Scott* and *Ableman v. Booth* increased federal authority vis-a-vis antislavery actions or desires. Finally, during the secession crisis the other "thirteenth amendment" of 1861 would have given irrepealable federal protection to slavery in the states. If Congress had power to propose that amendment, New York antislavery Democrat Moses Odell argued, it could also destroy slavery by constitutional amendment. The Thirteenth Amendment would give to Congress the first new grant of power since 1787, power that would be in support of fundamental human rights. Robert Kasson argued that the rights of whites and blacks were unsafe without the safeguarding of spouse, children, and personal liberty.[96]

Nature made all people free and equal before the law, Thomas T. Davis of New York argued. Liberty, as defined in the Declaration of Independence, gave vitality to the Constitution. It was the duty of government to reflect the natural order, just as conservatives argued. The primary law of nature, however, was not bondage but freedom. Blacks might not be equal with white in ability, Davis conceded, yet the laws must treat them equally because all were (or would be) free. And equality before the law could only occur when "every vestige of African slavery" was removed from the republic.[97]

Other reconstruction legislation complemented the constitutional amendment. As the House debated the Thirteenth Amendment, Republicans brought forward a new reconstruction bill. It was explicit in regard to freedmen's rights where the constitutional amendment, by its nature, was only general and implicit. Concepts of "equality before the law' and "equality of civil rights before the law" paralleled consideration of the amendment. Thomas D. Elliot of Massachusetts made the connection clear when he spoke in favor of the reconstruction bill and yet pointed to the constitutional dimension: "Let [the southern states] establish their constitutions; let it [sic] prohibit slavery; let them grant freedom and equality of rights, and we need nothing else."[98]

James Ashley called up the constitutional amendment on January 28 after a two week long debate. The final vote was scheduled for three days later, on January 31. On that day Ashley yielded the House floor to various northern Democrats who announced their conversion to abolition. New York Democrat Anson Herrick was typical in his reasoning. Many changes had occurred between June 1864 and this January day in 1865, chiefly Lincoln's stunning reelection victory. In light of the different circumstances, there was no virtue in maintaining an "imaginary consistency." At about four o'clock in the afternoon, with members of the Senate and Supreme Court in attendance, the House of Representatives reversed its decision of June 15 and approved the Thirteenth Amendment to the Constitution by a vote of 119 to 56, two more than the necessary two-thirds margin. With that solemn action, Congress sent the proposed amendment to the state legislatures for ratification. Its adoption and attendant social and legal support in three-fourths of the states would create a new reality for freedmen. It would, in Henry Wilson's words, prepare and welcome them for "the higher condition of life opening before them."[99]

It was true that the times had changed. War had done that. It was true that great advances toward freedom had occurred by January 1865. War had done that, too. Yet the war as well as the advance toward liberty were made up of thousands, millions, of individual affirmations that the conflict could be won, and that freedom was possible. Illinois Republican John F. Farnsworth's conclusion about the vote on the constitutional amendment was apt: "We are making history, and we are making it fast."[100]

NOTES FOR CHAPTER FIVE

1. *Official Opinions of the Attorneys General of the United States* (Washington: Government Printing Office, various volumes and years), 10:382-413.

2. *SAL*, 1:103-104, 2:809; *Annals of the Congress of the United States* (Washington: Gales and Seaton, 1853), 12:2, 937-40, 960, 1010, 1018-55, 1111, 1147. For a review of blacks employed as seamen on American shipping, see Patricia W. Romero, ed., *I too am America: Documents from 1619 to the Present* (New York: Publishers Company, 1968), 55-56; Harold D. Langley, "The Negro in the Navy and Merchant Service–1789-1860," *Journal of Negro History*, 52:275-76; Herbert Aptheker, *To Be Free: Studies in American Negro History* (New York: International Publishers, 2d edition, 1969), 114-15; Robert E. Perdue, *Black Laborers and Black Professionals in Early America, 1750-1830* (New York: Vantage Press, 1975), 89-90. Chief Justice Taney specifically cited the 1813 Seaman Act as a justification for his ruling in *Dred Scott v. Sandford* that blacks were not United States citizens, 19 Howard 393-633 (U. S. 1856); Don E. Fehrenbacher, *The Dred Scott Case: Its Significance in American Law and Politics* (New York: Oxford University Press, 1978), 360-61. That portion of the act that distinguished blacks from United States citizens, along with other discriminatory laws regarding citizenship were repealed in 1864, *Cong. Globe*, 38:1, 2837, 2866; *SAL*, 13:201-202.

3. Edwin C. McReynolds, *Missouri: A History of the Crossroads State* (Norman, Oklahoma: University of Oklahoma Press, 1962), 87-91; Duane Douglas Smith, "The Evolution of the Legal Concept of Citizenship in the United States," (unpublished Ph.D. dissertation, Ohio State University, 1936), 49, 52; Glover Moore, *The Missouri Controversy, 1819-1821* (Gloucester, Massachusetts: Peter Smith, 1967), 135, 142-44; *Annals of Congress*, 16:2, 23-24, 47-50, 78-80, 83-90, 100-102, 113, 571-73, 545-48, 555-57, 596, 613-15, 630-35; Kempes Y. Schnell, "Court Cases Involving Slavery: A Study of the Application of the Anti-Slavery Thought to Judicial Argument," (unpublished Ph.D. dissertation, University of Michigan, 1955), 114-18; Floyd C. Shoemaker, *Missouri's Struggle for Statehood, 1804-1821* (New York: Russell & Russell, 1969 reprint), 302-305; *Opinions Attorneys General*, 1:506-509.

4. Fehrenbacher, *Dred Scott*, 67-68, 72-73, 327-30, 332, 335-64, 419, 430; Carl B. Swisher, *Roger B. Taney* (New York: Macmillan, 1935), 151-55, 158; Schnell, "Court Cases," 139, 142, 144-47; Thomas D. Morris, *Free Men All: The Personal Liberty Laws of the North* (Baltimore: Johns Hopkins University Press, 1974), 169-73; Eric Foner, *Free Soil, Free Labor, Free Men: The Ideology of the Republican Party Before the Civil War* (New York: Oxford University Press, 1970), 97, 101-102, 292-93; Lincoln, *Coll. Works*, 2:401, 3:255; *North American Review* (April 1862), 94:448, and (October 1862), 95:509. For a thorough discussion of the evolution of United States citizenship, see James H. Kettner, *The Development of American Citizenship, 1608-1870* (Chapel Hill: University of North Carolina Press, 1978), passim. Kettner maintains that only after four years of war was it possible to affirm that blacks were citizens and eliminate many of the ambiguities of American citizenship, ibid., 333. For the ambiguity in treating blacks and citizenship before the *Dred Scott* decision, see Caleb Cushing to Jefferson Davis, May 25, 1854, Cushing Papers, DLC. Cushing reviewed two court martial cases in which blacks were allowed to

testify.

5. The quotation is from LeRoy P. Graff and Ralph W. Haskins, eds., *The Papers of Andrew Johnson* (Knoxville: University of Tennessee Press, 1976), 4:84-85, 99; *Opinions Attorneys General*, 10:387; Kirk H. Porter, *A History of Suffrage in the United States* (New York: Greenwood Press, 1969 reprint), 112-31. Aliens were allowed to vote in seven states until 1918, ibid., 121n.

6. Whiting, *War Power*, 25-26; *Opinions Attorneys General*, 10:382-89; Smith, "Evolution Citizenship," 114-21. The assertion of federal primacy in determining citizenship occurs, with Bates' opinion in 1862, much earlier than either Herman Belz or William Dunning had concluded. The 1866 Civil Rights Act confirmed Bates' 1862 opinion. Belz, *Emancipation and Equal Rights*, 67, 120; William A. Dunning, *Essays on the Civil War and Reconstruction and Related Topics* (New York: Macmillan, 1898), 96-98.

7. *Opinions Attorneys General*, 10:397-413; Cain, *Bates*, 222-25.

8. *Corfield v. Coryell* 4 Wash C. C. 371-81 (U.S.C.C., 1823); *Bennet v. Boggs* 3 Fed Cases 221 (U.S.C.C., 1830); Kettner, *Development American Citizenship*, 259-60; Schnell, "Court Cases," 124-27; New York *Times*, December 17, 1862; but see Bates to John D. De Free, December 17, 1862, for this: "There seems to be much curiosity to see [his opinion], and I am constantly asked for copies," DNA, M 699, roll 7; T. Farrar said that the Dred Scott opinion was the instance in which Taney "scandalizes all sound law, and all good sense," "State Rights", in *New Englander* (October 1862) 21:708, 721; N. H. Eggleston, "Emancipation," ibid., 813, for the separation of human and citizenship rights. See also William M. Wiecek, *Sources of Antislavery Constitutionalism in America, 1760-1848* (Ithaca, New York: Cornell University Press, 1977), 164-66, for a differing view of *Corfield v. Coryell*.

9. See Don E. Fehrenbacher, "Lincoln and the Constitution," in Cullom Davis, et al., eds., *The Public and Private Lincoln: Contemporary Perspectives* (Carbondale and Edwardsville, Illinois: Southern Illinois University Press, 1979), 132-33, for Republican reactions virtually nullifying the *Dred Scott* decision.

10. *Liberator*, January 9, 1863; Lincoln, *Coll. Works*, 6:28-30; *Opinions Attorneys General*, 10:389. Several months later the Speaker of the House, Schuyler Colfax, picked up Phillips' theme and reviewed the progressive, necessary steps of the war–emancipation in the District, confiscation, the Emancipation Proclamation, the use of black troops–as part of the "grand whole" from God to punish slavery, Colfax to James C. Conklin, printed in Indianapolis *Daily Journal*, September 7, 1863.

11. Lincoln, *Coll. Works*, 6:48-49.

12. Edward Everett Hale, "The Desert and the Promised Land; A Sermon," in Freidel, *Union Pamphlets*, 1:508; Welles, *Diary*, 1:212-13. For details on the final decree of emancipation, see Lincoln, *Coll. Works*, 6:24n-26n; Welles, *Diary*, 1:209.

13. Rev. M. French to Chase, January 2, 1863, Salmon P. Chase Papers, DLC; Ashley, *Duplicate Souvenir*, 243-44; Indianapolis *Daily Journal*, July 11, 1863; Welles, *Diary*, 1:212; Henry W. Bellows, "Unconditional Loyalty," in Freidel, *Union Pamphlets*, 1:512-13; Fisher, *Diary*, 447; Garrison, *Letters*, 5:143.

14. Lowrey, "Commander in Chief," in Freidel, *Union Pamphlets*, 1:499.

15. Ibid., first quotation, 486, second quotation, 480-81; Horace Bushnell,

"The Doctrine of Loyalty," in *New Englander* (July 1863) 22:580.

16. Fisher, *Diary*, 462.

17. Curtis quoted in Samuel F. B. Morse, et al., "The Constitution," in Freidel, *Union Pamphlets*, 1:535.

18. "Preogative Rights and Public Law," *Monthly Law Reporter* (January 1863) 129-50.

19. Washington *National Intelligencer*, January 3, 1863; Edward Archbold to Wade, February 15, 1863, Benjamin F. Wade Papers, DLC; Edward N. Crosby and Samuel F. B. Morse, "The Letter of a Republican . . . and Prof. Morse's Reply . . . , " in Freidel, *Union Pamphlets*, 2:639-45.

20. Charles J. Stillé, *How a Free People Conduct a Long War* (New York: Anson D. F. Randolph, 1863), 16; "Our Present Position: Its Danger and Duties," in *Continental Monthly* (April 1863) 3:492; Ashley, *Duplicate Souvenir*, 245; N. H. Eggleston, "Emancipation," in *New Englander* (October 1862) 21:791-92; Isaac Welch to Wade, January 31, 1863, Benjamin F. Wade Papers, DLC. See generally Silbey, *Respectable Minority*, and Christopher Dell, *Lincoln and the War Democrats: The Grand Erosion of Conservative Tradition* (Cranbury, New Jersey: Associated University Presses, 1975).

21. Johnson quoted in "The Great Union Meeting . . . ," in Freidel, *Union Pamphlets*, 2:581; Bushnell, "The Doctrine of Loyalty," in *New Englander* (July 1863) 22:577; Will S. Hays, "The Constitution as it is, the Union as it was," Indianapolis *State Sentinel*, July 17, 1863, stanzas one and three; Anonymous to Wade, October 5, 1863, Benjamin F. Wade Papers, DLC.

22. Wellsboro (Pennsylvania) *Agitator*, July 14, 1863; Peoria (Illinois) *Daily Transcript*, July 27, 1863.

23. Oates, *With Malice Toward None*, 331; Wood, *Black Scare*, 40-44, 52, and ch. 5; Mary F. Berry, *Military Necessity and Civil Rights Policy: Black Citizenship and the Constitution 1861-1868* (Port Washington, New York: Kennikat Press, 1977), 49-50, 56-60; Lincoln, *Coll. Works*, 6:56; F. P. Stanton, "The Third Year of the War, " in *Continental Monthly* (July 1863) 4:77; Fisher, *Diary*, 456' "Are Catholics Pro-Slavery and Disloyal?" in *Brownson's Quarterly Review* (July 1863) 4:367-71. See also Henry Wilson to Lincoln, October 25, 1863, Abraham Lincoln Papers, DlC, for continuing pressure on Lincoln to use black troops.

24. *Cong. Globe*, 37:2, 2100, 2671, 2675, 2717; ibid., 37:3, 525, 819-20, 1327, 1329-30, 1435; *SAL*, 12:805. The four Republicans voting "no" were Howe, Cowan, Lane (Indiana), and Anthony. David Donald, Constance Green, and Herman Belz do not consider the Washington-Alexandria extension act, Donald, *Sumner and the Rights of Man*, Green, *Secret City*, Belz, *Emancipation and Equal Rights*. For other efforts against discrimination on rail lines in Philadelphia and California, see *Liberator*, December 23, 1864, January 6, 1865, and *National Anti-Slavery Standard*, December 24, 1864, respectively.

25. "Are Catholics Pro-Slavery and Disloyal?" in *Brownson's Quarterly Review* (July 1863) 4:367-68; F. P. Stanton, "The Restoration of the Union," in *Continental Monthly* (October 1863) 4:450; Stanton, "The Third Year of the War," ibid. (July 1863) 4:77; Garrison, *Letters*, 5:143; Peoria (illinois) *Daily Transcript* July 15, 1863; Salmon P. Chase, *Going Home to Vote*, 29, in Salmon P. Chase Papers, DLC. Already in 1862 Elizur Wright warned against allowing the "stumps of slavery" to remain, and advocated the restructuring of southern society, Wright, *The Programme of Peace, by a Democrat of the Old*

School (Boston: Ticknor and Fields, 1862), 15. For more on the evolving acceptance of civil equality, see also *North American Review* (April 1863) 96:494-95; J. M. Sturtvevant, "The Destiny of the African Race in the United States, " in *Continental Monthly* (May 1863) 3:600-610; Edwin Wright, "The Sanction of Law, Divine," in *New Englander* (October 1863) 22:621; Chase, *Going Home to Vote*, 6-7, 18, 31, Salmon P. Chase Papers, DLC; Indianapolis *Daily Journal*, September 4, 1863.

26. Indianapolis *Daily Journal*, November 17, December 7, 1863; on the New York race riot, see Garrison, *Letters*, 5:165; Fisher, *Diary*, 457; and Adrian Cook, *The Armies of the Streets: The New York City Draft Riots of 1863* (Lexington, Kentucky: University of Kentucky Press, 1974); Wood, *Black Scare*, 23-24; Oates, *With Malice Toward none*, 341, 355-56, 359; Berry, *Military Necessity and Civil Rights*, 60-65; *North American Review* (October 1863) 97:348-55.

27. *North American Review* (October 1863) 97:338, 340, 341; Fisher, *Diary*, 443-44.

28. Leonard Bacon, "Reply to Professor [Joel] Parker," in *New Englander* (April 1863) 22:255; Chase, *Going Home to Vote*, 12-16, Salmon P. Chase Papers, DLC; Wilson's address at Abington, Massachusetts, August 1, 1863, in Abraham Lincoln Papers, DLC; Garrison, *Letters*, 5:170-72.

29. Indianapolis *Daily Journal*, November 18, 1863.

30. Lincoln, *Coll. Works*, 7:49, 51; Washington *National Intelligencer*, December 7, 1863. See also Washington *Daily Morning Chronicle* December 1, 7, 9, 1863.

31. Curtis, "The Bill of Rights as a Limitation on State Authority," (unpublished paper), 7-12 and passim; Raoul Berger, *Government By Judiciary* (Cambridge: Harvard University Press, 1977), 151-16; Schnell, "Court Cases, " 44-45. Note that Schnell observes that the antislavery crusade was "essentially a quest for the protection of the laws regarding traditional Anglo-American rights of man; first for the white man; later for the Negro," ibid., 45; Emerson, *Journals*, 9:459; Thomas H. McKee, *The National Conventions and Platforms of All Political Parties, 1789 to 1905* (Baltimore: Friedenwald Company, 1906), 113-14.

32. "Carnes on the Slave Power," in *North American Review* (April 1863) 96:495.

33. Herman V. Ames, *The Proposed Amendments to the Constitution of the United States during the first century of its History* (Washington: Government Printing Office, 1897), 22-23, 214, 353-66, 366-80; *Cong. Globe*, 38:1, 19, 20, 21; DNA, RG233, 38:1, Committee on Emancipation, H. R. 1. Elliot's bill established a bureau of emancipation so that " freedmen and the government of the United States shall be mutually protected, and their respective rights and interests duly determined and maintained."

34. *Cong. Globe*, 38:1, 145, 521-22, 1313; Donald, *Sumner and the Rights of Man*, 150-51; Bates' diary, February 10, 1864 entry, DLC. See also Hamilton, "Legislative and Judicial History of the Thirteenth Amendment," 7-8. For a brief review of the 1787 Ordinance, see *Journal of the Continental Congress*, 28:164-65, and Clarence E. Carter, ed., *The Territorial Papers of the United States* (Washington: Government Printing Office, 1934-1962), 2:49, 149; *Menard v. Aspasia*, 5 Peter 505; on the authorship of the 1787 Ordinance, see Merrill Peterson, *The Jefferson Image in the American Mind* (New York: Oxford University Press, 1960), 190-93, 197-98.

35. *Cong. Globe*, 38:1, 522-23; Bates diary, February 10, 1864 entry, DLC; Randall, *Constitutional Problems*, 391.
36. "International Law," in *Monthly Law Reporter* (November 1863) 13-14; "On Secession and State Rights," ibid. (December 1863) 70-77, 83; Morse, as quoted in *North American Review* (January 1864) 98:125.
37. John G. Fee to Chase, December 21, 1863, Salmon P. Chase Papers, DLC; G. T. Allen to Trumbull, February 16, 1864, Lyman Trumbull Papers, DLC.
38. "The President's Policy," in *North American Review* (January 1864) 98:253-54; C. S. Henry, "Retrospective," in *Continental Monthly* (January 1864) 5:3.
39. "The Federal Constitution," in *Brownson's Quarterly Review* (January 1864) 1:36-38; George P. Fisher, "Of the Distinction between Natural and Political Rights," in *New Englander* (January 1864) 23:7, 11-12, 21, 25-27.
40. *Cong. Globe*, 38:1, 553; Washington *National Intelligencer*, February 15, 18, March 2, 1864.
41. Washington *Daily Morning Chronicle*, January 23, February 6, 18, 27, 1864.
42. Washington *National Intelligencer*, March 17, 1864; Washington *Daily Morning Chronicle*, February 4, 1864, emphasis in the original.
43. *Cong. Globe*, 38:1, 694, 1130, 1283, 1313. On March 23, Finance Committee chairman William P. Fessenden remarked that S. No. 16 was "more important than any other business except the appropriation bills," ibid., 1130.
44. Ibid., 1313; Mark M. Krug, *Lyman Trumbull: Conservative Radical* (New York: A. S. Barnes and Company, 1965), 217-20.
45. *Cong. Globe*, 38:1, 1313-14.
46. Ibid., 1320, 1323-24, 1368-69.
47. Ibid., 1313-14.
48. Ibid., 1323, 1370, 1424. Publicist John Hancock reiterated the view that freedom secured citizenship, that changes in status brought "that class of our citizens . . . on [an] equal footing with the white population," Hancock, *The Great Question for the People! Essays on the Elective Franchise or Who has the Right to Vote?* (Philadelphia: Merrihew and Son, 1865), 20-25.
49. *Cong. Globe*, 38:1, 1346, 1361-64; Wood, *Black Scare*, 81. The only two Republicans to vote against Wilkinson's amendment were John Sherman and Lyman Trumbull.
50. *Cong. Globe*, 38:1, 1419-24, 1780-81, App., 118.
51. *Cong. Globe*, 38:1, 1366, 1417, 1425, 1444-47.
52. Ibid., 1447, 1456-57.
53. Ibid., 1462-63, 1465.
54. Ibid., 1482-83, 1488-89; Donald, *Sumner and the Rights of Man*, 150-51.
55. *Cong. Globe*, 38:1, 1481.
56. Ibid., 1486, 1489-90. The six negative votes were cast by Davis, Hendricks, McDougall, Powell, Riddle and Stansbury. McDougall objected to the vote on the ground that two-thirds vote of all senators (including the vacant seats of the seceded states) were necessary to pass a constitutional amendment. Vice-President Hannibal Hamlin ruled against the objection, saying that two-thirds of a quorom was all that was necessary.
57. *Liberator*, April 22, 1864; Washington *Daily Morning Chronicle*, March

11, 1864; "Abolition and Negro Equality," in *Brownson's Quarterly Review* (April 1864) 1:198, 202-204; "The Future Supply of Cotton," in *North American Review* (April 1864) 98:497.

58. Lincoln, *Coll. Works*, 7:243, 281-82.

59. *Liberator*, April 15, 22, 1864.

60. *Cong. Globe*, 38:1, 2612-15, quotation, 2615.

61. Abolitionists regularly acknowledged the hand of God working through the war as the chastisement of the nation for slavery. See *Liberator*, May 20, 1864.

62. *Cong. Globe*, 38:1, 2615, 2618, 2723; Washington *Daily Morning Chronicle*, April 15, 1864.

63. *Cong. Globe*, 38:1, App., 124-26.

64. *Cong. Globe*, 38:1, 2955.

65. Ibid., 2941-42, 2960, 2962.

66. *SAL*, 13:129, 200, 329. See especially, Henry Wilson, *History of the Antislavery Measures of the Thirty-Seventh and Thirty-Eighth United States Congresses, 1861-64* (Boston: Walker, Wise, and Company, 1864), 283, 307-12, 358-61, 373-76, for a review of the antislavery actions passed during the Civil War.

67. *Liberator*, May 20, 1864.

68. *Cong. Globe*, 38:1, 2979-80, 2989, 2991, 2995, 3357.

69. McKee, *National Conventions*, 123-26; Trefousse, *Radical Republicans*, 287-89; Davis to Wade, June 21, 1864, Benjamin F. Wade Papers, DLC. For the 1864 election, see generally Harold H. Hyman, "Election of 1864" in Arthur M. Schlesinger, Jr., ed., *History of American Presidential Elections, 1789-1968* (New York: Chelsea House, 1971), 2:1155-78. For the support of the antislavery amendment at the Republican-Union convention, see *Liberator*, June 24, 1864.

70. "The Legal Status of the Rebel States Before and After their Conquest," in *Monthly Law Reporter* (August 1864) 26:555-57.

71. "The Constitution and its Defects," in *North American Review* (July 1864) 99:123-24; Henry E. Russell, "The Constitutional Amendment," in *Continental Monthly* (September 1864) 6:315.

72. Russell, "The Constitutional Amendment," in *Continental Monthly* (September 1864) 6:320-24.

73. "The Constitution and its Defects," in *North American Review* (July 1864) 99:128-38, 142. See also Russell, "The Constitutional Amendment,;; in *Continental Monthly* (September 1864) 6:315: "Ought the idea of the nation to be now, at last, incorporated into the law of the nation, and so made a fixed fact of the nation's history?"

74. Joel Prentiss Bishop, *Secession and Slavery: or, The Effect of Secession on the relation of the United States to the Seceded States and to Slavery Therein* . . . (Boston: A. Williams and Company, 1864), 43-46, 50-54, 72-73.

75. Ibid., 95-97, 111-12.

76. Henry E. Russell, "Negro Troops," in *Continental Monthly* (August 1864) 6:194-98; Emerson, *Journals*, 10:71.

77. Wilson to Lossing, as quoted in Ernest McKay, *Henry Wilson: Practical Radical, A Portrait of a Politician* (Port Washington, New York: Kennikat Press, 1971), 189.

78. "Mr. Lincoln and Congress," in *Brownson's Quarterly Review* (October 1864) 1:429; "Abolition and Negro Equality," ibid., (April 1864) 1:193-

99; Alexander [Tap?] to Wade, September 8, 1864, Orson S. Murray to Wade, September 6, 1864, Benjamin F. Wade Papers, DLC; G. T. Allen to Trumbull, October 11, 1864, Lyman Trumbull Papers, DLC; Jonathan Hiertland to Stevens, May 29, 1864, Thaddeus Stevens Papers, DLC. See, for example, Tap to Wade on Lincoln's future course: "he will not dare to give up the Union, or to re-establish slavery, I hope."

79. *Liberator*, June 10, 1864.

80. "Lincoln Catechism," in Freidel, *Union Pamphlets*, 2:981-83, 988, 991.

81. Ibid., 1008-1009; George F. Comstock, "Let us Reason Together," 2:890-91, and Robert C. Winthrop, "The Principles and Interests of the Republican Party Against the Union," 2:1094-95, both in Freidel, *Union Pamphlets*; Francis Lieber, "Lincoln or McClellan," ibid., 1132. For the Democratic Party during the 1864 elections, see Silbey, *Respectable Minority*, 118-39.

82. "Abraham Lincoln," in Freidel, *Union Pamphlets*, 2:905-913. See also Chase's view: "God grant that [Lincoln's] name may go down to posterity with the two noblest additions historians ever recorded–Restorer and Liberator," Chase to Charles Sumner, October 9, 1864, Salmon P. Chase Papers, DLC.

83. Hyman, "Election of 1864," in Schlesinger, *History Presidential Elections*, 2:1175, quoting McClellan; United States Bureau of the Census, *Statistical History of the United States from Colonial Times to the Present* (New York: Basic Books, 1976), 1083. Congressional elections occurred throughout the year preceding the 39th Congress' opening in December 1865.

84. Fisher, *Diary*, 487.

85. G. T. Allen to Trumbull, December 19, 1864, Lyman Trumbull Papers, DLC; Wilson to Lincoln, November 24, 1864, Abraham Lincoln Papers, DLC. See also Charles Sumner to Chase, October 24, 1864, Salmon P. Chase Papers, DLC.

86. Rev. A. D. Mayo, "Progress of Liberty in the United States," in *Continental Monthly* (November 1864) 6:496. See also William H. Seward, *The Words of William H. Seward, edited by George E. Baker* (New York: Redfield, 1853-1872), 5:163: "The war is the principal force in a popular revolution against African slavery."

87. *Cong. Globe*, 38:2, 53; *National Anti-Slavery Standard*, December 24, 31, 1864; Ashley circular, December 25, 1864, Abraham Lincoln Papers, DLC. The total number of members voting was the key, since two-thirds of that number (assuming a quorum) was the constitutional majority. In this sense, a Democratic abstention was almost as good as a vote favoring the amendment.

88. Lawanda and John H. Cox, *Politics, Principles, and Prejudice, 1865-1866: Dilemma of Reconstruction America* (New York: Free Press of Glencoe, 1963), 6-25; Horowitz, *Great Impeacher*, Trefousse, Radical Republicans, 298-300, all of which inform my treatment; *Liberator*, December 16, 1864 for Charles Sumner's letter of praise, and *National Anti-Slavery Standard*, February 11, 1865.

89. George S. Denison to Chase, January 13, 1865, I. White to Chase, January 6, 1865, Salmon P. Chase Papers, DLC.

90. William M. Grosvenor, "The Law of Conquest: The True Basis of Reconstruction," in *New Englander* (January 1865) 24:111-15; Alex Twining, "President Lincoln's Proclamation of Freedom to the Slaves," in ibid., 24:184, 186.

91. *Cong. Globe*, 38:2, 138-41.
92. Ibid., 150-54, 216, 241-42.
93. Ibid., 177. Ward did not favor the amendment, believing that it would have little real effect on the freedmen's condition.
94. Ibid., 149-50, 194-95, 216.
95. Ibid., 170-71, 181. See also the speech of Kentucky Union Democrat Robert Mallory, 179-80, and William E. Friack (D, Ohio), ibid., 480. Fernando Wood (D, New York), was an exception to these statements, continuing a strick pro-slavery attitude, ibid., 194-95. For southern attitudes see George S. Denison to Chase, January 13, 1865, Salmon P. Chase Papers, DLC, and this quotation from the New Orleans *Tribune*, reprinted in the *Liberator*, December 23, 1864: "Slavery is dead! Would that we could add, that the prejudices engendered by the inhuman institution have ceased also to live!"
96. *Cong. Globe*, 38:2, 145-46, 174, 191-93. See also Arthur Bestor, "State Sovereignty and Slavery–A Reinterpretation of Proslavery Constitutional Doctrine, 1846-1860," *Illinois State Historical Society Journal* (1961) 54:117-80; Schnell, "Court Cases," 44-45 on antislavery as an effort to guard white and later black civil rights; J. White to Chase, January 6, 1865, Salmon P. Chase Papers, DLC.
97. *Cong. Globe*, 38:2, 154-55. For Republican expression of doubt about black ability and/or equality, see ibid., 202, 484-85, and *Liberator*, December 30, 1864.
98. *Cong. Globe*, 38:2, 234, 280-81, 300.
99. Ibid., 478, 488, 524, 531; Cox, *Politics*, 6-25; all eight abstentions were from Democratic members, Wilson, *History Antislavery Measures*, 384; on the war's effect, "Abraham Lincoln," in *North American Review* (January 1865) 100:13, and the review of Henry Wilson's *History Antislavery Measures*, ibid., 100:240; F. P. Stanton, "How the War Affects America," in *Continental Monthly* (April 1863) 3:420.
100. *Cong. Globe*, 38:2, 201.

VI

THE ESCAPE OF HISTORY

The Sabbath. February 12, 1865. The twelfth day past Congress' approval of the constitutional amendment prohibiting slavery and enshrining freedom; the time of celebration of joy.

The Sabbath. February 12, 1865. The Lord's day of rest from his great creation commemorated in his people's own rest from labor, from deeds done, from efforts made.

The Sabbath. February 12, 1865. Birthday of Abraham Lincoln, president and leader during four years of confusion, hurt, discovery, and invigoration.

It was a time of relative ease, almost contentment, as the new inauguration approached and the war showed signs of ending. The constitutional amendment had been available for ratification less than two weeks, and already thirteen states had assented.[1] The long battle against the slave power neared an end. The Congress continued consideration of a reconstruction bill, unsure as to how the constitutional amendment might shape the reality of reunion. The key question as yet had no answer–how must the peace be like the war, so that what had been achieved might be preserved and fostered?

The House chamber was overflowing as a black choir raised up hymns of praise. Then the crowd looked upon a sole black man standing at the Speaker's desk, praying a fervent prayer, his words an unction. The Reverend Henry Highland Garnet, the black pastor of Washington's Fifteenth Street Presbyterian Church preached before an assembly of whites and blacks there in the chamber of the House of Representatives.[2] Garnet explained his understanding of the end of slavery. Answering the rhetorical question of when the reformers' demands would finally end, when the abolitionists would finally be happy, Garnet said:

> When all unjust and heavy burdens shall be removed from every man in the land. When all invidious and proscriptive distinctions shall be blotted out from our laws, whether they be constitutional, statute, or municipal laws. When emancipation shall be followed by enfranchisement and all men holding allegiance to

> the government shall enjoy every right of American citizenship. When our brave and gallant soldiers shall have justice done unto them. When the men who endure the sufferings and perils of the battle-field in the defence of their country, and in order to keep our rulers in their places, shall enjoy the well-earned privilege of voting for them. When in the army and navy, and in every legitimate and honorable occupation, promotion shall smile upon merit without the slightest regard to the complexion of a man's face. When there shall be no more class-legislation, and no more trouble concerning the black man and his rights, than there is in regard to other American citizens. When, in every respect, he shall be equal before the law, and shall be left to make his own way in the social walks of life. . . .
>
> Upon the total and complete destruction of this accursed sin depends the safety and perpetuity of our Republic and its excellent institutions.
>
> Let slavery die. It has had a long and fair trial. God himself has pleaded against it. The enlightened nations of the earth have condemned it. Its death is signed by God and man. Do not commute its sentence. Give it no respite but let it be ignominiously executed.[3]

At a February 4 Boston meeting celebrating the passage of the Thirteenth Amendment, William Lloyd Garrison asserted that the Amendment was proof certain of God's favor and a sign that the cause of the Union had finally become the cause of liberty and the black. The Amendment was, in fact, the culmination of long years of antislavery and pro-liberty activity, efforts to secure in law the principles upon which America was founded. For Garrison, the Thirteenth Amendment was "the Declaration [of Independence] CONSTITUTIONALIZED."

Major General Benjamin F. Butler, recently relieved from the command of the Department of Virginia and North Carolina, addressed the same meeting and echoed Garrison's view. When ratified and made part of the Constitution, every black would be a citizen entitled to every "political and legal immunity and privilege. . . equal in right under the law."[4]

Garrison and Butler shared a high view of abolition's substance; freedom was more than the absence of slavery and necessarily secured equal rights and privileges. Some abolitionists, Gerrit Smith for one, differed, and therefore were already urging yet another constitutional amendment that would guarantee freedmen's rights and not just abolish the legal status of "slave." The consolidation of all antislavery measures into and under the Thirteenth Amendment, while never a unanimously approved idea, was still a discernable and plausible theory throughout the war years. By February 1865, with the Amendment only one step away from embodiment in the fundamental law, doubts and questions began to surface as to its efficacy, its catholic application, and power. Perhaps in recognition of the divergent views of abolitionists, perhaps merely as a tactical suggestion, Oliver Johnson's *National Anti-Slavery Standard* recommended the dissolution of antislavery societies. With the Amendment, their primary *raison d'etre* had been fulfilled. The effects of slavery did pose a problem with which abolitionists had to deal, but they could do so in different organizations and in combinations with new fellow-workers. In effect, Johnson agreed with Gerrit Smith and believed that the question of status was distinct from the question of rights. Even before the war's end, the radical-abolitionist alternative–the view that had won acceptance by passage of the Thirteenth Amendment–showed signs of decline.[5]

Abolitionists and radical congressmen did not differ on goals. If anything, the demand for specific guarantees for freedmen's civil and political rights came from the realization that freedmen must be more than mere ex-slaves. Massachusetts Governor John A. Andrew, addressing the state legislature early in January, had pointedly called for an end to discrimination. Color, long the badge of slavery, should "cease to be the badge of exclusion from any of the privileges of citizenship." Similarly, I. N. Tarbox believed voting distinctions based on color would only serve to invite "the Lord again to chastise us, and vex us with his sore judgment." Frederick Douglass and Wendell Phillips, speaking before the Massachusetts Anti-Slavery Society convention on January 26, both had stressed the necessity of black suffrage as the only sure means to safeguard liberty. "No emancipation is effectual, no freedom is real, which does not take that shape," said Phillips. Douglass put it squarely; the vote was the "all-important right."[6]

Gerrit Smith's desire for another constitutional amendment was not universally shared. Yet by focusing upon new goals, civil rights and suffrage, abolitionists became at once more radical, but more short-cited. Throughout the war each specific antislavery goals had been attained until the ultimate goal–abolition–had been accomplished. Now it had come, and rather than derive effects from the Thirteenth Amendment, abolitionists and radicals continued the heretofore successful pattern of seeking additional incremental goals. But if the abolition of slavery brought the fullness of freedom, then abolitionists' emphasis upon additional measures was not only unnecessary, but damaging to the Amendment. Continuing the war-born pattern of specific goals very nearly conceded the conservatives' argument that freedom was status and not substance.

Important specific changes were still occurring. On February 1, John S. Rock had become the first black lawyer admitted to practice at the bar of the Supreme Court. Three years before the same John Rock had visited Washington, D.C. in the wake of abolition there. A white mob had assaulted him. Now Charles Sumner had presented him to Chief Justice Salmon P. Chase, who had taken the post after Roger Taney's death in October, 1864. Rock's presence in the Supreme Court's chamber was a fitting symbol of the overthrow of Taney's legacy–an abolitionist sat in his chair, and a black man, whose rights no white man was bound to respect, stood before the bar with the same privileges as other lawyers.[7]

Taney's presence on the Court had been a chief reason that some feared for the Emancipation Proclamation and the freedman's future. Wendell Phillips had put it succinctly: "Now, God help the negro if he hangs on Roger B. Taney for his liberty!" With his replacement by Chase, antislavery men felt confident that the "cause," in congressman James Ashley's word, would be safe. The Court would be called upon to pass on many issues raised by the war. Chase's presence assured that "every department of the government is now raised out of the mire of slavery," according to one of the Ohioan's admirers. Oliver Johnson expressed the view that:

> Slavery will hereafter sue in vain for favour . . . and the humblest negro may enter the temple of American Justice in the full assurance of finding protection for his rights as a man and a citizen.[8]

In Congress deliberations continued on the House's reconstruction bill, H. R. 602. That bill contained a key provision, by James Ashley, guaranteeing freedom and equality of civil rights to all persons within each seceded state. Civil rights included the right to hold property, to sue and be sued, to testify in courts–in essence, to be treated fairly by the law and other citizens. Ashley, the floor manager of the recently passed constitutional amendment, made clear that H. R. 602 was aimed precisely at the remnants of slavery, state discriminatory legislation and black codes. Yet the bill's relation to the Thirteenth Amendment (when ratified) was not discussed, and as the congressional session neared its close, the bill was tabled and lost.[9] However, the constantly increasing number of freedmen prompted Congress to create the Freedmen's Bureau, charged among other things with the resettlement, education and general rehabilitation of slaves into free men.[10]

Correspondents of Salmon Chase and Benjamin Wade reported slow but constant progress in the people's thinking about slavery and related issues. New Orleans customs collector George S. Denison reported to Chase as early as November 1864 that opinion was moving toward acceptance of some black suffrage. Brevet Brigadier General James S.

Brisbin, superintendent of black troops in Kentucky, advised Wade that the Union should make more use of the Negro. Brisbin feared that the Confederacy might, in a last desperate gamble, arm as many as 250,000 slaves. Later, in February 1865, Brisbin confirmed that laws and constitutional amendment aside, "the problem of freedom can be worked out under army rules and Kentucky is now nominally free."[11]

Brisbin's "nominal" freedom was more tentative than he suggested.[12] Yet he was correct in his central statement: the war itself was the great emancipator. On the same day that Brisbin wrote Wade, congressman Henry Winter Davis predicted the war's end, possibly by July 4 and certainly by the close of the year. What effect the absence of war might have on the nation was a question often asked in the late winter of 1865.[13]

> Neither party expected for the war, the magnitude, or the duration, which it has already attained. Neither anticipated that the *cause* of the conflict should cease. Each looked for an easier triumph, and a result less fundamental and astounding.[14]

Lincoln summed up the history of his first term of office, the history of the war, and the history of the end of slavery. The Second Inaugural Address, remembered for its peroration, was anchored in two themes: the history of men's actions, and the God behind those actions. Within his brief four paragraph address, Lincoln displayed none of the ambiguity found in his earlier reflections upon the meaning of the war. Doubtless, ambiguity retreated as Union forces advanced. Yet, where Lincoln had once echoed the pleading of Job, he now expressed the acceptance that transcended resignation and submission, suggesting a deep trust in the working out of a divine plan:

> Fondly do we hope–fervently do we pray–that this mighty scourge of war may speedily pass away. Yet, if God wills that it continue, until all the wealth piled by the bondsman's two hundred and fifty years of unrequited toil shall be sunk, and until every drop of blood drawn with the lash, shall be paid by another drawn by the sword, as was said three thousand years ago, so still it must be said "the judgments of the Lord, are true and righteous altogether."[15]

Only with that understanding did Lincoln–could Lincoln–continue and express forgiveness and reconciliation: "With malice toward none; with charity for all, with firmness in the right, as God gives us to see the right, let us strive on to finish the work we are in; to bind up the nation's wounds."[16]

On March 23 Lincoln left Washington for City Point, Virginia, headquarters of General in Chief Ulysses S. Grant. While there Lincoln visited the front, communicating regularly to Secretary of War Stanton. Like successive hammer blows, events now quickly brought an end to the war and the era. On the night of April 2 Jefferson Davis and his government evacuated Richmond, leaving only hours before federal troops occupied the once capital of the Confederacy. Leaving Grant's headquarters, Lincoln travelled to Richmond on April 4, arriving barely a day after the city's capture. It was during this visit of April 4-5 that Lincoln encountered a group of new freedmen who, upon seeing the author of the Emancipation Proclamation, fell down before him. "You must kneel to God only," Lincoln told them.[17]

Four days later Robert E. Lee surrendered his once mighty Army of Northern Virginia, reduced now to barely 28,000 men, at Appomattox Courthouse. Almost to the day, the war had lasted four years. While other southerners still resisted (notably Joseph E. Johnston in North Carolina), Lee's capitulation marked the effective end of the war. Back in Washington, Lincoln greeted the news with satisfaction and public restraint. "Everything I say, you know, goes into print," he joked. "If I make a mistake it doesn't merely affect me nor you but the country."[18]

It was a time for caution, a time for measured words and actions. What would peace be like? Were the "splendid possibilities" created by the war temporary, or had they been permanently engrafted onto the American spirit? The question facing the country was squarely this: "What are we to do with the country our arms have regained?" The *North American Review* did not answer its question, but gave an astute observation: "With the end of the war the real trial of our statesmanship, our patriotism and our patience will begin."[19]

The President made what became his last public address on April 11. He spoke at length of the reconstructed government of Louisiana, reconstructed under his supervision and according to his plan. Radicals looked upon Louisiana with suspicion, worrying that the state's return to the Union had been so rapid that southern whites had not the opportunity nor the necessity to reform their thinking either about the Union or about blacks. Because of these suspicions, Lincoln emphasized the state's new constitution and its positive components. For the first time he committed himself publicly to some form of black suffrage, if only for the "very intelligent" and those who had fought for the Union. Most important, however, was the President's emphasis on the possibility for further change in the Louisiana constitution. The present status of blacks was not all that some wanted, he admitted, and not all that he might want. Yet the question was clear, and the President put it forcefully: "Will it be wiser to take it as it is, and help improve it; or to reject, and desperse it?"[20] The President had discerned and made his own a chief lesson of the war–change, even profound change, was possible given the right situation and an attitude open to change. Before peace could reign, the war must first end; secession and slavery must finally be vanquished.

Charleston, the site of the war's beginning, had fallen to federal forces on February 18. The President and Stanton had planned a flag-raising ceremony for April 14 even before Lee's surrender on April 9. With the Confederacy's collapse the celebration at Charleston would take on added meaning. Four years before Major Robert Anderson had commanded the federal garrison at Charleston. On April 14, 1865, Major General Anderson would raise the same Stars and Stripes he had lowered in surrender.

April 14, 1865. Good Friday. A crowd of about 3,000 gathered at Charleston harbor to hear Henry Ward Beecher's address marking the raising of the flag of the United States. Among the guests were Senator Henry Wilson, Supreme Court Justice Noah Swayne, English abolitionist George Thompson, and William Lloyd Garrison. Earlier that day Garrison had visited the grave of John C. Calhoun, South Carolina's most illustrious son and architect of much of what she had become. Four years before Garrison could not have travelled anywhere in Dixie. Now he came as the prophet proved true.

The President worked throughout the day at the White House, meeting with the Cabinet and finally leaving for the theater about 8:15 that evening. Two hours later he lay dying, shot once in the brain by the actor John Wilkes Booth.[21]

His countrymen recognized him as martyr, cementing the Union anew with his own blood. They recognized him as champion of the poor, "whose fetters God commissioned him to break." They saw and created a secular Christ, dying on Friday, in the hope of a national resurrection in Easter reconstruction.[22]

There was no need to make his importance in death greater than it was in life. He was absolutely interwoven in the history of those four years. At his death in the moment of victory, he took his place in that history–a word, a name, full of meaning, symbol of reality.

Sumter—Slavery—Freedom—Lincoln.

Now the war was over; now Andrew Johnson was President. Now was the "danger of success" at hand. Abolitionists had predicted that southerners would try to keep the substance of slavery even if they yielded its "shadow," or form. That was why, in the view of the *National Anti-Slavery Standard*, reconstruction had to "go down deep to the foundation of things, or it might about as well be let alone." The editor had in mind the redistribution of land, political rights for blacks, and a prolonged military occupation of the South. Much of this would have been difficult to secure even with Lincoln as president. In March Lincoln and his new attorney general James Speed had agreed to wait for subsidence of passion in the post-war South before instituting any proceedings to prosecute for treason. Nine days after Lincoln's death, Speed reaffirmed that the South was still controlled by the "rebellious spirit now rampant" and that civilian judicial proceedings could not yet be re-established. Yet two days earlier, a week after the assassination, Assistant Attorney General J. Hubley Ashton circulated a letter to the United States district attorneys in Missouri, Tennessee, and Kentucky, directing the suspension of new confiscation actions against rebel property. A month later, however, Speed directed confiscation proceedings to begin in Virginia and suggested that a Kentucky grand jury indict some rebel sympathizers for treason to demonstrate that the government had "ample and sufficient power to punish the guilty and defend the innocent." Conflicts of perception and action were evident, and it was unclear when the South would be ready for peace and the government willing to forgo war measures.[23]

Some had anticipated the ambiguity that accompanied the peace. In December 1863, Wendell Phillips declared that:

> [T]he nation owes the negro, after such a war, in which he has nobly joined, not technical freedom but substantial protection in all his rights. It should never admit state sovereignty between it and the negro, until both by constitutional guarantees and by natural laws it has insured him full, real liberty.

In June 1864, however, William Lloyd Garrison expressed considerably less optimism and worried publicly that "the disease of this people is yet unhealed; their sin is neither forsaken, nor repented of, nor acknowledged, nor even understood by themselves."[24] The disease–racism–had not died with the war, and the question became whether the leniency shown to Lee at his surrender, and by implication to all the seceded South, would make reconstruction more difficult.[25]

What was the freedman's future? Was he a free man or something less? What was the government's attitude toward him; what would it be? In March 1865 the *National Anti-Slavery Standard*'s Washington correspondent confidently predicted that Congress would continue to use the District of Columbia as its laboratory for legislation on freedmen. Chief Justice Chase and the editor of the *North American Review* had both pronounced freedmen citizens–in the words of the *Review*, "the necessary consequence, as it is the only effectual warranty of freedom."[26] Yet the ambiguity remained, in part because some Americans could not comprehend the changes war had effected.

They were left perplexed, as was Kentucky slaveholder W. R. McFerren. He had remained loyal throughout the war; a son had died in the Union's cause. Now, at age 72, McFerren wanted his five slaves to care for him. They had been bought in accordance with the Constitution and the law of Kentucky. Why, McFerren wrote Lincoln on April 9, could he not have them? Lincoln did not have the opportunity to answer, but the question remained, and as long as it did, the freedman's fate was uncertain. That was why freedom in name created more questions than it answered. Indeed, nominal freedom freed neither black nor white from slavery, as the *North American Review* observed:

> If we only emancipate him, he will not let us go free. We must do something more than merely this. While the sufferings from them is still sharp, we should fix it in our minds as a principle, that the evils which have come upon us are the direct and logical consequence of our forefathers having dealt with a question of man as they would with one of trade or territory. . . . It is well to keep this present in the mind, because in the general joy and hurry of peace we shall be likely to forget it again, and to make concession, or to leave things at loose ends for time to settle,–as time has settled the blunders of our ancestors.[27]

The South did not act much like a vanquished foe, at least with regard to its former bondsmen. Secession sentiment was still strong in Charleston, South Carolina, according to M. S. Littlefield, a correspondent of Lyman Trumbull's. The end of the war was really only an armistice, a respite in the fighting, Littlefield wrote. Given the chance, rebellion would flourish "if even a vestage of the slavery question be left unsettled." It was clear, Littlefield concluded, that the South intended to put the freedman "way out of the reach of Justice." His opinion was borne out by events in other ex-rebel states. Virginia passed a law to pay black laborers a ridiculously low $5.00 per month salary. Tennessee's proposed black code prohibited black testimony in judicial proceedings and created two sets of punishments for the same crime, one for whites, and another, harsher set for blacks. Similarly, discriminatory laws on the books before the war would in all likelihood remain in force during the post-war era.[28]

Conjoined with these disturbing facts were Andrew Johnson's first actions regarding reconstruction. Six weeks after assuming the presidency Johnson issued an amnesty proclamation granting a full return of civil rights to a broad class of southerners. The only conditions for the amnesty were that title to slaves had to be relinquished and the claimant had to take the oath of allegiance to the United States. Johnson also excluded from the proclamation terms fourteen categories of southerners in an effort to keep the pre-war leadership class from political power in the reconstructing state governments. Even so, the vast majority of ex-rebels (and potentially indictable traitors) were given the means to recover all their rights as American citizens.

On the same day Johnson returned citizenship rights to millions of ex-rebels, he withheld those rights from thousands of ex-slaves. The May 29 Amnesty Proclamation was a bitter pill for abolitionists to swallow because of its twin proclamation appointing William W. Holden as provisional governor of North Carolina, and calling a state convention for the purpose of establishing a new state legislature. In that second proclamation, Johnson explicitly limited the franchise to those voters who took the amnesty oath, and who were eligible to vote on May 20, 1861, the date of North Carolina's secession. This ruled out any balloting by freedmen since on May 20, 1861, no blacks could vote in North Carolina. Blacks were thus excluded from choosing delegates to the state convention, and effectively eliminated from participation in the reconstruction of North Carolina's government.[29]

The President followed his North Carolina action with rapid appointments of provisional governors for Mississippi, Georgia, Texas, Alabama, South Carolina, and Florida. By July 13 every former Confederate state was well on its way to reconstruction. Each governor issued a call for a state convention, and every call stipulated the same two criteria as Johnson's original: the amnesty oath, and suffrage qualifications as before secession.[30] Moreover, Johnson gave his provisional governors the power to pass on applications for special pardons of those otherwise excluded by the terms of the May 29 Amnesty Proclamation. Thus, on the governor's recommendation, prominent ex-Confederates might well be pardoned and admitted to political and civil rights.[31]

Johnson's first appointee, William W. Holden, made his attitude toward freedmen clear from the start. Addressing the freedmen Holden said: "It now remains for you, aided as you will be by the superior intelligence of the white race . . . to decide whether the freedom thus suddenly bestowed upon you will be a blessing to you or a source of injury." To North Carolina whites, Holden asserted that he would give education and legal marriage to freedmen, but "it remains for the people of this State in Convention and by legislative action to define the status of the emancipated race. . . . The extent of their further elevation belongs legitimately to the governing race."[32] Thus under Andrew Johnson's leadership reconstruction would be something done *to* blacks, with a preoccupation with their formal, controlled status.

The President had acted during the interregnum between the war's end and the congressional session of December 1865. Just as Lincoln had time to cope alone with the first months of war, so did Johnson take advantage of the congressional hiatus to deal exclusively with the first months of peace.[33] Johnson's actions were politically possible because the war's end brought a disinclination to press for further "radical" measures. With the war over, the necessity for novel approaches to problems appeared to have ended, too. At least many northerners hoped that was the case. Conservatives hoped that prewar political alliances might be rebuilt and played upon the latent conservatism of some Unionist members of Congress. Johnson himself would attempt shortly to create a National Union party coalition. Many commentators expected a major party realignment, suggesting that Republican-abolitionist answers for war were irrelevant for peace.[34]

Abolitionists and radicals in and out of Congress did not concede the struggle to Johnson and conservatism. The *National Anti-Slavery Standard* observed cogently that the question at issue was just who were the people. Johnson's instruction on voter qualifications for the reconstructing states' conventions decided the matter, and blacks were excluded *ipso facto*. The newspaper went on to term Johnson's policy "the last great crime of the Nation." One publicist judged the situation accordingly: "If the loyal black *may* not vote, the rebel white *must* not." Massachusetts senator Charles Sumner echoed the disbelief of many radicals when he wrote to Senator Ben Wade: "How easy it was to be right! The President seems to have made an effort to be wrong." In Sumner's view, Johnson could either have postponed the decision on reconstruction until Congress met, appointing temporary administrators only, or the President could have followed the principles of the Declaration of Independence and included freedmen in the eligible electorate. Instead, Johnson struck out on his own, and Sumner plaintively asked Wade, "What can be done?"[35]

Abolitionists' initial shock was short-lived. They rapidly began to organize to counter Johnson's policies. Sumner again wrote Wade, saying that the President could not stop the triumph of "the cause," though he might delay it some. Sumner urged Pennsylvania Republican Thaddeus Stevens to "arrest this fatal policy," suggesting that Stevens write or meet with Johnson to persuade him of the error he was committing. Sumner was determined to see "the cause" through, as was clear in his parting message to Stevens: "It is hard–very hard to be driven to another contest." The Massachusetts senator also wrote Chief Justice Chase declaring that unless the President acted upon the principles of 1776, his policies would be "unconstitutional . . . [and] . . . indecent."[36]

Chief Justice Chase was disappointed with Johnson's policy of not considering blacks as American citizens. Chase predicted that northerners would not tolerate disloyal southerners as the basis for reconstructed state governments. He suggested a solution to the situation, however: "[W]e must work for the constitutional amendment & having obtained that remand our appeal to the People, which in the end will obey the instincts of humanity & the voice of Justice."

Chase's views were significant; if the Thirteenth Amendment only had the object of affecting status, leaving rights out of the equation, its ratification could be no antidote to Johnson's reconstruction policies, or for southern intransigence. Yet the Amendment together with the "voice of Justice" were Chase's alternatives to policies that denied freedmen citizenship and political participation in reconstruction.[37] The Amendment secured freedom for blacks in name *and* substance. The "voice of Justice"–the voice of abolitionists–was the catalyst that would activate freedom.

The question facing the abolitionist-radical alliance in the summer of 1865 was the question that had been implicit all along: what did freedom mean? "Is the freedman a citizen? Shall he vote," asked one of Chase's many correspondents. "Should reconstruction be left at the hands of prejudiced Southern men?" The historian Benjamin Lossing warned Henry Wilson, author of much antislavery legislation:

> Your work is not yet done. The freedmen are citizens, but may not exercise the *privileges* of citizens. When they shall be in possession of those privileges, the great design of the "late war," as I apprehend it, will be fully accomplished, so far as the late bondsmen are concerned.[38]

The condition of freedmen in the South was not good. When given a chance to improve themselves, blacks surprised even their staunchest supporters with their ability to overcome years of "laziness" as slaves. Simultaneously with reports of the freedmen's poor conditions, the Johnson Administration curtailed war-related prosecutions. By September Attorney General Speed wrote that it was "not the wish of the Government to keep open the sores made in & by the late struggle." This leniency, combined with the amnesty policy, prompted Benjamin Wade to observe that Johnson was trying to imitate Lincoln's compassionate attitude toward the South. In this, Wade commented, Johnson was "the feeble copyist of a very feeble original." The co-author of the Wade-Davis bill of 1864 retained his antipathy toward what he conceived of as superficial reconstruction.[39]

Leniency toward southern whites appeared to doom the freedmen's place as a free person in southern civil and political life. Former congressman John Covode, just returned from a visit to New Orleans, reported that "the slave holders will have slavery in some form if they get control." Before the war southerners had often protested that they liked their Negroes. Back in 1864 New Orleans customs collector George S. Denison saw through that rhetoric to the reality: "This was all grammar. They liked the negro like I like my horse–a convenient beast of burden for my use & pleasure. But that a negro should have a voice or influence in Government, or any rights which a white man is bound to respect–this is intolerable." In mid-1865 Denison's observation was more apt than ever.[40]

The trouble with Andrew Johnson, in Chief Justice Chase's opinion, was that he looked to state constitutions to determine the rights of citizens. What the President forgot, Chase maintained, was that "the war had made all men free [;] the war has made all men citizens." Rather than look at the legal conditions five years in the past, Johnson ought to use the "*actual relations now*" as his standard. Loyal blacks were part of "the people," unquestionably so, according to Chase. And yet, despite his errors, Johnson did support the Thirteenth Amendment. Its ratification, Chase believed, would supply "a fulcrum of immense value. . . and progress."[41]

Doubtless, the fulcrum Chase envisioned would be used to support the idea of substantive freedom for blacks. Ohio congressman James A. Garfield posed the key concept to a July 4 crowd at Ravenna, Ohio:

> What is freedom? Is it mere negation? Is it the bare privilege of not being chained,–of not being bought and sold, branded and scourged? If this is all, then freedom is a bitter mockery, a cruel delusion. . . . But liberty is no negation. It is a substantial, tangible reality. It is the realization of those imperishable truths of the Declaration.[42]

Freedom had been so long undefined because there had never been the need for explicit definition. White men assumed an identity between themselves and free men, that is, citizens. Only the advent of four million freed black men and women created the condition that required reflection upon freedom's meaning.[43]

The battle was joined between substance and form. If high abolitionism won, substantive freedom would, at the very least, continue as the nation's goal. If, on the other hand, freedom as status prevailed, not only would blacks suffer, but the late seceded South would soon return to the Union in strength. And the supreme irony would be that southern representation in Congress would increase by the very blacks who, no longer counted as three-fifths, would become at once whole men, and empty.

That specter prompted invigorated political activity among radicals. The dreaded result was, in Benjamin Wade's words, "political suicide." Some abolitionists and politicians proposed, therefore, yet another constitutional amendment. This one would secure freedmen's civil rights and make those rights a matter of national definition. Henry Winter Davis, Maryland's Whig turned radical Republican, supported a new amendment, as did the *National Anti-Slavery Standard*. The newspaper made the call for a new constitutional amendment a continuing column heading from July onward. By supporting another constitutional amendment even before the Thirteenth Amendment was ratified, abolitionists unwittingly contributed to the decline of the expansive view of freedom. The Thirteenth Amendment's abolition of slavery confirmed the plenitude of freedom. If abolitionists now advocated yet another constitutional amendment to secure freedmen's civil rights, then the substantive view of freedom and the Thirteenth Amendment lost potency. If the Thirteenth Amendment confirmed the fullness of freedom, there was no need for another.[44]

Benjamin Butler gloomily appraised the situation in the nation, but expressed some hope for the future

> All is wrong [;] we are losing the first results of this four years struggle.
>
> The most [vivid] hope I have is that the rebels will behave so outrageously as to awaken the Government and the North once more out of the dream of brotherly union. . . . My ground for that hope is that heretofore under Providence whenever all looked gloomy for our cause, something of outrage or extravagant pretensions has been put forth on the part of the South which has brought our people to their senses–
>
> May it so happen again. I think it is happening.[45]

It was. Throughout the fall of 1865 southern conventions met to re-create their state legislatures as the first step in rectifying their relationship with the Union. Not far behind on the agenda, however, was the effort to define the freedman's status, his rights and place in the new society. In brief, the more post-war society resembled the pre-war system, the happier whites would be. The same Mississippi convention that emancipated the state's slaves (that is, repealed the state's slave code) was, in the view of one observer, bent on the use of vagrancy laws and other means "to restore all of slavery but its name." Once federal troops were withdrawn, the "poor freedom" that blacks enjoyed would soon vanish. "The utter want of all sense of justice, right [and] honor toward the negro is amazing," the writer remarked.

Other reports from the former Confederacy confirmed southern intentions–and northern fears–about the freedman's situation. Predictions were clear and in agreement: the black could expect the same, if not worse, conditions from "freedom" than he experienced under slavery. The South's intention was as the *National Anti-Slavery*

Standard described it: "Not only is slavery not dead, the rebellion is not dead. As it did not begin in 1861, it does not end in 1865."[46]

Northerners, particularly radicals, were angered by the arrogance ex-rebels showed toward the war's outcome. They were horrified at Johnson's policies that allowed (cultivated?) such a southern response. Radical leaders began to organize to prevent that initial summer trend in reconstruction from becoming the final answer to the question "what shall we do with the Negro." There were indications that Lyman Trumbull's Senate Judiciary Committee might investigate southern white actions and intentions toward the freedmen. "It was not enough to strike down the master," Charles Sumner told Massachusetts Republicans gathered in convention, "you must also lift up the slave." And Thaddeus Stevens said quite directly that if southern states would not bow before God and "embrace the Declaration of Independence," Congress would not recognize their reconstruction.[47]

That the spirit of slavery had not died was clear from the news reaching northerners during the summer and fall of 1865. Kentucky–loyal Kentucky–indicted an army officer for "aiding slaves to escape" during the war. Although no state black codes were enacted until November, the publication of South Carolina's proposed code in the New York *Tribune* stirred comment. Assistant Attorney General J. Hubley Ashton supplied the *Tribune* editor Horace Greeley with a copy of the code and the newspaper detailed the methods by which freedmen were to be reduced to near slavery. Extensive use and expansion of apprenticeship, abandonment, and vagrancy laws would allow South Carolina courts to order the "apprenticeship" of black children until majority if "abandoned" by their parents or if parental consent was given. So, too, would unemployment defined as vagrancy, allowing arrest and "hiring out" for up to a year.[48] Some commentators believed that the Thirteenth Amendment's ratification would make all such codes and freedmen regulations unconstitutional. The problem, however, would be to ensure that this was the universal interpretation placed on the Amendment. And southern states were notorious before the war for flouting constitutional obligations to protect free speech and free press rights of northern antislavery men. The trend in 1865 confirmed the fact that southerners had not appreciably changed their ways or attitudes. The irony was that the day before the New York *Tribune* published its published the proposed black code, South Carolina had ratified the Thirteenth Amendment.[49]

These were "troublesome times" with "dismal prospects" for freedmen. Earlier hopes that "sambo will come out all right" bespoke not only northern racism, but a remarkable detachment from reality.[50] In the last months of 1865 southern intentions were proved in ways that the North could not ignore if it was to maintain any semblance of commitment to the freedmen.

The Thirteenth Amendment initially made swift progress toward ratification. By April 14, 1865, twenty states had approved the Amendment. If the lately seceded states were counted toward the total number of states (a view not without controversy) then only seven more ratifications were needed for the Amendment's incorporation into the Constitution. Between Lincoln's assassination and November 1, however, only Connecticut, New Hampshire, and New York approved the proposal. None of the states reconstructed under Johnson's authority had even considered the Amendment, although all had met in state conventions and reorganized state legislatures. On October 7 Florida's provisional governor William Marvin wrote Secretary of State William Seward, who was charged with oversight of the ratification process. Marvin explained that Florida was reluctant to ratify since adoption of the Amendment would force abolition in Kentucky and Delaware, two loyal states that had rejected the Thirteenth Amendment. But if the President really wanted Florida's assent, Marvin told Seward he would try to move the legislature toward approval.[51] Five weeks later Marvin suggested that Florida would follow her southern sister states, but would not lead the Amendment's ratification. Whatever action Alabama, Georgia, and others took, Marvin assured Seward that Florida would follow suit.[52]

In the meantime South Carolina, under the guidance of its provisional governor Benjamin F. Perry, considered the constitutional amendment. The state had abolished its slave code and adopted a new constitution and was presently preparing a new code for the "protection of the Freedmen in all their rights of person and property." Under the circumstances, Perry wondered whether the Johnson Administration still thought ratification of the Thirteenth Amendment was necessary. The biggest impediment to ratification, according to Perry, was the "constant irritating local legislation on the part of Congress in reference to the freedmen." With that in mind Perry wrote Seward that section two of the Amendment was too much for South Carolina to swallow.[53]

On November 6 Seward telegraphed the governor assuring him that section two restrained rather than increased congressional power. Presumably, Seward attached special meaning to the word "appropriate" in section two: "Congress shall have power to enforce this amendment by appropriate legislation." Seward again wrote Perry three days later emphasizing Johnson's desire that South Carolina ratify the Amendment, calling her assent "particularly important and especially desirable."[54]

With Seward's interpretation of section two at hand, the South Carolina legislature passed the Thirteenth Amendment by a large majority. There was, however, a significant condition attached to its approval. Any congressional interference with civil or political relations within the state (that is, freedmen's rights) would be a violation of the Constitution, the legislature declared. Even when altered by the abolition amendment, the Constitution would prohibit "irritating local legislation" on freedmen's rights. The idea of substantive freedom was neatly disposed of with Seward's aid because South Carolina's symbolic acceptance of abolition was more important to the Administration than its real presence. After ratifying the Amendment, South Carolina's legislature immediately began consideration of the state's new black code.[55]

It was precisely this interpretation of section two of the Amendment that Benjamin Butler rejected so strongly in recommending a civil rights bill to Thaddeus Stevens. Congress must declare its intent "so that hereafter no sophistry can claim that the word 'appropriate' is a *restrained* word."[56]

Sewards's "sophistry" did not convince members of the Mississippi legislature. By late November they had enacted the state's new black code, allowing the apprenticeship of black minors and expanding the definition of vagrant to include all unemployed freedmen. By that definition, unemployed blacks were subject to arrest and "hiring out." Additional provisions legalized black marriages, prohibited freedmen from possessing firearms without a license, granted court access, and allowed black testimony only in cases in which blacks were principal parties. After passing the black code, the Mississippi legislature was ready to consider adoption of the Thirteenth Amendment.

A report from the legislature's Joint Committee on State and Federal Relations suggested Mississippi's acceptance of the Amendment was unnecessary. Since the state had already abolished its slave code, the Thirteenth Amendment could have no practical effect because "the absolute freedom of the African race is already assumed here." It was irrelevant but acceptable if the Administration wanted its passage. Section two of the Amendment, however, caused "more grave objection." The committee expected that no "possible good can result from its adoption," In a gesture of benevolence that fooled no one, the committee expressed its desire to "withdraw the negro from national and state politics; to quiet forever all subjects and questions connected with it . . . and prevent the outbreak of agitation hereafter." Because Mississippi could not anticipate what construction Congress might place on the Amendment's second section–what might be construed as "appropriate"–the committee recommended rejection of the entire constitutional amendment:

> This committee can hardly conceive of a more dangerous grant of power, than one which, by construction, might admit federal legislation in respect to persons, denizens and inhabitants of the state.[57]

Mississippi rejected the Thirteenth Amendment on December 2.[58] On the same day Alabama ratified the constitutional amendment but followed South Carolina's example and added the reservation that the new amendment gave no grant of power for Congress to legislate on the political status of the freedmen. A week later, Alabama adopted its black code, with provisions similar to those of Mississippi and South Carolina. With North Carolin'as ratification on December 1 and Georgia's on December 6 (part of Georgia's black code passed on December 15), twenty-seven states had approved the Thirteenth Amendment. While there had been some maneuvering for the honor of being the twenty-seventh state to ratify (Oregon passed the amendment on December 8), it was fitting that an ex-Confederate state should provide the necessary margin for the Amendment's adoption. Seward issued the formal promulgation on December 18, and the status of "slave" ceased to exist in American law.[59]

Reaction to the final abolition of slavery was muted in comparison to the fanfare that greeted Congress' approval of the Amendment on January 31. But the ten and a half intervening months had taught even the most enthusiastic supporter of abolition that substantive freedom was still only an ideal. Substantive slavery was a more accurate description of the emerging southern reality. The *National Anti-Slavery Standard* called the Amendment's promulgation a "sham ratification" and observed that the "sober opinion must be that the great work of Abolition still waits its legal completion." The more sanguine Washington *Daily Morning Chronicle* hoped all states would soon ratify so that "the life of Liberty will soon be chanted by an unbroken chorus of free American states." The New York *Times* criticized antislavery advocates because they did not rejoice with the Amendment's ratification, wanting instead to turn the moment into a "carnival of vengeance." In the *Times*' opinion, there was too much "botheration about the status of the negro."[60]

Although the abolition of slavery was now the fundamental law of the land, four of the ex-Confederate states either had rejected (Mississippi) or qualified their ratifications of the Amendment (South Carolina, Alabama, and Florida) because they feared the grant of power given to Congress by the measure.[61] Southern white intentions were revealed with the passage of black codes designed to keep freedmen as close to their former slave status as possible. When questioned about the freedmen's condition one southerner admitted that federal protection for the freedman was proper: "Yes, if the nigger is to be free, I reckon [the Freedmen's Bureau] is [a good idea]; but it's a mighty bitter thing for us." More important, white southerners made no commitment to respect the rights of freedmen, despite President Johnson's insistence that ratification of the Thirteenth Amendment was the *sine qua non* for re-admission into the Union. This philosophical gymnastic was immeasurably aided by Seward's perverse interpretation of the Amendment's second section. What was clearly a grant of new power to Congress became, at Seward's hands, a reassurance to southern whites that they retained control over black citizens. It was a great blow to the idea of expansive, substantive freedom.[62]

Rapid military demobilization after the war's end had reduced the number of Union men under arms to only 150,000, down from the 1,000,000 soldiers serving in April. With that reduced force, long-term, meaningful occupation of the South was impossible. In its place was Johnsonian leniency. The same lenient attitude that worked to exclude blacks from their rights, also produced the rapid reconstruction of white men's governments, controlled almost exclusively by former rebels. "My God," Brigadier General James S. Brisbin wrote to Thaddeus Stevens, "can any sane man look at the men who fill their so called state legislatures and then say that the states are loyal?" The issue, of course, centered in the definition of loyalty and loyalty's object. In a formal sense, ex-rebels were transformed into American citizens again when they subscribed to Johnson's amnesty criteria. To that extent, they were loyal to the United States, having pledged their allegiance. Loyalty's object, however, was a different story. To *what* America were the ostensibly rehabilitated white southerners loyal; was it the same America that northerners claimed? Or was it the "Union as it was?" The tendency to interpret away the idea of substantive freedom had already worked to create, as nearly as possible, "the Constitution as it was." While slavery as status was gone forever, slavery as substance remained and was fostered by the new southern black codes. Former Texas attorney general William Alexander wrote Chief Justice Chase in December 1865 that "as yet the great teachings of the war have not yet reached [Texans]." Had they reached anyone southward? After the fighting stopped in April 1865, the battle continued to determine exactly what those teachings were.[63]

On January 5, 1866 Lyman Trumbull introduced a civil rights bill to enforce the Thirteenth Amendment's abolition of slavery. Because Trumbull accepted the substantive view of slavery and freedom, a federal civil rights act was necessary and appropriate to ensure freedmen's rights. Together with an extension of the Freedmen's Bureau

Act, the Civil Rights Act would make explicit the high abolition view that freedom was more than the absence of slavery, and that civil equality between the races was the necessary consequence of abolition. Conservatives worried that the bill might be interpreted as conferring suffrage on blacks. Trumbull denied this conclusion and the Senate passed the bill on February 2.[64]

President Johnson vetoed the Freedmen's Bureau extension bill on February 19, and the Senate sustained his action the next day. (A nearly identical bill extending the Bureau's life was enacted on July 16.) In the wake of the veto, the House began consideration of the civil rights bill on March 1. Much discussion ensued about the power of Congress over civil rights. M. Russell Thayer of Pennsylvania declared that his intention in voting for the Thirteenth Amendment had been to give Congress the power to ensure freedmen's rights; that that was the purpose of the Amendment's second section. Others disagreed, however, with that interpretation. One of the most significant dissenters was John A. Bingham of Ohio. Long known as a radical, Bingham did not believe that Congress acquired power under the abolition amendment to touch state laws affecting freedmen's rights. To remedy that deficiency, Bingham proposed a new constitutional amendment specifically granting Congress authority to prohibit state abuse of citizens' civil rights.[65]

The House passed the civil rights bill on March 13, and on March 27 President Johnson vetoed it. After a vigorous debate the Senate overrode the veto on April 6. Three days later and after no debate, the House also overrode the veto, and the Civil Rights Act became law.[66]

The enactment of the Civil Rights Act of 1866 would have been an unambiguous endorsement by Congress of the idea of substantive freedom had not another measure been given simultaneous consideration–Representative Bingham's new constitutional amendment. Introduced on December 6, 1865, the new amendment sought the same end as the Civil Rights Act. But Bingham thought the civil rights measure was unconstitutional because he believed that the Thirteenth Amendment did not give Congress adequate power to enforce substantive freedom. The doubt Bingham raised convinced enough of his colleagues so that on June 13, 1866, the Congress passed another constitutional amendment, and sent it to the states for ratification. It would become the Fourteenth Amendment.[67]

To some the Fourteenth Amendment was an attempt to make "doubly sure" that the Civil Rights Act was constitutional. Yet by the perceived need to ensure the law's constitutionality, Congress conceded away much of the Thirteenth Amendment's power.

Moreover, by resorting to an explicit listing of some civil rights in the Fourteenth Amendment, Congress also conceded the idea that substantive freedom was included in the Thirteenth Amendment, thus acknowledging that freedom *per se* did not necessarily guarantee civil equality for blacks. A broadly based power to enforce the abolition of slavery was, in effect, set aside for the much more specific and circumscribed action proper under the proposed Fourteenth Amendment. Of course, the Fourteenth Amendment was part of the continuing attempt by Congress to teach the lesson of the war to recalcitrant southern whites. Just as slavery was of long duration, so "the settle [of slavery]," wrote General J. W. Phelps, "should be correspondingly thorough-going and final." And the black codes which were the target of the new amendment contained the "*deadly venom of slavery*."[68]

But there was no agreement about the war's lesson. Certainly, southerners rejected the idea that ex-slaves were entitled to civil equality or political rights. More important, northerners no longer supported the Thirteenth Amendment's absolute ban on slavery as an adequate corrective for post-war racial legislation. By adopting the Fourteenth Amendment, Congress retreated to a more familiar arena of specific, enumerated duties and responsibilities. In that respect the Fourteenth Amendment resembles mere law. The Thirteenth Amendment used the language of the Northwest Ordinance, but relied upon the Declaration of Independence for its meaning. From that perspective there could be no gradation in freedom. Freedom was the plenitude of rights, and slavery the negation of rights. But freedom held precedence, so that it was incorrect to reverse the order and make liberty the mere negation of slavery.[69] This was a lesson of the war abolitionists and radical proposed and fought for, and a key to understanding the scope of the Thirteenth Amendment. But only six months after the abolition amendment's ratification and incorporation into the Constitution, Congress sent the Fourteenth Amendment to the states, an amendment that would have been unnecessary had the ideal of substantive freedom been upheld. What was to have been the crowning achievement of antislavery, became instead the most modest of ornaments.[70]

How did this happen? What allowed the drift away from the broad view of freedom to the comparatively narrow focus of the Fourteenth Amendment? A clue is found in a letter of Charles H. Ray, former editor of the Chicago *Tribune* and a frequent correspondent of Lyman Trumbull's. Writing in February 1866, Ray reminded Trumbull that the country was changing. "You all in Washington must remember that the excitement of the great contest is dying out." The absence of war was the key. Ray recognized it, as did the leader of New England intellectuals, Ralph Waldo Emerson: "the energy of the nation seems to have expended itself in the war, and every interest is found as sectional and timorous as before."[71]

The war imposed many demands upon the leaders of the North, demands that were necessities if the Union was to be preserved. The need to strike at the rebellion's cause–slavery–was a lesson learned early by abolitionists and radicals in Congress. Eventually, Lincoln and the country as a whole agreed with abolition's necessity. What was not learned was the next logical step in the process of abolition. It was meaningless to abolish slavery if freedom was to be only negative. Despite repeated exhortations from radicals and repeated demonstrations from southerners in and out of the Union that they would not treat blacks as fellow citizens, Americans were all too willing to return to peace and forget the black. True, there was the Fourteenth Amendment, and there would also be a Fifteenth Amendment securing black suffrage. These subsequent amendments, however, were necessary only after substantive freedom lost its place in the nation's conscience. Once Congress retreated from an open-ended view of freedom, freedmen's rights were almost certainly doomed. No matter how precise subsequent amendments were, their very precision limited them. Prejudice could always find a loophole.

The other side of war-born necessity was war-born opportunity. Once the war ended, both necessity and opportunity faded away. The sobering conclusion about the relation between war and the abolition of slavery is this: that which was most awful was precisely that which was necessary. Without the horror of war, the horror of slavery could not have been abolished, nor could the idea of substantive freedom ever have emerged as a plausible alternative to racial discrimination. As it was, the impetus of history formed during the war became an anachronism. War was stronger than prejudice, but prejudice was stronger than peace. And so the lessons formed during the experience of war, because irrelevant during the time of peace. The obligations that the lessons imposed and the new opportunities that they envisioned were overthrown, and the United States of America escaped the history that had cemented its existence.

> For Jerusalem is ruined, and Judah is fallen; because their tongue and their doings are against the Lord, to provoke the eyes of his glory. The shew of their countenance doth witness against them; and they declare their sin as Sodom, they hide it not. Woe unto their soul! for they have rewarded evil unto themselves.
>
> (Isaiah 3:8-9)

NOTES FOR CHAPTER SIX

1. U. S. Bureau of Rolls and Library, *Documentary History of the Constitution* (Washington: Government Printing Office, 1894-1905), 2:522-635. Rhode Island, Illinois, Michigan, Maryland, West Virginia, Massachusetts, Pennsylvania, Maine, Kansas, Ohio, Virginia, and Missouri had ratified the Amendment.

2. *Cong. Globe*, 38:2, 643-44; Henry Highland Garnet, *A Memorial Discourse by the Rev. Henry Highland Garnet Delivered . . . February 12, 1865* (Philadelphia: Joseph M. Wilson, 1865), 65-67. See also Joel Schor, *Henry Highland Garnet: A Voice of Black Radicalism in the Nineteenth Century* (Westport, Connecticut: Greenwood Press, 1977), 205-207.

3. Garnet, *Memorial Discourse*, 85-86, 88.

4. *Liberator*, February 10, 1865.

5. Ibid., February 24, 1865; *National Anti-Slavery Standard*, February 11, 1865.

6. Andrew in *Liberator*, January 13, 1865; I. N. Tarbox, "Universal Suffrage," in *New Englander* (January 1865) 24: 165-66; Phillips and Douglass in *Liberator*, February 10, 1865.

7. *National Anti-Slavery Standard*, February 11, 18, 1865.

8. Phillips in *Liberator*, January 1, 1864; James Ashley to Lincoln, November 14, 1864, Abraham Lincoln Papers, DLC; A. Foster to Chase, December 10, 1864, Oliver Johnson to Chase, December 7, 1864, Salmon P. Chase Papers, DLC.

9. *Cong. Globe*, 38:2, 280-81, 967-68, 970-71.

10. *SAL*, 13:507-509; Donald G. Nieman, *To Set the Law in Motion: The Freedmen's Bureau and the Legal Rights of Blacks, 1865-1868* (Millwood, New York: KTO Press, 1979), xiii-xv. As an example of the problem, by August 1864 over 30,000 freedmen were reportedly in the District of Columbia, Mrs. Josephine Griffing to Trumbull, August 10, 1864, Lyman Trumbull Papers, DLC.

11. George S. Denison to Chase, November 25, 1864, Salmon P. Chase Papers, DLC; James S. Brisbin to Wade, February 10, 21, 1865, Benjamin F. Wade Papers, DLC. On March 13, 1865, the Confederacy enacted a law giving freedom to slaves who fought in the southern army, *OR*, Series IV, 3:1161. See also Robert F. Durden, *The Gray and the Black: The Confederate Debate on Emancipation* (Baton Rouge: Louisiana State University Press, 1972).

12. At the close of its session, Congress passed a law freeing the wives and children of slaves enlisted in the Union army. At the end of March one observer rejoiced at how well the law appeared to be working at ending the "damnable slave system in Kentucky." That it had not ended the system nor the love of it was seen some months later when one writer queried Attorney General James Speed whether the act applied to a woman whose husband died prior to the law's passage. Samuel May, Jr., to Wilson, March 31, 1865, Henry Wilson Papers, DLC; W. S. Yates to James Speed, July 19, 1865, DNA, RG60, Letters Received, Kentucky, Private Citizens, 1840-66.

13. *Cong. Globe*, 38:2, 969.

14. Lincoln, *Coll. Works*, 8:332-33.

15. Ibid., 333.

16. Ibid.

17. Ibid., 372-92; Long, *Civil War Day by Day*, 665-71; Lincoln quoted in

Peter J. Parish, *The American Civil War* (New York: Holmes & Meir, 1975), 569.

18. James G. Randall and David Donald, *The Civil War and Reconstruction* (Lexington, Massachusetts: D. C. Heath and Company, 1969), 526-29; Lincoln, *Coll. Works*, 8:394.

19. J. P. Thompson, "The Advancement of Christ's Kingdom by War," in *New England* (April 1865) 24:308; "Reconstruction," in *North American Review* (April 1865) 100: 541, 545, 556.

20. Lincoln, *Coll. Works*, 8:399-405, quotation, 403.

21. Long, *Civil War Day by Day*, 640; Lincoln, *Coll. Works*, 8:375, 375n-76n; *National Anti-Slavery Standard*, April 22, May 6, 1865; Oates, *With Malice Toward None*, 426-33.

22. Eulogy to the bar of the United States Circuit Court at Chicago, enclosed in William H. Bradley to Trumbull, April 18, 1865, Lyman Trumbull Papers, DLC; quotation from Wendell Phillips, *National Anti-Slavery Standard*, May 6, 1865. See also Forgie, *Patricide*, 288, 288n.

23. *National Anti-Slavery Standard*, April 1, 1865; James Speed to William Price, March 22, 1865, Speed to John G. Underwood, April 24, 1865, J. Hubley Ashton, April 22, 1865, Speed to Lucius H. Chandler, May 13, 1865, William Stewart [chief clerk of the Attorney General] to Cary Cox, May 31, 1865, DNA, M 699, roll 9, quotation from Stewart to Cox. The theme that peace was more dangerous than war was carried throughout the spring and summer of 1865. In June Rev. Samuel Johnson preached on "Peace and Peril," while an editorial in the *National Anti-Slavery Standard* of August 19 warned against "The Present Danger," *National Anti-Slavery Standard*, August 12, 19, 1865.

24. Phillips quotation, *Liberator*, January 1, 1864; Garrison, quoted in ibid., June 10, 1864.

25. Emerson, *Journals*, 10:93-94.

26. *National Anti-Slavery Standard*, April 1, 1865; Chase to Lincoln, April 12, 1865, Salmon P. Chase Papers, DLC; "Reconstruction," in *North American Review* (April 1865) 100:559.

27. W. R. McFerren to Abraham Lincoln, April 9, 1865, enclosed in McFerren to James Speed, April 9, 1865, DNA, RG60, Letters Received, Kentucky, Private citizens, 1840-66; "Reconstruction," in *North American Review* (April 1865) 100:549-50. A correspondent to Benjamin Wade reminded the senator "what you already know, that in Kentucky is the big battle over slavery to be fought." C. Clay Smith to Wade, May 12, 1865, Benjamin F. Wade Papers, DLC.

28. M. S. [Littlefield] to Trumbull, May 8, 1865, Lyman Trumbull Papers, DLC; *National Anti-Slavery Standard*, June 3, 10, 17, 1865; Neiman, *To Set the Law in Motion*, 4-5, 17-18, 24-28, 39-45.

29. The text of Johnson's May 29 Amnesty Proclamation and the proclamation appointing William W. Holden provisional governor of North Carolina are in Edward McPherson, *The Political History of the United States of America During the Period of Reconstruction, April 15, 1865-July 15, 1870* (New York: Da Capo Press reprint, 1972), 9-12.

30. Ibid., 12, 19-28. Louisiana, Arkansas, and Tennessee were already much advanced in reconstruction due to Lincoln's plans having gone into effect there before the war concluded. On May 9 Johnson recognized the Pierpont Administration located in Alexandria as the legitimate government

of all Virginia, ibid., 8.

31. James Speed to James Johnson [governor of Georgia], June 23, 1865, Speed to William Price [United States district attorney for Baltimore] June 28, 1865, DNA, M 699, roll 10. In September Speed queried Mississippi provisional governor William Sharkey asking if there were any members of the state legislature that Sharkey wanted pardoned so that they could take their seats, Speed to Sharkey, September 16, 1865, ibid.

32. William W. Holden, *Memoirs of W. W. Holden* (Durham, North Carolina: Seaman Printery, 1911), 2:49-50, 52.

33. Parish, *American Civil War*, 598.

34. Morton Keller, *Affairs of State: Public Life in Late Nineteenth Century America* (Cambridge: Belknap Press of Harvard University Press, 1977), 48-60.

35. *National Anti-Slavery Standard*, June 3, 24, 1865; John Hancock, *The Great Question for the People! Essays on the Elective Franchise or Who has the Right to Vote?* (Philadelphia: Merrihew & Sons, 1865), 4; Charles Sumner to Wade, June 9, 1865, Benjamin F. Wade Papers, DLC.

36. Charles Sumner to Wade, June 12, 1865, Benjamin F. Wade Papers, DLC; Sumner to Stevens, Jun 19, 1865, Thaddeus Stevens Papers, DLC; Sumner to Chase, June 25, 1865, Salmon P. Chase Papers, DLC.

37. Salmon P. Chase to Charles Sumner, June 25, 1865, Salmon P. Chase Papers, DLC. Earlier in June, Chase addressed a committee of blacks in New Orleans and declared his belief that executive and legislative actions during the war had made freedmen citizens of the United States and that they were entitled to claim their rights as citizens, *Liberator*, July 7, 1865.

38. A. Mot to Chase, June 30, 1865, Salmon P. Chase Papers, DLC; Benjamin Lossing to Wilson, June 19, 1865, Henry Wilson Papers, DLC. Lossing went on, however, to recommend attitude changes rather than "imperious laws" as the best way to secure freedmen their citizenship rights.

39. "Freedmen at Port Royal," in *North American Review* (July 1865) 101:1-28; J. Hubley Ashton to Robert B. Carnahan, July 25, 1865, James Speed to W. N. Grover, September 20, 1865, DNA, M 699, roll 10; Wade to Charles Sumner, draft dated July 29, 1865, Benjamin F. Wade Papers, DLC. New seizures for confiscation were stopped in Virginia since the inhabitants there were being "unnecessarily vexed" by the execution of the confiscation laws, James Speed to L. H. Chandler, September, 1865. DNA, M 699, roll 10.

40. John Covode to Wade, July 11, 1865, Benjamin F. Wade Papers, DLC; George S. Denison to Chase, October 8, 1864, Salmon P. Chase Papers, DLC.

41. Chase to Mr. Shuckers, July 7, 1865, Salmon P. Chase Papers, DLC.

42. James A. Garfield, *The Works of James Abram Garfield, edited by Burke A. Hinsdale* (Boston: J. R. Osgood and Company, 1882-83), 1:86.

43. See Edward Bates' opinion of November 1862: "Eighty years of practical enjoyment of citizenship, under the Constitution, have not sufficed to teach us either the exact meaning of the word [citizen], or the constituent elements of the thing we prize so highly," *Opinions Attorneys General*, 10:383.

44. Wade to Charles Sumner, draft dated July 29, 1865, Benjamin F. Wade Papers, DLC; Charles Sumner to Stevens, July 12, 1865, Thaddeus Stevens Papers, DLC; Parish, *American Civil War*, 595; *National Anti-Slavery Standard*, July 22, 1865.

45. Benjamin F. Butler to Wade, July 26, 1865, Benjamin F. Wade Papers, DLC.

46. C. E. Lippincott to Trumbull, August 24, 1865, Charles H. Fox to Trumbull, September 26, 1865, Lyman Trumbull Papers, DLC; Bvt. Major General E. M. McCook to Wade, September 25, 1865, Benjamin F. Wade Papers, DLC; *National Anti-Slavery Standard*, August 5, 1865. See also Charles Sumner's remark before the Massachusetts Republican state convention, September 14: "As there is still a *quasi* Rebellion, so is there still a *quasi* Slavery," quoted in ibid., September 23, 1865.

47. Speech of Thaddeus Stevens, September 7, 1865, Thaddeus Stevens Papers, DLC; Charles Sumner to Wade, August 3, 1865, Benjamin F. Wade Papers, DLC; Charles H. Fox to Trumbull, September 26, 1865, Lyman Trumbull Papers, DLC; Sumner quotation in *National Anti-Slavery Standard*, September 23, 1865; Stevens quotation, Speech of Thaddeus Stevens at Gettysburg, October 2, 1865, Thaddeus Stevens Papers, DLC.

48. John M. Palmer to James Speed, November 28, 1865, DNA, RG60, Letters Received, Kentucky, Misc. Federal Officials, 1863-66; J. Hubley Ashton to Horace Greeley, November 18, 1865, DNA, M 699, roll 10; New York *Tribune*, November 14, 1865.

49. W. M. Grosvenor, "The Rights of the Nation and the Duty of Congress," in *New Englander* (October 1865) 24:756-63, 769-71. See also Benjamin F. Butler to Stevens, November 30, 1865, for the view that the Thirteenth Amendment gave citizenship to blacks and proposing that Congress pass a civil rights bill to enforce the Amendment, Thaddeus Stevens Papers, DLC. South Carolina ratified the Thirteenth Amendment on November 13, 1865, with the proviso that Congress did not gain power to interfere with state definitions of civil or political arrangements, DNA, RG11, Records of Constitutional Amendments, Thirteenth, South Carolina (hereafter, Recs., Thirteenth Amendment). See also *Senate Document 240*, 71 Congress, 3 Session, 4, for a complete listing of the dates and votes of all state actions regarding the Thirteenth Amendment.

50. Letter to the Editor, dated October 27, 1865, with headline "Troublesome Times and Dismal Prospects," New York *Times*, November 13, 1865; James Smith to Trumbull, October 26, 1865, Lyman Trumbull Papers, DLC. For northern post-war racial attitudes, see Fredrickson, *Black Image*, 165-71, 175-83, and Wood, *Black Scare*, 1-11. And for a general overview of conditions in the South during this time, see Carl Schurz, *The Reminiscences of Carl Schurz* (New York: Doubleday, Page and Company, 1909), 3:150-209.

51. *Senate Document 240*, 71:3, 4; William Marvin to William Seward, October 7, 1865. Seward responded on November 1 saying that Florida's action was "indispensible to the return of peace and harmony throughout the Republic." DNA, RG11, Recs., Thirteenth Amendment, Florida. Delaware finally assented to the abolition of slavery on February 12, 1902, ibid., Delaware.

52. William Marvin to William Seward, November 12, 1865, ibid., Florida. The Governor noted that the state convention had failed to recognize explicitly that freedom existed without distinction of color. Although the convention abolished slavery in Florida, black witnesses testify in court only when blacks were involved as the major parties, ibid. Florida's black code was formally adopted January 1, 1866, *Senate Executive Document 6*, 39th Congress, 2 Session, 174-76.

53. Benjamin F. Perry to William Seward, November 4, 1865, DNA,

RG11, Recs., Thirteenth Amendment, South Carolina.

54. William Seward to Benjamin F. Perry, November 6, 9, 1865, ibid. The New York *Times* called South Carolina's fear of federal interference "natural and proper," New York *Times*, November 16, 1865.

55. South Carolina ratification dated November 13, 1865, DNA, RG11, Recs., Thirteenth Amendment, South Carolina; *Senate Document 240*, 71:3, 4. South Carolina's black code contained provisions similar to those in Mississippi, described below, *Senate Executive Document 6*, 39:2, 202-219. See also Theodore B. Wilson, *The Black Codes of the South* (University, Alabama: University of Alabama Press, 1965), 61-80.

56. Benjamin F. Butler to Thaddeus Stevens, November 20, 1865, Thaddeus Stevens Papers, DLC.

57. For the text of Mississippi's black code, see *Senate Executive Document 6*, 39:2, 190-96; Report of the Joint Standing Committee on State and Federal Relations [of Mississippi], DNA, RG11, Recs., Thirteenth Amendment, Mississippi.

58. The Joint Committee's report, recommending rejection, was adopted by the Mississippi House on November 27 and by the state Senate on December 2. The action was taken precisely because of the Thirteenth Amendment's second section, ibid.

59. Alabama ratification, ibid., Alabama; *Senate Executive Document 6*, 39:2, 170-71, 179; *Senate Document 240*, 71:3, 4. On the rivalry for being the twenty-seventh state to ratify, see L. E. Parson [Alabama governor] to William Seward, December 4, 1865, Addison Gibbs [Oregon governor] to Seward, August 14, 1865, DNA, RG11, Recs., Thirteenth Amendment, Alabama, Oregon, respectively.

60. *National Anti-Slavery Standard*, December 23, 1865; New York *Times*, December 20, 1865; second *Times*' quotation from *Times*, November 17, 1865; Washington *Daily Morning Chronicle*, December 19, 1865. See also New York *Tribune*, December 19, 1865.

61. Florida ratified the Amendment on December 27, 1865, with similar reservations as South Carolina and Alabama, DNA, RG11, Recs., Thirteenth Amendment, Florida; *Senate Document 240*, 71:3, 4; Howard D. Hamilton, "The Legislative and Judicial History of the Thirteenth Amendment," (unpublished thesis, University of Illinois, 1950 [?]), 29-30.

62. John T. Trowbridge, *The Desolate South, 1865-1866, edited by Gordon Carroll* (Boston: Little, Brown and Company, 1956), 156; Berry, *Military Necessity and Civil Rights*, 89-90. Sumner was reported to have remarked about Seward: "He never understood *our war*," as quoted in Keller, *Affairs of State*, 56.

63. John Hope Franklin, "Reconstruction and the Negro." in Harold M. Hyman, ed., *New Frontiers of the American Reconstruction* (Urbana, Illinois: University of Illinois Press, 1966), 69-70; James S. Brisbin to Stevens, December 29, 1865, Thaddeus Stevens Papers, DLC; William Alexander to Chase, December 21, 1865, Salmon P. Chase Papers, DLC.

64. *Cong. Globe*, 39:1, 129, 209, 211, 340, 475, 599, 606-607; Benedict, *Compromise of Principle*, 147-49; Horace E. Flack, *The Adoption of the Fourteenth Amendment* (Baltimore: The Johns Hopkins Press, 1908), 17-25. See also Robert Kohl, "The Civil Rights Act of 1866," *Virginia Law Review*, 55:274-76, 283-92; Sidney G. Buchanan, "The Quest for Freedom: A Legal History of the Thirteenth Amendment," *University of Houston Law Review*,

12:15-21; Hyman, *More Perfect Union*, 454, 457-60; Hamilton, "Legislative and Judicial History of the Thirteenth Amendment," 52-57.

65. McPherson, *Political History, 1865-1870*, 74-78; Flack, *Adoption Fourteenth Amendment*, 17-19, 25-32; *Cong. Globe*, 39:1, 14, 1115, 1151-53.

66. *Cong. Globe*, 39:1, 1367, 1809, 1861; Flack, *Adoption Fourteenth Amendment*, 35-40; McPherson, *Political History, 1865-1870*, 68-72, 74-78; *SAL*, 14:27-30. Johnson's vetoes were greeted with the "laudations of the rebel grey everywhere," according to one report, W. H. Smith to D. H. Bingham, DNA, RG233, Records of the House of Representatives, Joint Committee on Reconstruction, 39th Congress, 1st Session.

67. Flack, *Adoption Fourteenth Amendment*, 55-70, 74-97; *Cong. Globe*, 39:1, 14, 3149. Thaddeus Stevens also considered a plan for a new constitutional amendment. See his undated memorandum, Thaddeus Stevens Papers, DLC.

68. *Cong. Globe*, 39:1, 2498; Benedict, *Compromise of Principle*, 169-70 for the Fourteenth Amendment's essential conservatism and narrow definition; J. W. Phelps to Stevens, February 13, 1866, John Binny to Stevens, January 5, 1866, Thaddeus Stevens Papers, DLC. See also Binny to Stevens, December 18, 21, 23, 25, 1865, and February 20, 1866, and John G. Hertwig to Stevens, May 11, 1866, ibid.

69. Rose, *Rehearsal for Reconstruction*, 305-306; Randall, *Constitutional Problems*, 386-88; Hyman, *More Perfect Union*, 420-22.

70. Notable because they are exceptions are *Bleyew v. U.S.* and *In re: Turner*.

71. Charles H. Ray to Trumbull, February 7, 1866, Lyman Trumbull Papers, DLC; Emerson, *Journals*, 10:116.

SELECTED BIBLIOGRAPHY

Public Documents

National Archives:

Record Group 11, Records of Constitutional Amendments
Record Group 46, Records of the U.S. Senate
Record Group 60, Records of the Department of Justice
Record Group 233, Records of the U.S. House of Representatives
Micropublication M 433, Records of the U.S. District Court for the District of Columbia Relating to Slaves, 1851-1863
Micropublication M699, Letters Sent by the Department of Justice, General and Miscellaneous, 1818-1904

US *Federal Cases*
US *Supreme Court Reports*
US *Journals of the Continental Congress*
US *Annals of the Congress of the United States*
US *Congressional Globe*
US *House of Representatives Journal*
US *Senate Executive Document 6*, 39th Congress 2nd Session
US *Senate Document 240*, 71st Congress 3d Session
Official Opinions of the Attorney General of the United States (Washington: Government Printing Office, various volumes and years)
The Statutes at Large ... of the United States of America (Boston: Little, Brown and Company, 1863-1866)

Newspapers and Contemporary Periodicals

Indianapolis *Daily Journal*
Indianapolis *State Sentinel*
The *Liberator*
The *National Anti-Slavery Standard*
New York *Times*
Peoria (Illinois) *Daily Transcript*
Philadelphia *American*
Philadelphia *Legal Intelligencer*
Washington, D. C. *Daily Morning Chronicle*
Washington, D. C. *National Intelligencer*
Wellsboro (Pennsylvania) *Agitator*

Manuscript Collections: Library of Congress

Edward Bates Papers

Salmon P. Chase Papers
Caleb Cushing Papers
Abraham Lincoln Papers
Thaddeus Stevens Papers
Lyman Trumbull Papers
Benjamin F. Wade Papers
Henry Wilson Papers

Other Primary Sources

Adams, Henry. *Letters of Henry Adams*, edited by Worthington C. Ford (Boston: Houghton Mifflin, 1930-38).

Ashley, James M. *Duplicate Copy of the Souvenir from the Afro-American League of Tennessee to Hon. James M. Ashley of Ohio ... edited by Benjamin W. Arnett* (Philadelphia: Publishing House of the A. M. E. Church, 1894).

Bates, Edward. *The Diary of Edward Bates, 1859-1866, edited by Howard K. Beale* (New York: Da Capo Press, 1971).

Belmont, August. *Letters, Speeches and Addresses of August Belmont* (New York: Private, 1890).

Beecher, Henry Ward. *Patriotic Address in America and England, from 1850 to 1885 ... edited by John R. Howard* (New York: Fords, Howard, and Hulbert, 1887).

Biographical Dictionary of the American Congresses, 1774-1961 ([Washington]: Government Printing Office, 1961).

Bishop, Joel Prentiss. *Secession and Slavery: or, The Effect of Secession on the relation of the United States to the seceded States and to slavery therein ...* (Boston: A. Williams and Company, 1864).

Blaine, James G. *Twenty Years in Congress* (Norwich, Connecticut: Henry Bill Publishing Company, 1884).

Butler, Benjamin F. *Private and Official Correspondence of General Benjamin F. Butler ...* (Norwood, Massachusetts: The Plimpton Press, 1917).

British and Foreign Anti-Slavery Society. *The Anti-Slavery Reporter* (London: Kraus Reprint, 1969), 3d series.

Carter, Clarence E., ed. *The Territorial Papers of the United States* (Washington: Government Printing Office, 1934).

Chase, Salmon P. *Going Home to Vote; Authentic Speeches of Salmon P. Chase* (Washington: W. H. Moore, 1863), in Salmon P. Chase Papers, Library of Congress.

———— *Inside Lincoln's Cabinet: The Civil War Diaries of Salmon P. Chase, edited by David Donald* (New York: Longmans, Green and Company, 1954).

Curtis, Benjamin R. *Executive Power* (Boston: Little, Brown and Company, 1862).

Dennett, John R. *The South As it is: 1865-1866, edited by Henry M. Christman* (New York: Viking Press, 1965).

Dickinson, Daniel S. *Speeches, Correspondence, etc., of the late Daniel S. Dickinson of New York* (New York: G. P. Putnam & Sons, 1867).

Dictionary of American Biography, edited by Allen Johnson (New York: Charles Scribner's Sons, 1964).

Emerson, Ralph Waldo. *Journals of Ralph Waldo Emerson, with Annotations*. Edited by Edward Waldo Emerson and Waldo Emerson Forbes (Boston and New York: Houghton Mifflin Company, 1913-1914).

Fisher, Sidney George. *A Philadelphia Perspective: The Diary of Sidney George Fisher, Covering the Years 1834-1871, edited by Nicholas B. Wainwright* (Philadelphia: Historical Society of Pennsylvania, 1967).

Freidel, Frank M. comp. *Union Pamphlets of the Civil War, 1861-1865* (Cambridge: Belknap Press of Harvard University Press, 1967).

Garfield, James A. *The Works of James Abram Garfield, edited by Burke A. Hinsdale* (Boston: J. R. Osgood and Company, 1882-1883).

Garnet, Henry Highland. *A Memorial Discourse by Rev. Henry Highland Garnet delivered . . . February 12, 1865* (Philadelphia: Joseph M. Wilson, 1865).

Garrsion, William Lloyd. *The Letters of William Lloyd Garrison, edited by Walter M. Merrill* (Cambridge: Belknap Press of Harvard University Press, 1979).

Goddard, Samuel A. *The American Rebellion: Letters on the American Rebellion* (London: Simpkin, Marshall and Company, 1870).

Hancock, John. *The Great Question for the People! Essays on the Elective Franchise or Who has the Right to Vote?* (Philadelphia: Merrihew and Son, 1865).

Hay, John. *Lincoln and the Civil War in the Diaries and Letters of John Hay, edited by Tyler Dennett* (New York: Dodd, Mead and Company, 1939).

Hayes, Rutherford B. *The Diary and Letters of Rutherford Birchard Hayes* ([n.p.]: Ohio State Archaeology and Historical Society, 1924).

Holden, William W. *Memoirs of W. W. Holden* (Durham, North Carolina: Seeman Printery, 1911).

Johnson, Andrew. *The Papers of Andrew Johnson*, edited by LeRoy P. Graf and Ralph W. Haskins (Knoxville, Tennessee: University of Tennessee Press, 1976).

Lincoln, Abraham. *The Collected Works of Abraham Lincoln, edited by Roy P. Basler* (New Brunswick, New Jersey: Rutgers University Press, 1953).

Lowell, James Russell. *Political Essays* (Boston and New York: Houghton Mifflin Company, 1888).

McPherson, Edward. *The Political History of the United States of America During the Great Rebellion, 1860-1865* (New York: Da Capo Press, 1972).

———— *The Political History of the United States of America, During the Period of Reconstruction, April 15, 1865-July 15, 1870* (New York: Da Capo Press, 1972).

Motley, John L. *The Causes of the American Civil War* (New York: J. G. Gregory, 1861).

Owen, Robert Dale. *The Wrong of Slavery, the Right of Emancipation, and the future of the African Race in the United States* (Philadelphia: J. B. Lippincott and Company, 1864).

Perkins, Howard C., ed. *Northern Editorials on Secession* (New York: D. Appleton-Century Company, 1942).

Perry, Thomas S., ed. *The Life and Times of Francis Lieber* (Boston: J. R. Osgood, 1882).

Phillips, Wendell. *Speeches, Lectures, and Letters* (Boston: Lee and Shephard, 1870).

Pierce, Edward L. *Enfranchisement and Citizenship: Addresses and Papers* (Boston: Roberts Brothers, 1896).

Schurz, Carl. *The Reminiscences of Carl Schurz* (New York: Doubleday, Page and Company, 1909).

Seward, William H. *The Works of William H. Seward, edited by George E. Baker* (New York: Redfield, 1853-1884, 1972 reprint).

Stillé, Charles J. *How a Free People Conduct a Long War* (New York: Anson D. F. Randolph, 1863).

Sumner, Charles. *The Works of Charles Sumner* (Boston: Lee and Shephard, 1872-1883).

Thorndike, Rachel S., ed. *The Sherman Letters: Correspondence Between General and Senator Sherman from 1837 to 1891* (New York: Charles Scribner's Sons, 1894).

Trowbridge, John T. *The Desolate South, 1865-1866, edited by Gordon Carroll* (Boston: Little, Brown and Company, 1956).

U.S. Bureau of Census. *Statistical History of the United States, from Colonial Times to the Present* (New York: Basic Books, 1976).

U.S. Bureau of Rolls and Library. *Documentary History of the Constitution* (Washington: Government Printing Office, 1894-1905).

The War of the Rebellion. A Compilation of the Official Records of the Union and Confederate Armies ... (Washington: Government Printing Office, 1894-1905).

Welles, Gordon. *Diary, edited by Howard K. Beale* (New York: W. W. 1960).

Whiting, William. *The War Powers of the President and the Legislative Powers of Congress in relation to Rebellion, Treason and Slavery* (Boston: John L. Shorey, 1863), 4th edition.

Wilson, Henry. *History of the Antislavery Measures of the Thirty-Seventh and Thirty-Eighth United States Congresses, 1861-64* (Boston: Walker, Wise and Company, 1864).

[Wright, Elizur]. *The Programme of Peace. By a Democrat of the Old School* (Boston: Ticknor and Fields, 1862).

Secondary Sources: Books and Periodicals

Abbott, Richard H. *Cobbler in Congress: The Life of Henry Wilson, 1812-1875* (Lexington, Kentucky: University of Kentucky Press, 1972).

Ames, Herman V. *The Proposed Amendments to the Constitution of the United States During the First Century of its History* (Washington: Government Printing Office, 1897), Volume II of the *Annual Report of the American Historical Association*, 1896.

Aptheker, Herbert. *To Be Free: Studies in American Negro History* (New York: International Publishers, 1969).

Barnes, Gilbert H. *The Antislavery Impulse, 1830-1844* (New York: D. Appleton-Century, 1933).

Baxter, Maurice G. *Orville H. Browning, Lincoln's Friend and Critic* (Bloomington, Indiana: Indiana University Press, 1957).

Belz, Herman. *Emancipation and Equal Rights: Politics and Constitutionalism in the Civil War Era* (New York: W. W. Norton, 1978).

——— *A New Birth of Freedom* (Westport, Connecticut: Greenwood Press, 1976).

——— "Protection of Personal Liberty in Republican Emancipation Legislation of 1862," *Journal of Southern History* (1976) 42:385-400.

——— *Reconstructing the Union: Theory and Policy During the Civil War* (Ithaca, New York: Cornell University Press, 1969).

Benedict, Michael Les. *A Compromise of Principle* (New York: W. W. Norton, 1974).

——— "Preserving the Constitution: The Conservative Basis of Radical Reconstruction," *Journal of American History* (1974)

61:65-90.

Berdahl, Clarence A. *War Powers of the Executive of the United States* ([n.p.]: University of Illinois Studies in Social Sciences, volume IX, Nos. 1 & 2, 1921).

Berger, Raoul. *Government by Judiciary: The Transformation of the Fourteenth Amendment* (Cambridge: Harvard University Press, 1977).

Berry, Mary F. *Military Necessity and Civil Rights Policy: Black Citizenship and the Constitution, 1861-1868* (Port Washington, New York: Kennikat Press, 1977).

Bestor, Arthur F. "State Sovereignty and Slavery: A Reinterpretation of Pro-slavery Constitutional Doctrine, 1846-1860," *Illinois State Historical Society Journal* (1961) 54:117-80.

Bloss, G. M. D. *Life and Speeches of George H. Pendleton* (Cincinnati: Miami Printing and Publishing Company, 1868).

Brock, William R. *An American Crisis: Congress and Reconstruction, 1865-1867* (London: Macmillan & Company, 1963).

Bryan, Wilhelmus B. *A History of the National Capital; from its foundation through the period of the adoption of the organic act* (New York: Macmillan Company, 1916).

Buchanan, G. Sidney. "The Quest for Freedom: A Legal History of the Thirteenth Amendment," *Houston Law Review*, volume 12, Nos. 1-5.

Cain, Marvin. *Lincoln's Attorney General: Edward Bates of Missouri* (Columbia, Missouri: University of Missouri Press, 1965).

Cherry, Conrad, ed. *God's New Israel: Religious Interpretations of American Destiny* (Englewood Cliffs, New Jersey: Prentice-Hall, 1971).

Cook, Adrain. *The Armies of the Streets: The New York City Draft Riots of 1863* (Lexington, Kentucky: University of Kentucky Press, 1974).

Cox, Lawanda. *Lincoln and Black Freedom* (Columbia, South Carolina: University of South Carolina Press, 1981).

Cox, Lawanda and John H. *Politics, Principles, and Prejudice, 1865-1866: Dilemma of Reconstruction America* (New York: Free Press of Glencoe, 1963).

Curry, Leonard D. *Blueprint for Modern America: Non-Military Legislation of the First Civil War Congress* (Nashville, Tennessee: Vanderbilt University Press, 1968).

Curtis, Michael K. "The Bill of Rights as a Limitation on State Authority," (unpublished paper).

Davis, Cullom et al., eds. *The Public and Private Lincoln: Contemporary Perspectives* (Carbondale and Edwardsville, Illinois:

Southern Illinois University Press, 1979).

Dell, Christopher. *Lincoln and the War Democrats: The Grand Erosion of Conservative Tradition* (Cranbury, New Jersey: Associated University Presses, 1975).

Donald, David. *Charles Sumner and the Rights of Man* (New York: Alfred A. Knopf, 1970).

Dubois, James T. and Gertrude S. Matthews. *Galusha A. Grow, Father of the Homestead Law* (Boston: Houghton Mifflin, 1917).

Dumond, Dwight L. *The Secession Crisis, 1860-1861* (New York: Macmillan, 1931).

Dunning, William A. *Essays on the Civil War and Reconstruction and Related Topics* (New York: Macmillan Company, 1898).

Durden, Robert F. *The Gray and the Black: The Confederate Debate on Emancipation* (Baton Rouge, Louisiana: Louisiana State University Press, 1972).

Durham, Harriet F. "Lincoln's Sons and the Murfan Syndrome," *Lincoln Herald* (1979) 79:67-71.

Engs, Robert F. *Freedom's First Generation: Black Hampton, Virginia, 1861-1890* ([n.p.]: University of Pennsylvania Press, 1979).

Fairman, Charles. *Reconstruction and Reunion, 1864-1888, Part One* (New York: Macmillan Company, 1971).

Fehrenbacher, Don E. *The Dred Scott Case: Its Significance in American Law and Politics* (New York: Oxford University Press, 1978).

———— "Only His Step-Children: Lincoln and the Negro," *Civil War History* (1974) 20:293-310.

Finkleman, Paul. *An Imperfect Union: Slavery, Federalism, and Comity* (Chapel Hill, North Carolina: University of North Carolina Press, 1981).

Flack, Horace E. *The Adoption of the Fourteenth Amendment* (Baltimore: The Johns Hopkins University Press, 1908).

Fladeland, Betty L. "Compensated Emancipation: A Rejected Alternative," *Journal of Southern History* (1976) 42: 169-186.

Foner, Eric. *Free Soil, Free Labor, Free Men: The Ideology of the Republican Party Before the Civil War* (New York: Oxford University Press, 1970).

———— *Politics and Ideology in the Age of the Civil War* (New York: Oxford University Press, 1980).

Forgie, George B. *Patricide in the House Divided: A Psychological Interpretation of Lincoln and His Age* (New York: W. W. Norton, 1979).

Fredrickson, George M. *The Black Image in the White Mind: The Debate on Afro-American Character and Destiny, 1817-1914* (New

York: Harper and Row, 1971).

——— *The Inner Civil War: Northern Intellectuals and the Crisis of the Union* (New York: Harper Torchbook edition, 1968, c1965).

Garrison, Wendell P. *William Lloyd Garrison, 1805-1879* (New York: The Century Company, 1885-1889).

Gerteis, Louis S. *From Contraband to Freedman: Federal Policy Toward Southern Blacks, 1861-1865* (Westport, Connecticut: Greenwood Press, 1973).

Green, Constance M. *The Secret City: A History of Race Relations in the Nation's Capital* (Princeton, New Jersey: Princeton University Press, 1967).

Hamlin, Charles E. *The Life and Time of Hannibal Hamlin* (Cambridge, [Massachusetts]: Riverside Press, 1899).

Horowitz, Robert F. *The Great Impeacher: A Political Biography of James M. Ashley* (New York: Brooklyn College Press, 1979).

Hyman, Harold M. *A More Perfect Union* (New York: Alfred A. Knopf, 1973).

——— (ed.), *New Frontiers of the American Reconstruction* (Urbana, Illinois: University of Illinois Press, 1966).

Ingle, Edward. *The Negro in the District of Columbia* (Baltimore: The Johns Hopkins Press, 1893).

Jordan, Winthrop D. *White Over Black: American Attitudes Toward the Negro, 1550-1812* (Chapel Hill, North Carolina: University of North Carolina Press, 1968).

Keller, Morton. *Affairs of State: Public Life in Late Nineteenth Century America* (Cambridge: Belknap Press of Harvard University Press, 1977).

Kettner, James H. *The Development of American Citizenship, 1608-1870* (Chapel Hill, North Carolina: University of North Carolina Press, 1978).

Kirwan, Albert D. *John J. Crittenden: The Struggle for the Union* (Lexington, Kentucky: University of Kentucky Press, 1962).

Kohl, Robert. "The Civil Rights Act of 1866: Its Hour Come Round at Last: Jones *v.* Alfred H. Mayer Co." *Virginia Law Review* (1969) 55:272-300.

Krug, Mark M. *Lyman Trumbull: Conservative Radical* (New York: A. S. Barnes and Company, 1965).

Langley, Harold D. "The Negro in the Navy and Merchant Service–1798-1860," *Journal of Negro History*, 52:273-286.

Lee, R. Alton. "The Corwin Amendment in the Secession Crisis," *Ohio Historical Quarterly* (1961) 70:1-26.

Long, E. B. *The Civil War Day by Day: An Almanac* (Garden City,

New York: Doubleday and Company, 1971).

Lucie, Patricia M. L. "Confiscation: Constitutional Crossroads," *Civil War History* (1977) 23:307-321.

Mabee, Carelton. *Black Freedom: The Nonviolent Abolitionists from 1830 Through the Civil War* ([New York]: Macmillan Company, 1970).

McKay, Ernest. *Henry Wilson: Practical Radical: A Portrait of A Politician* (Port Washington, New York: Kennikat Press, 1971).

McPherson, James M. *The Struggle for Equality: Abolitionists and the Negro in the Civil War and Reconstruction* (Princeton, New Jersey: Princeton University Press, 1964).

McReynolds, Edwin C. *Missouri: A History of the Crossroads State* (Norman, Oklahoma: University of Oklahoma Press, 1962).

Moore, Glover. *The Missouri Controversy, 1819-1821* (Gloucester, Massachusetts: Peter Smith, 1967).

Morris, Thomas D. *Free Men All: The Personal Liberty Laws of the North* (Baltimore: The Johns Hopkins University Press, 1974).

Nevins, Allan. *Frémont: Pathfinder of the West* (New York: Frederick Ungar Publishing Company, 1961 reprint).

——————— (ed.), *Lincoln and the Gettysburg Address: Commemorative Papers* (Urbana, Illinois: University of Illinois Press, 1964).

——————— *The War for the Union* (New York: Charles Scribner's Sons, 1971).

Nicolay, John G. and John Hay. *Abraham Lincoln: A History* (New York: The Century Company, 1890).

Nieman, Donald C. *To Set the Law in Motion: The Freedmen's Bureau and the Legal Rights of Blacks, 1865-1868* (Millwood, New York: KTO Press, 1979).

Oates, Stephen B. " 'The Man of Our Redemption': Abraham Lincoln and the Emancipation of the Slave," *Presidential Studies Quarterly* (1979) 9:15-25.

——————— *With Malice Toward None: The Life of Abraham Lincoln* (New York: Harper and Row, 1977).

Paludan, Philip S. "The American Civil War Considered as a Crisis in Law and Order," *American Historical Review* (1972) 77:1013-1034.

Papers of the Abraham Lincoln Association, volume II.

Parish, Peter J. *The American Civil War* (New York: Holmes and Meier, 1975).

Perdue, Robert E. *Black Laborers and Black Professionals in Early America, 1750-1830* (New York: Vantage Press, 1975).

Peterson, Merrill. *The Jefferson Image in the American Mind* (New

York: Oxford University Press, 1960).

Pole, J. R. *The Pursuit of Equality in American History* (Berkeley, California: UCLA Press, 1978).

Porter, Kirk H. *A History of Suffrage in the United States* (New York: Greenwood Press, 1969 reprint).

Potter, David M. *Lincoln and His Party in the Secession Crisis* (New Haven, Connecticut: Yale University Press, 1962).

Quarles, Benjamin. *Lincoln and the Negro* (New York: Oxford University Press, 1962).

Randall, James G. *Constitutional Problems Under Lincoln* (Urbana, Illinois: University of Illinois Press, 1964), revised edition.

———— *Lincoln and the South* (Baton Rouge, Louisiana: Louisiana State University Press, 1946).

———— "Some Legal Aspects of the Confiscation Acts of the Civil War," *American Historical Review* (1912) 18:79-96.

Randall, James G. and David Donald. *The Civil War and Reconstruction* (Lexington, Massachusetts: D. C. Heath and Company, 1969), 2d edition.

Reynolds, Donald E. *Editors Make War: Southern Newspapers in the Secession Crisis* (Nashville, Tennessee: Vanderbilt University Press, 1970).

Romero, Patricia W., ed. *I, Too, Am America: Documents from 1619 to the Present* (New York: Publishers Company, 1968).

Rose, Willie Lee. *Rehearsal for Reconstruction: The Port Royal Experiment* (Indianapolis, Indiana: Bobbs-Merrill, 1964).

Roske, Ralph J. *His Own Counsel: The Life and Times of Lyman Trumbull* (Reno, Nevada: University of Nevada Press, 1979).

Salter, William. *The Life of James W. Grimes* (New York: D. Appleton and Company, 1876).

Schlesinger, Arthur M., Jr., ed. *History of American Presidential Elections, 1789-1968* (New York: Chelsea House, 1971).

Schor, Joel. *Henry Highland Garnet: A Voice of Black Radicalism in the Nineteenth Century* (Westport, Connecticut: Greenwood Press, 1977).

Shapiro, Henry D. *Confiscation of Confederate Property in the North* (Ithaca, New York: Cornell University Press, 1962).

Sherwin, Oscar. *Prophet of Liberty: The Life and Times of Wendell Phillips* (New York: Bookman Associates, 1958).

Shoemaker, Floyd C. *Missouri's Struggle for Statehood, 1804-1821* (New York: Russell and Russell, 1969).

Silbey, Joel H. *A Respectable Minority: The Democratic Party in the Civil War Era, 1860-1868* (New York: W. W. Norton, 1977).

Smith, Edward C. *The Borderland in the Civil War* (New York: AMS

Press, 1970).
Smith, Willard H. *Schuyler Colfax, the Changing Fortunes of a Political Idol* (Indianapolis, Indiana: Indiana Historical Bureau, 1952).
Stampp, Kenneth. *And the War Came* (Baton Rouge, Louisiana: Louisiana State University Press, 1950).
Swisher, Carl B. *Roger B. Taney* (New York: Macmillan, 1935).
ten Broeck, Jacobus. *Antislavery Origins of the Fourteenth Amendment* (Berkeley, California: University of California Press, 1951).
Trefousse, Hans L. *Benjamin Franklin Wade: Radical Republican from Ohio* (New York: Twayne Publishers, 1963).
——— *Lincoln's Decision for Emancipation* (Philadelphia: J. B. Lippincott Company, 1975).
——— *The Radical Republicans: Lincoln's Vanguard for Racial Justice* (Baton Rouge, Louisiana: Louisiana State University Press, 1968).
White, Horace. *The Life of Lyman Trumbull* (Boston: Houghton Mifflin Company, 1913).
Wiecek, William M. *Sources of Antislavery Constitutionalism in America, 1760-1848* (Ithaca, New York: Cornell University Press, 1977).
Wilson, Theodore B. *The Black Codes of the South* (University, Alabama: University of Alabama Press, 1965).
Wood, Forrest G. *Black Scare: The Racist Response to Emancipation and Reconstruction* (Berkeley and Los Angeles, California: University of California Press, 1968).

Unpublished Theses

Allen, Patricia M. "Freedom and Federalism, Congress and Courts, 1861-1866." Ph.D. dissertation, University of Glasgow, 1972.
Cochrane, William G. "Freedom without Equality: A Study of Northern Opinion and the Negro Issue, 1861-1870." Ph.D. dissertation, University of Minnesota, 1957.
Hamilton, Howard D. "Legislative and Judicial History of the Thirteenth Amendment." Thesis, University of Illinois, 1950.
Henry, George S. "Radical Republican Policy Toward the Negro, 1862-1872." Thesis, Yale University, 1968.
Lucie, Patricia M. L. See Allen, Patricia M.
Schnell, Kempes Y. "Court Cases Involving Slavery: A Study of the Application of Anti-Slavery Thought to Judicial Argument." Ph.D. dissertation, University of Michigan, 1955.

Smith, Duane D. "The Evolution of the Legal Concept of Citizenship in the United States." Ph.D. dissertation, Ohio State University, 1936.

Syrett, John G. "The Confiscation Acts: Efforts at Reconstruction During the Civil War." Ph.D. dissertation, The University of Wisconsin, 1971.